CAMBRIDGE

Official Cambridge Exam Preparation

CB129887

PREPARE

STUDENT'S BOOK WITH EBOOK

B2

LEVEL 7

James Styring
Nicholas Tims
Helen Chilton

Second Edition

Cambridge University Press
www.cambridge.org/elt

Cambridge Assessment English
www.cambridgeenglish.org

Information on this title: www.cambridge.org/9781009032476

First published 2015
Second Edition 2020
Second Edition update 2021

20 19 18 17 16 15 14 13 12 11

Printed in Dubai by Oriental Press

A catalogue record for this publication is available from the British Library

ISBN 978-1-009-03247-6 Student's Book with eBook
ISBN 978-1-009-03248-3 Workbook with Digital Pack
ISBN 978-1-009-03249-0 Teacher's Book with Digital Pack

CONTENTS

Key to symbols:
✅ *B2 First for Schools* exam task ▶ Video

LISTENING	SPEAKING	WRITING	VIDEO
		An essay (1) Writing Part 1	Creative minds
Five opinions about wearing a school uniform Listening Part 3	Talking about yourself Speaking Part 1		Fashion
			Influencers
		An informal letter or email Writing Part 2	
Five opinions about stress Listening Part 3	Offering help		
		An article (1) Writing Part 2	
Eight short conversations Listening Part 1	Generalising		
			The meaning of colours
		A story Writing Part 2	Stories
A talk about a new skate park Listening Part 2	Comparing photographs (1) Speaking Part 2		Where we live
		An essay (2) Writing Part 1	
A radio interview about a surprise Listening Part 4	Expressing surprise		Surprises!
			Sensing language

Key to symbols:
✅ *B2 First for Schools* exam task ▶ Video

WELCOME TO PREPARE

LEARN ABOUT THE FEATURES IN YOUR NEW STUDENT'S BOOK!

PREPARE FOR THE EXAM
Easy to find exam tasks to get you ready for the exam

ABOUT YOU
Start each unit by talking about you, your life and the unit topic

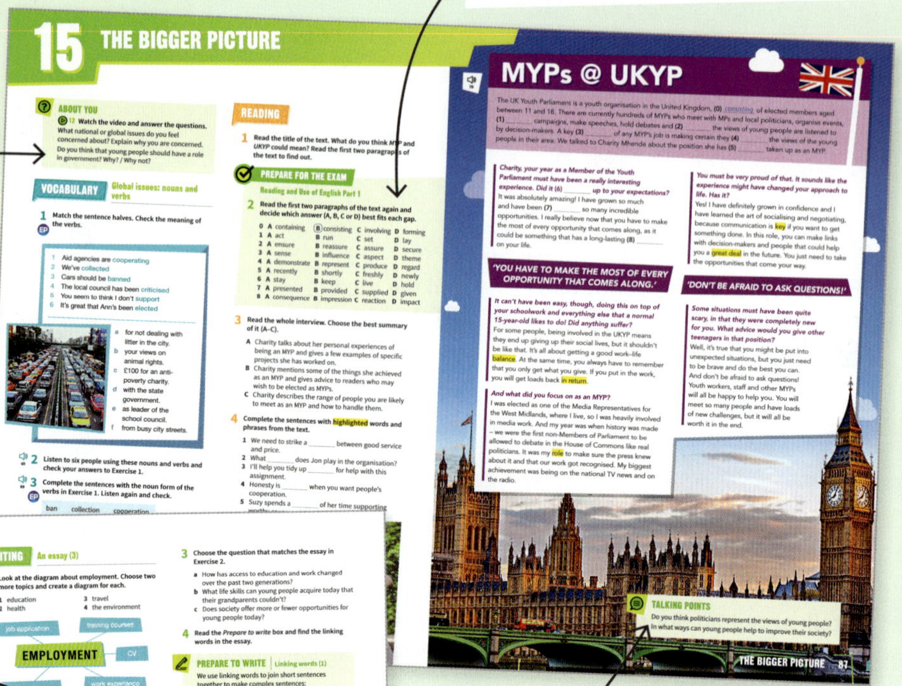

PREPARE TO WRITE
Learn useful tips to help you prepare, plan and check your writing

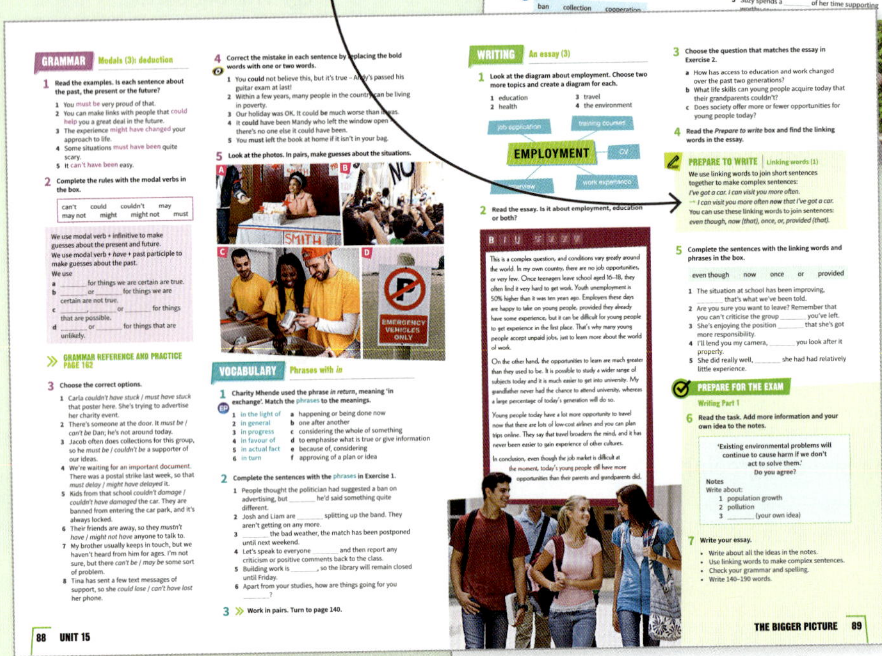

TALKING POINTS
Say what you think about the topic in the text

PREPARE TO SPEAK
Learn useful words and phrases for effective communication

VIDEO
Watch interviews with teenagers like you

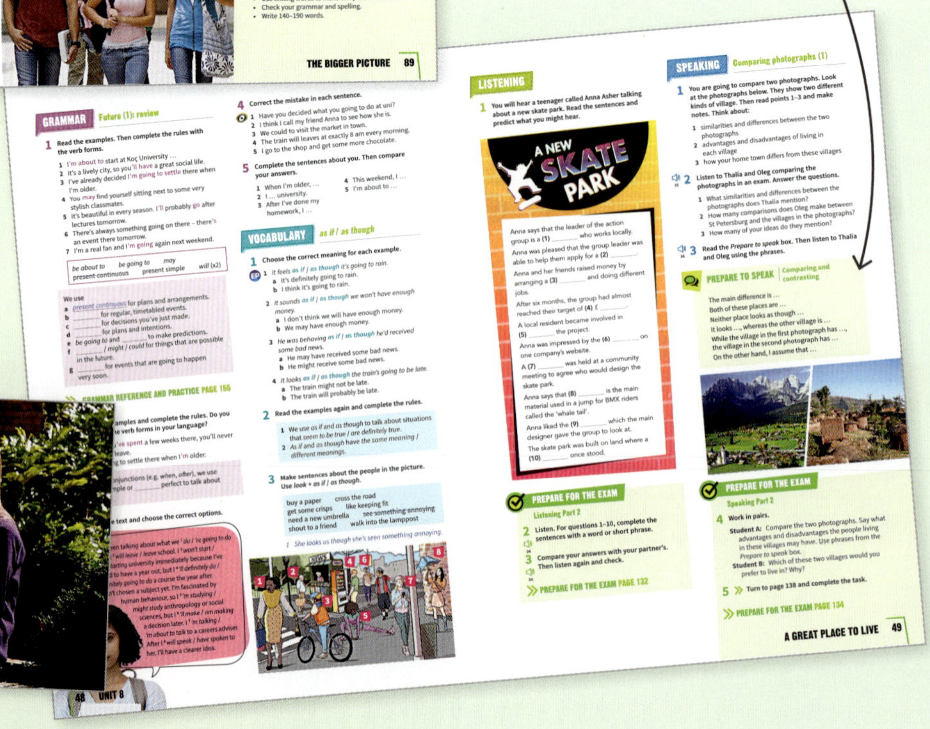

LIFE SKILLS

Develop important skills that you can use in your daily life

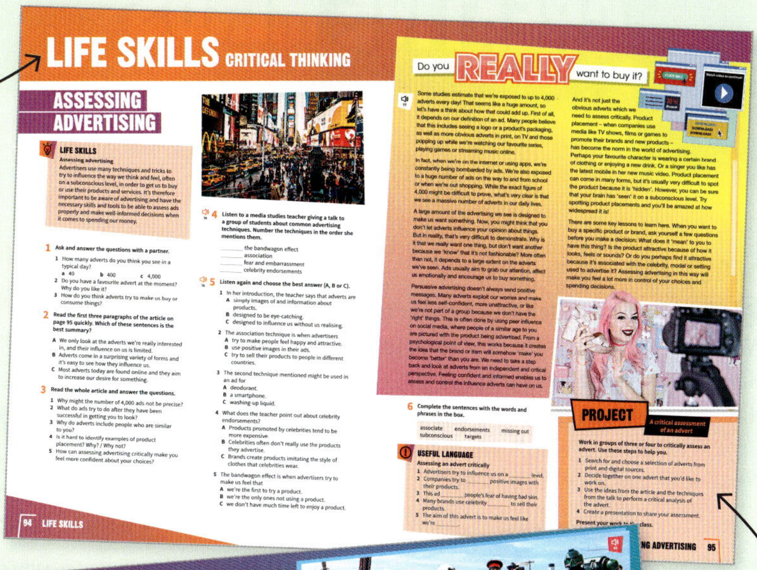

CULTURE

Learn about the culture of English-speaking countries and the wider world

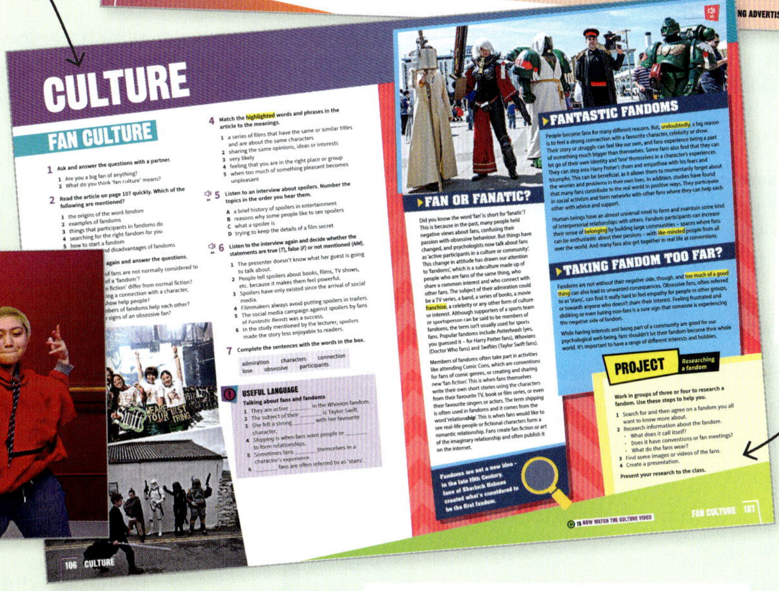

VIDEO

Watch interesting documentaries about the culture topics

PROJECT

Work together to create something fun and expand your learning

PREPARE FOR THE EXAM

Read useful tips, learn exam techniques, then try a practice exam task

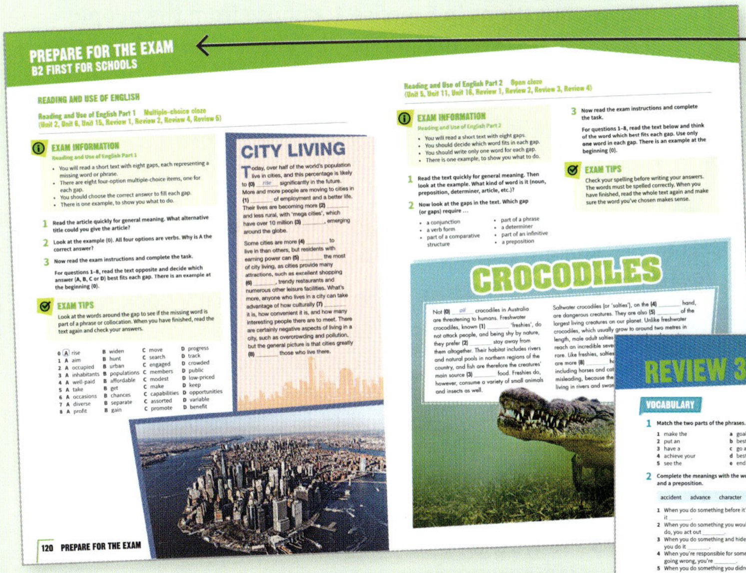

REVIEW

Check your progress

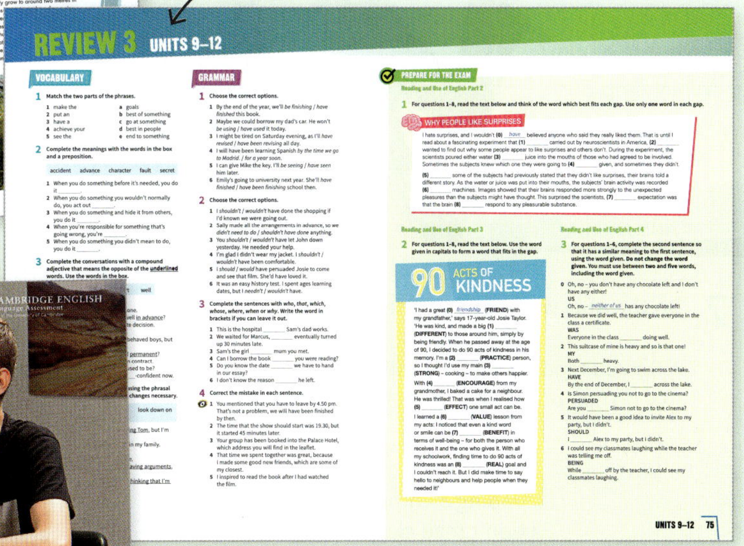

VIDEO

Watch teenagers doing speaking tasks in an exam situation

1 CREATIVE MINDS

ABOUT YOU

01 **Watch the video and answer the questions.**

What do you spend most of your time doing?
Have you ever been in a play?
Have you ever composed a piece of music?
Do you think people are naturally talented and creative or can they learn to be?

VOCABULARY Arts and media

EP **1** **Read the quiz. Check the meaning of the words.**

MEDIA QUIZ

1. Does your favourite TV show have an all-star **cast** or unknown actors?
2. Do you ever learn the lyrics to songs that are in **the charts**?
3. Do you read modern **bestsellers**, or do you prefer the **classics**?
4. What's your favourite **series** of books?
5. Have you ever seen a film being **shot**?
6. Do you have a favourite **piece** of art?
7. Have you ever seen someone famous make a public **appearance**?
8. Which channel **broadcasts** the best shows in your country?
9. What **track** do you listen to most on your favourite album?
10. Which app or website do you use to **stream** music?

2 **Do the quiz with your partner.**

Do you read modern bestsellers, or do you prefer the classics?

I like to read modern bestsellers. I'm reading a crime novel at the moment. I don't read classics very often.

READING

PREPARE FOR THE EXAM

Reading and Use of English Part 7

1 **Read the questions. Then read text A about a talented young person. Which two questions relate to text A?**

Which person

1. rapidly learned something they were interested in?
2. developed an interest after experiencing the work of others?
3. took up a new hobby so that they would understand something better?
4. has a clear idea of what they will do in the future?
5. became popular for sharing their everyday experiences?
6. felt confident that they would do well?
7. has a parent who was initially unsure about their child's ideas?
8. has a talent which was recognised in the media?
9. enjoys trying to help other people?
10. achieved an online record with their activity?

2 **Read the whole article. For the remaining questions in Exercise 1, choose from the people (B–D). The people may be chosen more than once.**

» PREPARE FOR THE EXAM PAGE 128

3 **Complete the sentences with the highlighted words and phrases from the article.**

1. I'm ________ the main character in my book ________ my sister, Charlie.
2. Lucy is ________ she can sing, but her voice is awful!
3. What ________ of novels do you like best? I love science fiction.
4. Have you sent in your ________ to the publisher yet?
5. Sonya's got a real ________ composing. She'll be famous one day.

THE ONES TO WATCH

01

A Nancy Yi Fan

When Nancy Yi Fan moved to the US from China, aged seven, she spoke hardly any English. Already an enthusiastic reader and writer in her native Chinese, she learned English by reading the classics, she says. It took her two years to write her first novel, *Swordbird*. When she had finished it, she emailed a copy to several leading publishers in the USA. Without an agent, book proposals are rarely read, but Nancy believed in her ability to succeed. And she did – a year later, at the age of 12, she was a published novelist with a bestseller. Now, Nancy has not only completed all three books in the *Swordbird* series, but also translated them into Chinese herself. The story is about a world full of birds, at war over a lack of food. Nancy even trained in martial arts in order to write the fight scenes more accurately. Hopefully they'll shoot a film version of the series in the future!

B Sigrid

Sigrid, a young singer-songwriter from Norway, has always loved music, and was inspired at an early age by artists such as Joni Mitchell and Adele. When she was 17, Sigrid, whose full name is Sigrid Solbakk Raabe, started a band, called Sala Says Mhyp, with her sister, Johanne, naming it after a pet cat called Sala they'd had as youngsters. Sigrid wrote the lyrics of her debut track *Sun*, which was released in 2013, and just three years later, in 2016, she signed with Island Records. Soon her music had reached the top of the charts in Norway, Australia and the UK, where she was so popular with critics that one national newspaper suggested she could be headlining at the UK's most famous music festival, Glastonbury, in the near future. Sigrid has won several music awards and is fulfilling her dream of touring the world.

C Tom Cassell

Tom Cassell, better known as Syndicate, is an entrepreneur who turned a hobby into a living. A massive fan of gaming, Tom had the idea of filming a game and commenting on the action while he was playing. He started uploading his videos to his YouTube channel *TheSyndicateProject*, and the genre became a huge hit. Tom also operates a second YouTube channel called *Life of Tom*, in which he vlogs about what he gets up to in his daily life. His father wasn't convinced it would be successful, but by 2017, *Life of Tom* had over 2.5 million subscribers and 390 million views. Tom also runs a Twitch channel, and he became the first person in the website's history to reach a million followers. In 2017, *TheSyndicateProject* reached 10 million subscribers. He now travels widely, promoting his videos, and is a well-known figure in the video-gaming world.

D Tenith Adithyaa

At the age of eight, Tenith Adithyaa started to study software languages, mastering nine of them in no time. As he grew up, Tenith discovered a passion for finding solutions to problems, coming up with the adjustable electricity extension board (which allows multiple plugs to be connected to the same point) and banana leaf preservation technology (which preserves banana leaves for a year without using any chemicals and allows environmentally friendly cups and plates to be made from them rather than plastic). These are just a few of his many successes, and, by the age of 15, he had already produced 17 useful innovations, not to mention winning several prestigious awards. Tenith wants nothing more than to improve people's lives through his work. He is currently running Altruu, the social network he founded, and plans to spend the coming years making the site a success. He also makes appearances as a motivational speaker and as a judge for invention competitions.

TALKING POINTS

How do you think people could become more creative?

What other qualities do young people need in order to succeed?

GRAMMAR Simple, continuous or perfect

1 Match the examples to the meanings.

1 Sigrid **has** always **loved** music.
2 By the age of 15, he **had** already **produced** 17 useful innovations.
3 He **is** currently **running** Altruu, the social network he founded.
4 He now **travels** widely, promoting his videos.
5 Tom had the idea of commenting on the action while he **was playing**.
6 She **emailed** a copy to several leading publishers.

a an action in progress in the present
b an action in progress in the past
c an action that started in the past and continues into the present
d a fact or state in the present
e a single completed action in the past
f an action that took place before another time in the past

2 Complete the rules with *continuous*, *perfect* or *simple*.

We use the
a present or past .... for permanent states and for regular or completed actions.
b present or past .... for actions or states that are/were in progress or unfinished.
c present or past .... for actions or states that connect two time periods.

» GRAMMAR REFERENCE AND PRACTICE PAGE 148

3 Choose the correct sentence or response. Can you explain your choices?

1 We didn't have time to speak to Jack for long.
   a When we arrived, he had left.
   b When we arrived, he was leaving.
2 I did nothing yesterday.
   a I spent the entire day sleeping.
   b I've spent the entire day sleeping.
3 What are you up to at the moment?
   a I often review films online.
   b I'm reviewing a film online.
4 I'm looking forward to the next book in the series.
   a I read all the others.
   b I've read all the others.
5 This actor is often in police thrillers.
   a Yes, he's playing lots of characters like this.
   b Yes, he plays lots of characters like this.

4 Choose the correct options.

1 Tonight, I *am going* / *go* to a concert with my friends.
2 They often *shoot* / *are shooting* films in our town because it's so beautiful.
3 Krishan *has written* / *writes* a bestseller about his childhood in India.
4 My dad *is having* / *has* a job at a recording studio.
5 What *are you reading* / *do you read* at the moment?
6 I *don't decide* / *haven't decided* what I want to do when I finish my studies.

5 Complete the sentences with your own ideas.

1 I have always listened to …
2 By the age of four, I had learned to …
3 I'm currently reading …
4 I often stream …

VOCABULARY Creative jobs

1 Match the creative jobs to the definitions.

EP

comedian	critic	editor	novelist
producer	programmer	TV presenter	

Someone who
1 gives their opinion of a book, play, film, etc.
2 corrects and changes text or film, or someone in charge of a newspaper.
3 is in charge of making a film, show or musical recording.
4 writes fictional books.
5 introduces a show.
6 produces apps or computer software.
7 entertains people by telling jokes.

02 **2 Listen to five people talking about their jobs. Match each speaker to a job in Exercise 1.**

02 **3 Listen again and make notes about each job. Then discuss the questions.**

1 Which job do you think is the easiest/hardest? Why?
2 Which job do you think is the most interesting? Why?

WRITING An essay (1)

1 Discuss the questions.

1 What creative subjects do you do at school?
2 Do you spend as much time on creative subjects as academic subjects?

2 Read the task. What question do you have to answer?

In your English class you have been talking about different school subjects. Now your English teacher has asked you to write an essay for homework.
Write your essay using **all** the notes and giving reasons for your point of view.

> **'Subjects such as drama and music are just as important as maths and languages.'**
> **Do you agree?**
>
> **Notes**
> Write about:
> 1 which subjects are important in your country
> 2 which subjects are useful for a career
> 3 .... (your own idea)

3 Read the *Prepare to write* box and the paragraphs of the essay (A–D). Match the paragraphs to the plan.

PREPARE TO WRITE | Organising essays

You can use four paragraphs to write an opinion essay about a statement or question.

- **Paragraph 1**: an introduction, possibly a statement about the current situation
- **Paragraph 2**: one or more arguments for or against the statement, possibly with an example from your own knowledge or experience
- **Paragraph 3**: one or more contrasting arguments, possibly with an example from your own knowledge or experience
- **Paragraph 4**: a conclusion, your opinion of the statement

A To sum up, it is clearly necessary for everyone to study academic subjects, but, at the same time, creative subjects are often ignored by schools. They deserve a more significant role in children's education.

B This is an interesting question which many people hold strong opinions about. In most schools in my country, students have far more lessons in subjects like maths and languages than creative subjects such as drama and music. Furthermore, many students study no creative subjects after the age of 15.

C However, others feel that without music and drama, students may never get to express their creative sides. They might never discover their talent for singing, playing musical instruments or acting. Many of the highest academic achievers have a creative side. For instance, Einstein loved music as much as he loved physics.

D Most people agree that academic subjects are important. Almost everyone will need maths and foreign language skills in their future working life. In contrast, few people will be lucky or talented enough to earn a living as a professional musician or an actor.

4 Which of the highlighted expressions in the essay introduces the following ideas? Give examples of more expressions that you could use.

a a general opinion
b an additional idea
c a different idea
d an example
e the conclusion

5 Read the task and answer the questions.

In your English class you have been talking about the role of education. Now your English teacher has asked you to write an essay for homework.
Write your essay using **all** the notes and giving reasons for your point of view.

> **'Schools should teach a range of skills, such as how to manage money and apply for jobs, as well as academic subjects like science and history.'**
> **Do you agree?**
>
> **Notes**
> Write about:
> 1 academic subjects
> 2 practical skills
> 3 .... (your own idea)

1 Do you agree or disagree with the statement?
2 What arguments support the statement?
3 What arguments can be used against the statement?
4 What is your own idea for note 3?

PREPARE FOR THE EXAM

Writing Part 1

6 Write your essay.

- Use your answers to the questions in Exercise 5.
- Organise your essay into the paragraph plan in the *Prepare to write* box.
- Use the expressions in Exercise 4.
- Check your spelling and grammar.
- Write 140–190 words.

» PREPARE FOR THE EXAM PAGE 130

2 ADDICTED TO FASHION

ABOUT YOU

02 Watch the video and answer the questions.

What do you take into account when you buy clothes?

Do you think that clothing affects people's moods?

Why do you think some people are so concerned about fashion?

Do you think people will judge you according to what you wear?

VOCABULARY Personality: adjective + preposition

1 Read what four young people say about fashion. Match the sentence halves from the extracts. Listen and check.

03 EP

EMMA

1 I'm aware of what's in fashion
2 I'm easily impressed by
3 I'm pretty adventurous with

a my taste in clothes, but I'd never wear fur.
b designer labels. My favourite is Prada.
c because I read fashion blogs.

AHMED

4 I'm addicted to shopping
5 I do need to be cautious about spending
6 I'm absolutely hopeless at making

a decisions about clothes.
b for clothes. I just can't stop!
c too much, though.

DAN

7 I'm not all that bothered about what
8 You shouldn't be critical of the way
9 I've never been mean about a friend's

a dress sense. People can be very sensitive about their appearance.
b others think of my dress sense. I just wear whatever I like.
c others dress. It's up to individuals to choose how they want to look.

SARA

10 There's no point in being loyal to a
11 I certainly wouldn't be jealous of a friend
12 I'm fairly decisive about

a what to buy. I don't waste time worrying about what else might be available.
b just because they had an expensive brand of trainers.
c particular brand. You should feel free to wear anything that looks good.

2 Answer the questions. Listen again and check.

03

1 Where does Emma buy most of her clothes?
2 What did Ahmed have to do when he accidentally spent too much?
3 Why does Dan like wearing conventional clothes?
4 What does Sara think of brands and labels?

3 Which statements in Exercise 1 are true for you? Discuss your answers.

READING

1 Do you enjoy shopping for clothes in a market? Why? / Why not?

2 Read the article quickly. Which 'big question' are all the people answering?

A Do people worry too much about fashion?
B Does fashion actually matter?
C Are you aware of the latest fashions?

PREPARE FOR THE EXAM

Reading and Use of English Part 1

3 Read the first paragraph of the article again and decide which answer (A, B, C or D) best fits each gap.

	A	B	C	D
0	A select	B agree	(C) settle	D establish
1	A disturbed	B bothered	C troubled	D stressed
2	A constant	B immediate	C latest	D current
3	A smoother	B calmer	C easier	D plainer
4	A hunting	B viewing	C looking	D exploring
5	A extended	B extreme	C expanded	D extensive
6	A deliver	B present	C supply	D provide
7	A budget	B limit	C economy	D bargain
8	A hope	B passion	C desire	D feeling

» PREPARE FOR THE EXAM PAGE 120

THE BIG QUESTION: ______________?

04

However you answer the question, you still have to **(0)** *settle* on something to wear each day. But what do you base your choices on? Perhaps you're someone who isn't particularly **(1)** ________ about keeping up to date with **(2)** ________ trends, but you wear what's in fashion because it's **(3)** ________ to do so, and you aren't especially interested in **(4)** ________ alternatives. Maybe you're a 'quality not quantity' kind of person, preferring to spend your cash on a few great designer pieces than own an **(5)** ________ collection of cheaper items. Or perhaps you do your best *not* to follow fashion because you're keen to **(6)** ________ an image as far from the mainstream as possible: in other words, you don't want to do what everyone else is doing and would rather stand out from the crowd. It might also be your **(7)** ________ that determines your choices, or a strong **(8)** ________ to fit in with your friends.

Here's how some of our readers answered the question …

4 REPLIES 9 LIKES 2 SHARES

Of course, and I like to be adventurous with what I wear, but I'm more worried about other people's terrible dress sense! I've been reading an article about the history of fashion. It made some interesting points, like who says blue is for boys and pink is for girls? In fact, 100 years ago, pink was a boys' colour and blue was for girls! And what about skirts for men? They're comfortable and functional, but men in the West rarely wear them.

We tend to think of fashion as fast-moving, but it actually changes really slowly. Men have been wearing shirts, ties and suits for centuries. Similarly, women's dress has changed very little during the past few hundred years, except for the introduction of trousers in the 1950s. You see some weird stuff on the catwalks, but in real life, clothes are boring. I reckon it's time for a fashion revolution!

Arslan, 17 Ankara

Not really. I can't stand designer labels. Everyone at my school seems to be impressed by them, but I can't understand why people are willing to pay a fortune for top brands when cheaper ones are really no different! It's hard to know what to do at school! If you have cheap clothes, people might be mean about it, but if you have really expensive clothes, there's always the worry that someone might be jealous of them. The point is, logos and brands cause all kinds of problems.

Olivia, 16 Glasgow

Yes. Clothes actually make me happy – up to a point! I have clothes to suit every mood, occasion and season. Fashion is important because it helps people to express their individuality and identity. 'High' fashion – the clothing supermodels wear on the catwalk – is associated with Paris, Milan, New York and London, but every country has developed its own fashion industry and its own look. I'm cautious about spending loads of money on fashion – there's no point. Most good malls sell clothes that are inspired by the catwalk, so you can still buy clothes that look stunning but cost ten times less. With fashion, there's something for everyone.

Camila, 16 Madrid

I think it does, actually. Some people aren't interested in how they look, but everyone wears *some* form of clothing and their clothes make a statement. I think clothes matter because your choice of clothes influences how others think of you. Take me, for example. I'm really into 'alternative' clothing. I avoid chain stores in malls. I'm loyal to a few small, independent shops in my town and get second-hand clothes from markets. I collect badges. I've been looking for some 1950s American badges, but they're all much too expensive. So what do my clothes say about me? They say I'm an individual. I think independently. I'm original. I have my own style.

Natalia, 17 León

What do YOUR clothes say about YOU?

REPLY

4 **Are the sentences true or false? Correct the false sentences.**

1 One particular colour has always been associated with girls. (Arslan)
2 It is worth paying more for a good brand. (Olivia)
3 People might make fun of you for wearing fashionable items. (Olivia)
4 Your clothes can change the way you feel. (Camila)
5 Cheap clothes don't look as good as more expensive items. (Camila)
6 Clothes can tell other people about the wearer. (Natalia)

5 **Match the highlighted words and phrases in the article to the meanings.**

1 partly
2 pieces of metal or plastic with words or a picture on them that you wear on your clothing
3 ability to dress well
4 a particular style of clothes
5 long, narrow stage which models walk on in a fashion show

TALKING POINTS

Why do you think some people enjoy having designer clothes? In what ways do you think the clothes someone wears show their personality?

GRAMMAR Present perfect simple and continuous

1 **Match the examples to the rules.**

1 Men **have been wearing** shirts, ties and suits for centuries.
2 Every country **has developed** its own fashion industry and its own look.
3 Women's dress **has changed** very little during the past few hundred years.
4 I**'ve been relaxing** at home, so I'm wearing something casual.

We use the present perfect simple for
a a past action with a present result.
b an action that happened in a time period that continues until now.
We use the present perfect continuous for
c an action that started in the past and is still continuing.
d an action (still continuing or just completed) that explains a present situation.

» GRAMMAR REFERENCE AND PRACTICE PAGE 149

2 **Choose the correct ending for each sentence.**

1 *Vogue* magazine has published …
2 *Vogue* magazine has been publishing …
a only one super-long magazine. It was 916 pages long!
b fashion magazines since 1892.

3 My wardrobe's almost empty. I've been getting rid …
4 I used to have loads of jackets, but I've got rid …
a of them all, sorry.
b of lots of old clothes recently. It's a nice feeling!

5 Anna works for Gucci. She's been designing …
6 Anna works for Gucci. She's designed …
a handbags for 15 years.
b hundreds of beautiful bags.

3 **Correct the mistake in each sentence.**

1 We're sitting outside without jackets all evening and I'm really cold now.
2 Stella McCartney produces some really interesting designs during her career.
3 I haven't been hanging your clothes outside yet. It looks like it might rain.
4 Look! Jen buys some new shoes! They're gorgeous.
5 I'm reading your blog all week. It's brilliant and I can't wait for tomorrow's update!
6 I've never been seeing such long queues in a clothes shop.

4 **Make five sentences with the present perfect simple or continuous form of the verbs in the box. Compare your sentences with your partner's.**

blog	buy	chill out (with)	learn
live (in)	play	watch	wear

I haven't been blogging for long. I think I wrote my first post about three months ago.

VOCABULARY Verb + preposition

1 **Complete the sentences with the correct form of the phrases in the box.**

EP

apologise for	compare with	cope with	
depend on	do without	~~heard of~~	laugh at

0 I haven't *heard of* *Teen Vogue*. What is it?
1 You still haven't ________ losing my scarf.
2 I hate it when people ________ my uniform.
3 Clothes these days are very comfortable ________ a century ago.
4 I hate ________ my parents for money to buy clothes.
5 Marta can't ________ going to crowded shopping centres.
6 I haven't got much money left this month, so I'll have to ________ that new pair of jeans I wanted.

2 **In pairs, ask and answer the questions using verb + preposition phrases.**

0 Is there anything that you can't do without?

Is there anything that you can't do without?

I definitely can't do without my sunglasses.

1 Could you cope with not having the latest fashions?
2 When was the last time you apologised for something you did?
3 What's the strangest fashion trend you've seen or heard of?
4 How stylish are you compared with your friends?
5 Who do you depend on for advice about fashion?
6 Would you ever laugh at someone because of what they were wearing?

LISTENING

05 **1** **You will hear a girl talking about wearing a school uniform. Read the sentences carefully. Then listen and decide which of the sentences (A–H) expresses her opinion about wearing a school uniform.**

A It makes everyone feel equal.
B It gives me a sense of belonging.
C It helps students focus on their work.
D It isn't as expensive as other clothing.
E I don't need to worry about damaging my clothes.
F I don't have to think about what to wear every day.
G It's more comfortable than some of the other clothes I wear.
H It has a positive effect on how students behave outside school.

2 **Read the reasons why A–D in Exercise 1 are true or not true for the girl. Work in pairs and decide why E–H are not true.**

A Not true. She says, 'Not that I'm saying it makes us all the same – far from it.'
B Not true. She does not refer to a sense of belonging.
C True. She says, 'If there's nothing to distract us in class, … we can all get on with what we're meant to be doing.'
D Not true. She does not refer to expense.

PREPARE FOR THE EXAM

Listening Part 3

3 06 **You will hear four more teenagers talking about wearing a school uniform. For speakers 2–5, choose from the list (A–H) what opinion each speaker expresses about school uniform. Use the letters only once. There are three extra letters which you do not need to use.**

Speaker 1 ___C___
Speaker 2 ________
Speaker 3 ________
Speaker 4 ________
Speaker 5 ________

» PREPARE FOR THE EXAM PAGE 132

4 **Discuss the questions.**

1 Do you think schools and colleges are right to ban some items of clothing or accessories, such as jewellery? Why? / Why not?
2 What are the good and bad points about uniforms at work?

SPEAKING Talking about yourself

07 **1** **Listen to an interview with Miguel and Vika. Write the questions which they are asked.**

07 **2** **Read the** ***Prepare to speak*** **box. Then listen again. Who uses each phrase? Write M (Miguel) or V (Vika).**

PREPARE TO SPEAK | Introducing an opinion

To be honest, …
To tell the truth, …
I guess …
Personally speaking …
I would say …

3 **Prepare for a short conversation about yourself.**

- Make notes on your answers to the questions in Exercise 1.
- Review your answers. Think about what tenses and relevant vocabulary you can use for each answer.

PREPARE FOR THE EXAM

Speaking Part 1

4 **Work in pairs. Ask each other questions.**

- Ask the questions from Exercise 1.
- Answer using phrases from the *Prepare to speak* box.

» PREPARE FOR THE EXAM PAGE 134

CULTURE

THE BRITISH FASHION SCENE

Victoria and David Beckham

Katharine Hamnett

Kim Jones

Cara Delevingne

1 Ask and answer the questions with a partner.

1 Do you know what a fashion influencer is? Can you name any?
2 What other jobs and professions are related to the world of fashion?

2 Read the article on page 19 quickly. Choose the best alternative title for the article.

A The growing French influence on the London fashion scene
B The French influencer bringing her unique style to the British capital
C British influencer makes her mark on the French fashion scene

3 Read the article again and answer the questions.

1 Why does the writer consider Freddie to be a London fashion influencer rather than a Paris fashion influencer?
2 What qualities does the writer admire about Freddie?
3 How did Freddie feel when she wore clothes that other people would like?
4 What recognition has Freddie received for her work?
5 Apart from her writing and videos, how else does Freddie interact with people?
6 According to the writer, what does Freddie's success demonstrate?

4 Match the highlighted words and phrases in the article to the meanings.

1 meetings where people learn about a subject
2 caused a person to notice something
3 uncertain and having little confidence
4 all the people and things connected with an activity
5 belief and confidence in your own ability

08 **5 Look at the photos. Do you know how these people are connected to fashion? Listen and check your ideas.**

08 **6 Listen again and choose the correct options.**

1 The British Fashion Council gave out *one award* / *two awards* / *five awards* in 1984.
2 The Fashion Awards began in *1984* / *1989* / *2018*.
3 Kim Jones has won the *Best Menswear* / *Trailblazer* / *Shaping Fashion* award once.
4 *David* / *Victoria* Beckham's fashion brand is named after *himself* / *herself*.
5 Clare Waight Keller has won the *Outstanding Achievement* / *Designer of the Year* / *Luxury Fashion* award.
6 Kate Moss and Cara Delevingne have both won the *Best Fashion Model* / *Emerging Talent* / *Designer of the Year* award.

7 Complete the sentences with the words in the box.

clients	look	made	modelling	names

USEFUL LANGUAGE

Talking about people in the world of fashion

1 She .... a name for herself in modelling.
2 His .... can be described as 'expensive luxury meets street style'.
3 Her .... include Selena Gomez and Meghan Markle.
4 He is one of the up-and-coming .... in fashion.
5 Her .... career began when she was ten.

LONDON FASHION WITH A FRENCH ACCENT

09

Freddie Harrel is one of our favourite London fashion influencers. Well, actually, she was born in Paris, but after nearly a decade in London, she's completely in love with the British capital and its fashion **scene**! She began her career in the marketing department of the popular online fashion retailer ASOS. She then became a personal stylist, helping people decide on every aspect of their appearance, from hair to clothes to make-up, and later started her own fashion blog.

What we really like about Freddie, apart from her amazing style, is her honesty and openness. She has often talked about her low **self-esteem**, the difficulties she has faced in life, and how these have helped her become the person she is today. There is so much more to her than just fashion and stylish clothes. But it is through fashion that she has chosen to develop her self-confidence and to demonstrate it to the world.

At the start of her career in fashion, Freddie often dressed in clothes that she thought other people would like, following a traditional idea of what is considered beautiful and attractive. But she found that dressing in that way only made her feel **insecure** about her appearance. It was then that she decided to start to dress in clothes that were bright, bold and that **caught her eye**. Freddie realised how curious and creative she was, and that she could use clothes to reflect different aspects of her personality and feelings.

Freddie regularly writes for a range of fashion magazines, has her own blog and also creates videos about her unique style. She's got hundreds of thousands of followers on social media, and that number will only continue to grow as more and more people discover her. She's also attracted the attention of fashion-industry experts, winning several awards, including being named fashion influencer of the year by the well-known fashion magazine *Cosmopolitan*.

Freddie Harrel

Apart from her online presence as an influencer, Freddie also has her own company making hair products, and she runs **workshops** about style and self-confidence. During the workshops, she shares her personal experiences and tips to fight worries and insecurities. She also talks about how clothes and style are an excellent way to show your true personality. We think it's great that the world is listening to influencers like Freddie, as it shows that being a fashion influencer doesn't just have to be about fashion and that influencers can have a positive impact on people's lives in many different ways.

PROJECT *A fashion profile*

Write a profile of a fashion designer or influencer. Use the questions below to help you.

1. Where is the designer from?
2. What do his/her designs look like?
3. When did he/she start in fashion?
4. Does he/she have a particular look?
5. Has he/she won any awards?
6. Is he/she involved in any other activities?

Present your profile to the class.

03 NOW WATCH THE CULTURE VIDEO

3 ALL IN THE MIND

ABOUT YOU

What things are you naturally good at?
What things have you learned to be good at?
Do you think people can learn to be good at anything?

VOCABULARY Abstract nouns

10 **1 Read the paragraph about a podcast called *The debate*. Choose the correct words. Listen and check.**

EP

THE DEBATE

Is there finally [1] ***agreement*** / ***problem-solving*** in the debate over nature v nurture? Here's what the experts have to say.

One [2] ***success*** / ***belief*** is that we are born with a personality that never changes, with a fixed amount of intelligence and skills, such as being good at [3] ***development*** / ***problem-solving*** or communication. In other words, our [4] ***success*** / ***agreement*** in life is dictated by our genes: this is the 'nature' argument.

The other idea is that we start life as a blank sheet, and that our social and intellectual [5] ***development*** / ***success*** comes from our life experiences: this is the 'nurture' view.

New research appears to suggest that both sides in the debate are right to a certain extent.

11 **2 Listen to Clara and Yusuf talking about *The debate*. Are the sentences true or false?**

1 Yusuf has already listened to *The debate*.
2 According to the podcast, everyone has the genes to become a professional footballer.
3 You need the right genes and the right environment to be successful.
4 According to the podcast, people can become more intelligent by working hard.

11 **3 Complete the sentences with the abstract nouns in the box. Listen again and check.**

ambition	drive	luck	thought

1 You need the ________ to be born with the right genes.
2 You need more than just ________ to become a professional footballer.
3 Students who have the ________ to study hard can actually become more intelligent.
4 Maybe the same is true for your sporting ability. I'll give that some ________!

4 Complete the sentences with the correct abstract nouns from Exercises 1 and 3.

1 Have you got the necessary ________ to work hard and be successful?
2 I'm sure you'll win. I wish you good ________!
3 Are we in ________ that you can't be successful if you don't work hard?
4 Some people think ________ means having a big house and a fancy car.
5 It's important to give your future some ________ so you can prepare well for it.
6 I'm not very good at ________. I usually ask someone else what to do.
7 Chico's not very confident and he doesn't have a lot of ________ in himself.
8 I think personal ________ is really important – we should keep improving ourselves.
9 Katya's ________ is to become a physicist, but first she'll need to improve her maths.

5 Discuss the questions.

1 What is your opinion of the nature v nurture debate?
2 What do you think are signs of success?

READING

1 Look at the photos and read the title of the article. In what ways do you think that humans are smarter than other species? Read the article quickly and check your ideas.

PREPARE FOR THE EXAM

Reading and Use of English Part 6

2 Six sentences have been removed from the article. Read sentences A–G and notice the underlined words. What do you think they might refer to?

A Some psychologists have trained one to recognise over 1,000 words for things such as this.
B However, research suggests that they can't put individual words together to form complex sentences.
C It was using a rock to crack open a shell containing one of its favourite foods.
D It is the moment when they realise that the image they see is actually of themselves.
E It has got a bigger brain, but brain size doesn't equal intelligence.
F This happens whether or not they belong to the same family, and they will even help outsiders.
G This involves being able to imagine what it must be like to be in someone else's situation.

HUMANS: THE SMARTEST SPECIES?

12

Many animals are said to be intelligent, and some live up to this reputation in surprising and charming ways: whales sing, dolphins enjoy showing off with toys, parrots pick up language and, apparently, an octopus has even learned to take the lid off a jar! This demonstrates a certain amount of drive and determination, but does it mean animals are as intelligent as humans?

There are five commonly recognised signs of intelligence: the ability to make and use tools; problem-solving; the ability to communicate and understand; the capacity for abstract thought (for example, adding numbers up); and the psychological qualities of self-awareness and empathy, among others. The first of these psychological qualities is the ability to realise that you are an individual who is separate from other individuals. Most children start to show basic signs of empathy at an early age. [1] .... For example, they understand that a friend who has lost his favourite toy must feel upset.

Our ancestors started using stone tools more than 2.5 million years ago. Scientists used to believe that only humans possessed this skill, but we now know that some animals also use tools. Chimpanzees make some unusual ones, from stick brushes for collecting ants to pointed sticks for weapons. Brown bears rub stones against themselves to remove dirt and dead skin from their fur. Even a crab was filmed recently with a tool! [2] ....

Both understanding and producing language are obvious signs of intelligence. Although a dog can't talk, it can understand the names of objects in instructions such as 'Fetch the ball!'. [3] .... It can also understand verb + noun commands in English, like 'Pick the toy up!', including combinations of verb + noun that it hasn't heard before. This is similar to the understanding of a human child, aged two.

Most animals make sounds to communicate with each other; dolphins make clicking noises, dogs bark and so on. When some parrots hear human language, they can pick it up and repeat it, often to great comic effect. [4] .... Some chimpanzees 'talk' to humans using sign language, but what they are able to say is fairly limited. Only humans are able to use language with detailed grammar.

There is an interesting test for self-awareness: the mirror test. For humans, the 'mirror stage' occurs around 15–18 months old. [5] .... To test this with animals, scientists draw a coloured spot on an animal's face. An animal that recognises itself in a mirror always tries to touch or remove the spot. Most animals can't recognise themselves in the reflection in a mirror. Only a small number of animals, including elephants, dolphins and great apes (chimpanzees, gorillas and orangutans) realise they are looking at themselves.

Perhaps the hardest intelligence test of all is for empathy. Empathy is extremely rare in animals, though elephants appear to display it. They are aware of others, care for each other when they are ill, and work together to protect young ones. [6] .... This kind of behaviour is fascinating, but it is the chimpanzee that is by far the cleverest in the animal kingdom. Some baby chimps have even beaten people in a memory test of numbers! But even though chimpanzees are good at problem-solving and abstract thought, they still can't light fires, cook food or make clothes, which means they are still behind humans when it comes to being the smartest species on Earth.

3 Read the example answer. Notice how the underlined words can help you to decide which is the correct answer.

1G: 'This' refers to 'empathy' before the gap. The missing sentence provides a definition of empathy, and an example is provided in the sentence following the gap.

4 Choose from the sentences A–F the one which fits each gap (2–6). Use the underlined words to help you decide. There is one extra sentence which you do not need to use.

» PREPARE FOR THE EXAM PAGE 126

TALKING POINTS

In which ways do you think human beings are not especially smart?

To what extent do humans depend on animals?

Does mankind show animals enough respect? How? / Why not?

GRAMMAR The grammar of phrasal verbs

1 Underline the phrasal verbs in the examples.

1 Some animals live up to this reputation in surprising ways.
2 Dolphins enjoy showing off.
3 They care for each other when they are ill.
4 They have the capacity for abstract thought (for example, adding numbers up).
5 When some parrots hear human language, they can pick it up and repeat it.

2 Match the phrasal verbs in Exercise 1 to the types of phrasal verb in the rules.

There are four types of phrasal verb:

a phrasal verbs without an object
Our car broke down last night.

b separable phrasal verbs with an object
I switched off the TV.
OR *I switched the TV off.*
I switched it off. (NOT ~~*I switched off it.*~~)

c inseparable phrasal verbs with an object
Can you deal with this problem?
Can you deal with it?
(NOT ~~*Can you deal this problem/it with?*~~)

d inseparable three-part phrasal verbs
I'm looking forward to the weekend.

» GRAMMAR REFERENCE AND PRACTICE PAGE 150

3 Read the email. Choose the correct phrasal verbs. In one answer, both options are possible.

I have some bad news about my visit. I'm really sorry, but I need to [1] *put off it / put it off* again. It's my best friend's birthday party the same weekend and I'm helping to organise it. I can't really [2] *get it out of / get out of it*. It's such a pity, as I've been [3] *looking forward to it / looking it forward to*. I'm sorry to [4] *let down you / let you down*. I've even bought my train tickets! I can't get a refund, so I'll have to [5] *throw them away / throw away them*, which is a bit annoying! Are you free on 30th May instead? I think I can get away then. I'd love you to [6] *show around me / show me around* the city. Maybe you could [7] *book us in / book in us* at a restaurant? I will be there, I promise! By the way, please [8] *pass on my thanks / pass my thanks on* to your brother for the book he lent me. It was great!

4 Correct the mistake in each sentence.

1 It's interesting that elephants care each other for when they are sick.
2 I hope this restaurant lives up its reputation!
3 The bus broke it down on the way to the airport.
4 Have you finished with the computer? Don't switch off it – I'll use it now.
5 Please pass my good wishes to your mum!

VOCABULARY Phrasal verbs: learning and thinking

1 Read the sentences and match the phrasal verbs to the meanings (a–f). Which phrasal verb does not need an object?

1 Don't make any sudden decisions about that job offer. **Think** it **through** carefully before you decide.
2 My brother wanted to go to the University of Durham, but he didn't **get in**.
3 Have you **backed up** your work yet? You wouldn't want to lose it all.
4 You've got to **face up to** it sometime. The problem won't go away.
5 Mateo always **mixes up** the words *Tuesday* and *Thursday* in English.
6 Please **focus on** your work, everyone – no chatting!

a make an extra copy of something held on a computer
b confuse two people or things
c succeed in being chosen for a team or educational institution
d give a lot of attention to
e accept that a difficult situation exists
f carefully consider the possible results of doing something

2 Are the phrasal verbs separable (S) or inseparable (I)? Which sentences have a mistake? Correct the mistakes.

1 I just can't focus anything on today. I've got a headache.
2 I'm going to think my plan through and check I haven't forgotten anything.
3 My cousin is having a party because he got King's College into.
4 You have to face your problems up to. They won't go away on their own.
5 I'm just backing my work up. I'll be with you in a minute.
6 You've mixed our books up. That one's mine.

3 Discuss the questions.

1 Which university is the most difficult to get into in your country?
2 Are you good at focusing on your homework?
3 Which words do you mix up in English?
4 Have you ever come up with a great solution to a problem?

WRITING An informal letter or email

1 Discuss the questions.

1 What new skills have you learned recently?
2 What is the best way to learn a new skill?

2 Read the task, then read Rob's email. Has Rob answered all Alex's questions?

You have received this email from your friend Alex.

> Can you help me with my class project? I have to write about the ways in which people learn a new skill. Please tell me about a skill you have picked up recently. How have you developed this skill? What aspects of it have you found difficult? Would you recommend that other teenagers take up the same skill?
>
> Thanks, Alex

Write your **email**.

Hi Alex

It's great to hear from you. Actually, I got a lifeguard qualification earlier this year, so now I'm spending most Saturdays down at the beach. We're there to help swimmers and surfers who get into difficulties, and this could be pretty scary without any training.

Anyway, to get qualified, I did a course at my local pool. I thought it through carefully before I signed up for it. I'm a strong swimmer and I've always been quite fit, so I got through the physical parts of the course fine, but I found all the stuff on first-aid techniques really challenging. I'm fine with it all now though, and I've picked up loads of practical tips from the more experienced guys I'm working with.

You need to be 15 for lifeguard training. Plus you must be in good shape. The thing is, other people will be relying on your strength and fitness in risky situations and you can't let them down.

Keep in touch!

Rob

3 Read the *Prepare to write* box, and read Rob's email again. Find:

a an opening expression
b a closing expression
c four phrasal verbs
d four other examples of informal language

PREPARE TO WRITE Informal letters and emails

In informal letters and emails

- use an informal opening expression.
  How nice to get your news!
  It's great to hear from you.
  Thanks for your email.
- use informal expressions to add ideas.
  To start with, … *Also …* *Plus …*
- use informal language and phrasal verbs.
  I reckon … *Anyway, …* *The thing is …*
  I pick things up quickly.
- use contracted forms.
  don't *can't* *wouldn't*
- use an informal closing expression.
  Take care *Write soon* *Love*
  Keep in touch

4 Find informal sentences and expressions in the email to match the formal sentences and expressions below.

1 It was very pleasing to receive your email.
2 Our job is to assist swimmers and surfers who experience difficulties.
3 This could be rather daunting without training.
4 It is also important that you have a good level of fitness.

5 Rob has not answered the final question in the task. Write a fourth paragraph to Rob's email, answering this question.

PREPARE FOR THE EXAM

Writing Part 2 (An informal letter or email)

6 Read the task and plan your answer.

This is part of an email you received from your English-speaking penfriend, Toni.

> I'd like to learn a language because I can only speak English. Do you think language learning is easy? What's the best way to learn new words? I'd like to learn your language. Can you suggest how I should start learning your language?
>
> Write back soon!
>
> Toni

Write your **email**.

7 Write your email to Toni.

- Answer all of Toni's questions.
- Use the tips in the *Prepare to write* box.
- Check your grammar and spelling.
- Write 140–190 words.

4 TAKE IT EASY

ABOUT YOU

Which of these situations typically make you feel stressed?

the amount of homework you have
not having enough money
getting ready for parties
arguing with friends/family

Can you think of other situations?

VOCABULARY Stress

13 **1** **Listen to eight situations and match them to the photos.**

2 **Match the words and phrases to the photos.**

EP

faint feel dizzy get in a panic
go over and over something in your mind
have difficulty sleeping have an upset stomach
lose your temper lose your appetite

3 **Discuss the questions.**

1 When was the last time you lost your temper?
2 Do you ever get in a panic about exams?
3 Have you ever had difficulty sleeping? When?

READING

1 **Read the headings for an article about stress. Do you agree or disagree? Compare your answers in pairs.**

A Stress is for adults, not people my age.
B A bit of stress helps me to get things done.
C It's not my fault that I get stressed.
D I know how to deal with stress.
E Everyone gets stressed from time to time. It's no big deal.

2 **Read the article quickly. Match the headings in Exercise 1 to parts 1–5 of the article. Use the sentence(s) in bold at the end of each paragraph to help you choose the heading that follows.**

3 **Read the article again. Complete the sentences with one or two words in each gap.**

1 The article suggests that most teenagers have fewer reasons to ________ than adults.
2 The author believes that stress is about more ________ deadlines.
3 Hormones released in stressful situations can both ________ and ________ our energy levels.
4 The article strongly recommends finding time in your day-to-day life ________ and also to relax.
5 Psychologists advise people to try and see the ________ in stressful situations.

14 UNDER PRESSURE?

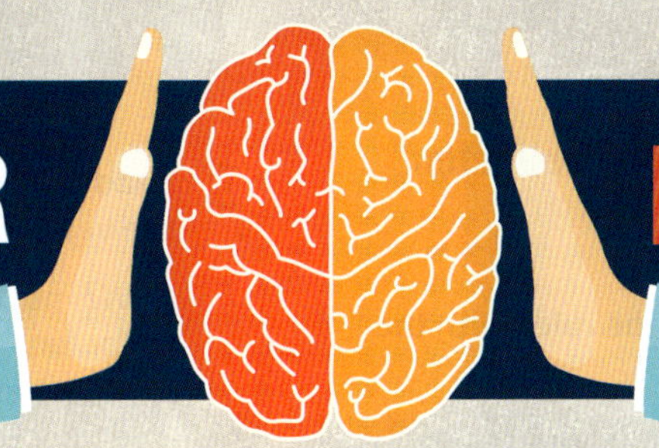

1 *A Stress is for adults, not people my age.*

Which of these two types of people is more stressed: a parent who has to go to work to earn money to pay bills and bring up a family, or a teenager who has to go to school to study? Surveys report that 75% of adults say they feel stressed on at least three occasions every week. However, an astonishing 85% of teenagers between 14 and 17 say the same thing. What's more, a third of the girls and half of the boys believe the pressure is there every single day. In this age group, the three most frequent causes of stress are schoolwork, parents and problems with friends. **But isn't this just part of life?**

2 ____________________

Very few of us would say we never get stressed. But what does stress mean to you? Is it a piece of work you need to finish for school? Perhaps it's a class you mustn't be late for. If stress was just about deadlines, we would probably be able to keep it under control. However, for most people, it's bigger than this. And it can be a very big deal. But could we get rid of it from our lives? **Do we actually want to?**

3 ____________________

When we are stressed, our body responds to the danger by releasing chemicals called *hormones*. They temporarily increase our heart rate and boost our energy levels. Thousands of years ago, we used this energy to avoid getting attacked by wild animals. So, in small doses, many people find that stress can motivate them. But constant stress can have the opposite effect, leading to feelings of anxiety. At this point, hormones actually lower our energy levels and we risk suffering from a whole range of health problems, such as having difficulty sleeping or losing your appetite. **So how do we avoid this?**

4 ____________________

Most of us know the basics of how to handle stress: we should take regular exercise and eat healthily. Sleep is also important. According to some reports, teenagers ought to get over nine hours of sleep every night. But fighting stress needn't be boring. We must also make some time in our schedule for fun, preferably with friends, and also a little quiet time, when we can relax. We should spend time around positive people, who don't get us down. Helping other people can help us feel less stressed, too, which is why volunteering is a good idea. And if you're getting in a panic, stop what you are doing and take several deep breaths. Pause for a moment and think about all the good things in your life. **Have you tried that? Is everything (or everyone) still stressing you out?**

5 ____________________

A common belief is that our stress comes from all the things we have to do because of *other* people. However, some psychologists believe it's more helpful to think of stress as how we *react* to the things that stress us. The reason is that these things are beyond our control, but we *can* control how we react to them. We've just got to find the right way. One thing we can do is to look for the positive in situations. When your parents say you can't go away with your friends for the weekend because it's too expensive, think of it as an opportunity to do something at home instead. You don't have to choose something boring, like organising your wardrobe: you could spend a day practising that new skateboarding trick or catching up on your favourite TV programmes. Of course, there may be things you *do* have to do before you can go and enjoy yourself. Do you have a tricky essay to write that's due in next week? You'd better do *that*, **but maybe you could see it as a challenge rather than a chore.**

TALKING POINTS

Do you think teenagers get stressed as much as adults?

What do you think is the best way to deal with stress?

GRAMMAR Modals (1): necessity, obligation, prohibition and advice

1 **Read the examples. Then complete the rules with the verbs in the examples.**

1 You **don't have to** choose something boring.
2 We **should** take regular exercise.
3 Teenagers **ought to** get over nine hours of sleep every night.
4 Fighting stress **needn't** be boring.
5 Is it a piece of work you **need to** finish for school?
6 Do you have a tricky essay to write that's due in next week? You**'d better** do that.

We use
a ________, *had better* or *ought to* for advice.
b ________ for necessity.
c ________, (*haven't got to*) or *needn't* for lack of obligation.

» GRAMMAR REFERENCE AND PRACTICE PAGE 151

PREPARE FOR THE EXAM

Reading and Use of English Part 4

2 **Complete the second sentence so that it has a similar meaning to the first sentence, using the word given. Do not change the word given. You must use between two and five words, including the word given.**

0 Getting plenty of sleep is necessary when you're very busy. **SHOULD**
You *should get a* lot of sleep when you're very busy.

1 Clare knew that she had to complete all her homework by Friday. **NECESSARY**
Clare knew that ________ her to complete all her homework by Friday.

2 'You need to get to my party on time!' said Daisy. **HAD**
'You ________ late for my party!' said Daisy.

3 There's no need to attend the extra classes. **HAVE**
You ________ to the extra classes.

4 'You needn't wear your uniforms for the school trip,' said the teacher. **DO**
'You ________ wear your uniforms for the school trip,' said the teacher.

5 It would be a good idea if I went to bed early tonight. **OUGHT**
I ________ to bed early tonight.

6 There's no need for me to help my dad. **GOT**
I ________ help my dad now.

» PREPARE FOR THE EXAM PAGE 123

3 **Read the examples and complete the rules with the verbs.**

1 We **must** also make some time in our schedule for fun.
2 Our stress comes from all the things we **have to** do because of other people.
3 It's a class you **mustn't** be late for.
4 We**'ve** just **got to** find the right way.

We use
a ________ for prohibition.
b ________, ________ or ________ for obligation.
c *must* or *have got to* when the obligation is our personal opinion.
d ________ when the obligation is not our personal opinion.

4 **Correct the mistake in each sentence.**

1 Simon must to control his temper more.
2 You don't have to use my things without asking first!
3 I really think you can take regular exercise because it's good for you.
4 I'll meet you later because I should go to the doctor's at 3 pm.
5 I haven't done any exercise for ages. I've better do some this week.
6 You haven't eat too much when you're studying or you'll feel sleepy.

5 **Complete the sentences with your own ideas.**

1 I really should …
2 Every day, I have to …
3 At school, we don't have to …
4 Tomorrow, I must …
5 Students mustn't …
6 My parents say I ought to …

VOCABULARY Phrasal verbs: health

1 **Match the phrasal verbs to the meanings.**

EP 1 I **threw up** after that meal. I think I'm allergic to shellfish!
2 It's taken me weeks to **get over** this flu.
3 Arguing with my friends really **gets** me **down**.
4 I slowly **came round** after the operation.
5 We all **came down with** food poisoning in the evening, so we couldn't go out.
6 When I lose my temper, I find it difficult to **calm down** quickly.

a feel less annoyed or stressed
b make someone feel unhappy
c feel better after an illness or an unhappy event
d be awake again after being unconscious
e become ill
f vomit/be sick (informal)

2 » **Work in pairs.** **Turn to page 138.**

LISTENING

15 **1 You will hear a boy talking about stress. Read the sentences carefully. Then listen and decide which of the sentences (A–H) is true for the boy.**

A I don't suffer badly from stress.
B Schoolwork and family make me stressed the most.
C I have a range of ways to deal with stress.
D The future is my biggest cause of stress.
E Physical activity is my main way of fighting stress.
F I don't like how I behave when I'm stressed.
G I followed advice on a technique for dealing with stress.
H Arguing with other people makes me stressed.

2 Read the reasons why A–D in Exercise 1 are true or not true for the boy. Work in pairs and decide why E–H are not true.

A Not true. He says he does get stressed.
B Not true. Exams stress the boy, but he only mentions talking to his parents.
C True. He says he does a variety of things to keep stress under control.
D Not true. He doesn't mention the future.

PREPARE FOR THE EXAM

Listening Part 3

16 **3 You will hear four more teenagers talking about stress. For questions 2–5, choose from the list (A–H) what each speaker says about it. Use the letters only once. There are three extra letters which you do not need to use.**

Speaker 1 ...C...
Speaker 2 ....
Speaker 3 ....
Speaker 4 ....
Speaker 5 ....

SPEAKING Offering help

17 **1 Listen to the conversation. What is Ben going to do for Olivia?**

17 **2 Listen again and complete the phrases.**

like	need	shall	sure

1 .... I take the games for you?
2 Are you ....? That'd be fantastic, thanks.
3 I'll text you when I leave here if you ....
4 Thanks, but there's no ....

18 **3 Listen to a conversation between Noah and his mother. Answer the questions.**

1 Who offers to help who?
2 What offers are made?
3 What does Noah's mother really want him to do?

18 **4 Read the *Prepare to speak* box. Then listen again. Which phrases do Noah and his mother use?**

PREPARE TO SPEAK | Making offers

Making offers
Would you like me to ... ?
Shall I ... ?
Let me ...
I'll ... if you like.

Refusing offers
It's OK, I can do it myself.
No, don't worry. I can manage that.
Thanks, but there's no need.

Accepting offers
It'd be great if you could.
Are you sure? That'd be fantastic, thanks.

5 Write down all the things you need to do this week. Which of them could someone else help with?

6 Work in pairs. Then change roles.

Student A Tell Student B about your list.
Student B Make offers to Student A.
Student A Respond to the offers appropriately.

I've got to finish a project, get some new trainers and buy a birthday present for my dad.

Let me help you with your dad's birthday present.

It'd be great if you could.

LIFE SKILLS LEARNING TO LEARN

TIME MANAGEMENT

LIFE SKILLS

Time management

Life can be very busy! Balancing your school life with your social life and free-time activities can often be tough. Managing your time effectively is a key skill to develop and has many benefits, such as reducing anxiety, performing better at school, and finding it easier to make decisions.

1 **Ask and answer the questions with a partner.**

1. How often do you feel that you don't have enough time to do everything you need to do? Why?
2. How do you feel when you finish work at the last minute or do things late?
3. What kind of things distract or interrupt you when you're trying to concentrate?

2 **Look at the headings and the three photos in the article on the opposite page. Match photos A–C to three of the headings 1–5. Read the article quickly and check your ideas.**

3 **Read the article again and answer the questions.**

1. Is making a list of distractions enough to deal with them? Why? / Why not?
2. What does organisation involve, apart from having everything tidy and in order?
3. What are some of the main reasons for putting something off?
4. Why is it a good idea to start with short periods when you first try using 'timeboxes'?
5. Why shouldn't we do things we like all the time?

4 **Match the highlighted words and phrases in the article to the meanings.**

1. deciding to delay something until a later time
2. a time by which something must be done
3. dealt with something or a situation
4. blocks or pieces of something
5. a very difficult task which requires a big effort

5 **Which of the time management tips from the article do you think are the most useful? Can you think of any other time management tips?**

19 **6** **Look at the chart. How could this be used to help your time management? Listen to a talk on time management for university students and check your ideas.**

URGENCY (HIGH ← → LOW); **IMPORTANCE** (HIGH ↑ ↓ LOW)

	HIGH urgency	LOW urgency
HIGH importance	**1** Important **and** urgent. You should **do it now.**	**2** Important but **not** urgent. **Do it later.**
LOW importance	**3** Urgent but **not** important. **Ask** someone else **to do it.**	**4** **Not** urgent and **not** important. **Don't waste your time!**

19 **7** **Read the following notes, which a student made in the talk. Listen again and complete them with one or two words in each gap.**

Planning

- is a crucial [1] ______
- creating a study schedule is a [2] ______
- include weekly plan & long-term goals
- helps establish a [3] ______

Study patterns

- pay attention to your own unique study [4] ______
- work out optimum study methods
- have a designated [5] ______
- experiment with study patterns
- alternate between [6] ______ and [7] ______ tasks

Prioritising

- focus on what [8] ______
- balance multiple demands
- use a time matrix to [9] ______ from 1 to 4 by urgency & importance

8 **Complete the sentences with the words in the box.**

behind	commitments	meet	minute	stick

USEFUL LANGUAGE

Talking about time management

1. I'm getting ______ with my project.
2. This will help you to ______ deadlines.
3. A study planner will help you to ______ to a schedule.
4. Don't leave things until the last ______!
5. Prioritising tasks will ensure that you meet your ______.

TOP FIVE TIME MANAGEMENT TIPS

20

The majority of adults find managing their time a struggle, and your teenage years can be just as challenging. Trying to split your time between different demands – academic, social, family – can often be a real headache. Learning how to manage your time well will help you to avoid getting behind with your work and to feel calmer and less stressed. Here are our top five tips to get you started.

1 DEAL WITH DISTRACTIONS

Try making a list of all the ways you get distracted. Looking at your phone will be on it, but there will be lots of other things, too. Next, decide how you can control each of the distractions on your list. For example, keeping your phone out of reach or putting it away while you're doing your homework will help you finish a lot faster. You'll be amazed at how much more productive you can be when you've dealt with distractions.

A

B

2 GET ORGANISED

Everything is so much quicker and easier with good organisation. So, before you start studying, make sure that you've got your books, notes and anything else you'll need at hand. Being organised is also about estimating how long tasks or projects will take before you begin them, and making sure that you'll have enough time to dedicate to them. And if you haven't left yourself enough time, always ask for an extension in advance so that your teachers know you need more time to complete something. Never wait until a deadline to announce a delay.

3 DON'T PUT THINGS OFF

Not finishing your work on time, being late, or leaving things until the last minute are all signs of putting things off. Learning to start early enough is a key time management skill. We often avoid starting tasks that we think will be difficult, stressful or unpleasant. But in fact, when we actually start them, we almost always discover that they are not quite as bad as we thought. And often we even end up enjoying doing the thing that we were putting off!

C

4 TIMEBOX

So you've tackled distractions, got yourself organised and stopped putting things off, but are you still finding it difficult to manage your time? Well, it sounds like it's time to try 'timeboxing'. The basic idea here is to set a fixed period of time, or a 'timebox', which you use to do a planned activity. Limiting the number of minutes you work on something will help you break tasks down into manageable chunks and allow you to divide your time between different demands. Start with realistic timeboxes of 5, 10 or 15 minutes and you'll soon see the results.

5 WORK FIRST, PLAY LATER

There's usually something else you'd prefer to be doing instead of studying, like trying to improve your score on the latest game, chatting to friends, or watching a series you're hooked on. Of course, we enjoy these things and they make us feel good. But we also know that we can't do them all the time because then they wouldn't be special any more. So try keeping some things you enjoy doing as a reward for when you finish your work, or complete a number of timeboxes. You'll feel much happier with yourself because you've worked hard for it!

PROJECT

A time management poster

Work in groups of three or four to talk about your own time management. Use these steps to help you.

1. Tell your group about the areas of time management which you find most challenging.
2. Choose time management tips from the article and university tutorial which you would like to try.
3. Don't just think about the present. Which tips and strategies would you like to develop now that could be useful for you in the future?
4. Search online for other time management tips and advice and share what you find with your group.
5. Design a mini-poster with personalised time management tips. Place the poster inside the cover of your notebook or use it as a desktop image.

Present your poster to the class.

REVIEW 1 UNITS 1–4

VOCABULARY

1 Match the words to the meanings.

bestseller broadcast cast
the charts shoot track

1 show a programme on TV, radio or online
2 all the actors in a film, play or show
3 one song or piece of music on an album
4 an official list of the most popular songs each week
5 use a camera to record a film or take a photo
6 a very popular book that many people have bought

2 Complete the conversations. Use the word pairs in the box in the correct form and the correct order.

bothered / cope jealous / compare critical / do
hopeless / decisive impressed / adventurous

1 **A:** Would you say you are a ________ person? I mean, do you make your mind up quickly about things?
B: Not really! In fact, I'm completely ________ at deciding what to do.
2 **A:** I think our football manager is quite ________ of us – we never seem to do anything right!
B: I know. We could ________ without his negative comments.
3 **A:** People often ________ me with my 'clever' sister.
B: Do you ever get ________ of her?
4 **A:** Sofia has never had trouble ________ with exam stress.
B: No, but she never gets ________ about anything.
5 **A:** I was really ________ by Alex's art project.
B: Yes, he's been really ________ with colour, hasn't he?

3 Match the phrasal verbs in the box to the meanings.

back up face up to focus on
get through mix up think through

1 make an extra copy of something held on a computer
2 succeed, e.g. in an exam
3 confuse two people or things
4 give a lot of attention to
5 carefully consider the possible results of something
6 accept that a difficult situation exists

4 Choose the correct verb to complete each phrase.

1 *catch / have / feel* an upset stomach
2 *drop / lose / forget* your temper
3 *take / think / go* over and over things in your mind
4 *lose / feel / be* your appetite
5 *have / get / feel* difficulty sleeping
6 *have / go / get* in a panic

GRAMMAR

1 Choose the correct options.

Tavi Gevinson was just 11 when she [1] *started / had started* her fashion blog, *Style Rookie*. On it, she [2] *posted / was posting* pictures of herself and wrote descriptions of her clothes. At first, people thought the site was fake and that a fashion expert [3] *set / had set* it up. But within a few years, Tavi's site [4] *is attracting / was attracting* thousands of readers. *Rookie*, an online magazine Tavi [5] *has been running / is running* since she was 15, grew from the blog. Tavi [6] *has acted / acted* in several roles in the last few years and has been named one of the most influential teens in the world.

2 Complete the sentences with the present perfect simple or continuous form of the verbs in the box. Use the same verb in each pair of sentences.

do ring run try

1 a I can come out now. I ________ my revision.
b I ________ homework for three hours.
2 a You look hot. ________ you ________?
b ________ you ever ________ a marathon?
3 a Dan ________ to help me with this maths for hours, but I still don't understand it.
b I ________ doing more exercise, but it doesn't seem to help.
4 a Clare ________ you several times today.
b Where have you been? I ________ you all morning.

3 Rewrite the underlined part of the sentences with the correct form of the phrasal verbs in the box and a pronoun if necessary.

come across come down with hand out
look after ~~make up~~ pass out throw away

0 No way! I think you <u>invented it</u>! *made it up*
1 Look at this old computer. I <u>found it</u> in the garage.
2 He <u>lost consciousness</u> when he saw the blood.
3 The teacher gave me the papers and asked me to <u>distribute them</u>.
4 I've got a cold. I <u>became ill with it</u> yesterday.
5 My brother's 11. I <u>take care of him</u> sometimes.
6 I don't have any DVDs. I <u>got rid of them</u> recently.

4 Correct the mistake in each sentence.

1 You don't have to get in a panic. It will only make things worse.
2 You needn't be more adventurous with food. Just try things!
3 We have better get going or we'll miss the flight.
4 I'm exhausted. I shouldn't go to bed earlier!
5 I know that your birthday is next week. You mustn't remind me.

PREPARE FOR THE EXAM

Reading and Use of English Part 1

1 **For questions 1–8, read the text below and decide which answer (A, B, C or D) best fits each gap.**

WANNA BE A FILM CRITIC?

You don't have to have a degree in film studies to **(0)** *review* films. Anyone can be a critic: all you need is to watch the latest **(1)** ________ at the cinema and write about them somewhere online, perhaps through a blog or social media page. However, **(2)** ________ a qualification in the field will make people **(3)** ________ what you have to say more seriously.

What is the day-to-day life of a critic like? Well, he or she may **(4)** ________ several films a day. It may sound like fun, but for every film they see, a critic must **(5)** ________ careful attention to the acting **(6)** ________, the soundtrack, the photography and the costumes. Critics have to make notes at the same time, and may even watch the same film over and over again! They will almost certainly discuss the **(7)** ________ in their critique, and, once it's **(8)** ________, deal with feedback from people who disagree with what they've written. It isn't as easy as it sounds!

	A	B	C	D
0	**(A)** review	**B** remark	**C** reflect	**D** respond
1	**A** versions	**B** updates	**C** releases	**D** episodes
2	**A** winning	**B** obtaining	**C** collecting	**D** establishing
3	**A** take	**B** get	**C** hold	**D** catch
4	**A** glance	**B** regard	**C** observe	**D** view
5	**A** place	**B** bring	**C** pay	**D** note
6	**A** performances	**B** displays	**C** presentations	**D** shows
7	**A** editor	**B** presenter	**C** novelist	**D** director
8	**A** broadcast	**B** published	**C** reported	**D** announced

Reading and Use of English Part 2

2 **For questions 1–8, read the text below and think of the word which best fits each gap. Use only one word in each gap.**

Fast fashion

If you **(0)** *have* ever bought a trendy T-shirt from a high street shop for £5, then you already know what fast fashion is: cheap clothing that you wear a few times before it wears **(1)** ________. So many of us are addicted **(2)** ________ shopping, and with such bargains to be found, it's no wonder. It's great to be able to show off our purchases to friends and, even better, to tell them **(3)** ________ little we paid for it! And, of course, fast fashion seems a great idea when you're a student and haven't **(4)** ________ earning much while you study.

Unfortunately, we need to face **(5)** ________ to the fact that 'cheap' refers not only to the price, but the wages, too. Fast fashion, as its name suggests, **(6)** ________ produced quickly, and in order to achieve this quick 'turnaround', people **(7)** ________ to sit at machines for long hours, for little pay. We must respond to what's happening in the industry and buy more expensive items **(8)** ________ last for longer.

Reading and Use of English Part 4

3 **For questions 1–6, complete the second sentence so that it has a similar meaning to the first sentence, using the word given. Do not change the word given. You must use between two and five words, including the word given.**

0 It's been four years since I started to write this blog. **BEEN**
I *have been writing* this blog for four years.

1 Simon has got flu, so can't play in today's match. **COME**
Simon has ________ flu, so can't play in today's match.

2 It's been a long time since I spoke to Jo. **FOR**
Jo and I ________ a long time.

3 Have you figured out the maths problem yet? **UP**
Have you ________ solution to the maths problem yet?

4 Seeing a doctor is something you should do if you aren't feeling well. **OUGHT**
You ________ a doctor if you aren't feeling well.

5 'I'm sorry I was late,' said James. **APOLOGISED**
James ________ late.

6 Wearing a uniform isn't necessary for students at my school. **NEED**
Students at my school ________ a uniform.

5 PAST TIMES

ABOUT YOU

Which periods of history have you studied at school?
Which periods of history do you find interesting? Why?
What do you know about the history of your local area?

VOCABULARY History

EP **1** **Read the quiz. Check the meaning of the words.**

21 **2** **Do the quiz with your partner. Listen and check. What extra information do you hear?**

3 **Discuss the questions.**

1. In which decade and century were you born? What about your parents?
2. Do women in your country have the vote? When did they get it?
3. Which town/state/region/country are you an inhabitant of?

HISTORY Quiz

1. On which continent did our earliest ancestors live?
   a Africa b America c Asia
2. What was New York City called when it was founded in 1624?
   a New London b New Paris c New Amsterdam
3. Which tribe of women from an ancient myth gave their name to a South American river?
   a the Amazons b the Centaurs c the Titans
4. In which century was the car invented?
   a the 18th century b the 19th century c the 20th century
5. In 1900, which country had the most citizens?
   a Russia b India c China
6. Which city had the most inhabitants in 1900?
   a New York b Tokyo c London
7. In which decade was television first broadcast to the public?
   a 1930s b 1950s c 1970s
8. When did all women over 21 get the vote in the UK?
   a 1900 b 1918 c 1928

READING

PREPARE FOR THE EXAM

Reading and Use of English Part 2

1 **Read the example answer (0) in the first paragraph of the text. What other word could you use instead of *if*?**

2 **For questions 1–8, read the first paragraph of the text and think of the word which best fits each gap. Use the ideas below to help.**

- Look at the words before and after each gap.
- Use only **one** word in each gap.
- There may be more than one correct answer.

» PREPARE FOR THE EXAM PAGE 121

3 **Read the questions and discuss possible answers.**

1. What alternatives can you think of to an eight-hour sleep?
2. How did sleeping habits change after the invention of artificial lighting?
3. How do the sleep patterns of different cultures and different age groups compare?
4. What is a 'siesta'?
5. What is a 'body clock'?

4 **Read the rest of the text and check your answers.**

5 **Complete the sentences with highlighted words and phrases from the text.**

1. How long do you ________ sleep at night?
2. I often have a quick ________ after lunch – eating makes me tired!
3. I never realised, but it ________ that we are at the same school.
4. Did you know that watching TV immediately before bed ________ your sleep?
5. The use of screens in bed is quite ________, but negatively affects sleep.

WE USED TO
SLEEP TWICE A NIGHT ...

22

What happens **(0)** *if* you wake up in the middle of the night? Do you have difficulty falling asleep again? Perhaps you're someone **(1)** .... becomes frustrated because you can't get back **(2)** .... sleep straightaway. Then you might begin to get in a panic about being tired the next day, or about problems you **(3)** .... experiencing, and you go over and over things in your head. Or perhaps you **(4)** .... woken up after a nightmare and the negative images are still in your mind. Whatever your sleeping habits, in **(5)** .... 21st century, being awake at night is generally regarded as problematic. This is logical, of course: there's **(6)** .... point being awake when everyone else is asleep. And if you end up being awake all night, you'll be **(7)** .... tired to cope well the following day. Even **(8)** .... in most parts of the world a 'good night's sleep' means more or less eight hours without interruption, it turns out that the concept of an eight-hour sleep is fairly recent.

Naturally, history textbooks tend to only record memorable accounts of wars and empires, of love and death, or bravery and determination. Sleep is something we take for granted, so it rarely comes up. You may have heard that our ancestors used to have two 'sleeps'. This isn't a myth. Historians have noticed references to a 'first sleep' and a 'second sleep' in documents covering several centuries, and in reference to different countries. The first sleep started after sunset and lasted until around midnight. Then people would lie awake for a while and chat or pray. Some neighbours even used to take the opportunity to visit each other between sleeps. After a few hours, they would have their second sleep, which lasted until dawn. In countries with long hours of daylight in summer, people would start work as early as four or five o'clock in the morning.

Artificial lights weren't common a few centuries ago. Only the rich could afford candles and, without electricity, nobody could do anything when it was dark. By the end of the 19th century, lighting had become more widespread as cities installed gas streetlights and domestic gas lamps appeared. All of a sudden, most people had lights and could stay up late if they wanted to. By the time electric lighting was introduced just a century ago, the two-sleep pattern had disappeared.

It's a pity we lost the two-sleep habit because, whether we like the idea or not, being awake for a period at night is both natural and healthy. It follows the body's natural energy and sleep rhythms. It is beneficial psychologically, too: the period between the two sleeps was the perfect time to think about the day ahead and plan for it. The nearest we get to two sleeps these days is the 'siesta', the short mid-afternoon nap still enjoyed in some parts of the world.

The two-sleep habit used to be quite widespread, but it wasn't universal. Sleep patterns have always varied between cultures and still depend on things like light, temperature and health. Hunter-gatherer tribes, for example, only need five or six hours' sleep because they have a much healthier lifestyle than most of the world. Other cultures don't have a fixed time for sleeping, but have much more informal sleep patterns, where individuals sleep for short periods throughout the day or night, whenever they feel tired.

Sleep patterns also vary according to age. While older adults and pre-teens are happy with early mornings in general, teenagers often go to bed later and get up later, too. Either pattern is fine, as long as the person in question gets enough sleep. However, many people are constantly checking their phones, and don't even stop when they go to bed. The blue light emitted by screens disrupts the production of sleep hormones, meaning it is harder to get to sleep and stay asleep. Experts therefore recommend switching screens off two hours before you want to go to sleep. This enables us to listen to our body clock and sleep when our body tells us it's time to do so.

TALKING POINTS

What is 'a good night's sleep' for you?
What difficulties might someone have if they work at night and sleep during the day?
Do you like the idea of living in a 24/7 society?

GRAMMAR Present and past habits

1 Read the examples. Then complete the rules with the verb forms in the box.

1 Between sleeps, people **would lie** awake for a while and chat.
2 The two-sleep habit **used to be** quite widespread.
3 Some neighbours even **used to take** the opportunity to visit each other between sleeps.
4 My brother **was always waking** me **up** early when I was younger.
5 Many people **are constantly checking** their phones.
6 Individuals **sleep** whenever they feel tired.
7 I**'m sleeping** a lot because I'm getting over an illness.

past continuous	present continuous (x2)
present simple	*used to* *would*

We use
a ________ for present habits and states.
b ________ (without an adverb) for temporary present habits.
c ________ + *always/constantly* for annoying present habits.
d ________ for past habits and states.
e ________ for past habits (but not past states).
f ________ + *always/constantly* for past habits, especially to criticise or complain.

» GRAMMAR REFERENCE AND PRACTICE PAGE 152

2 Read the text and choose the correct verb forms.

BREAKFAST: HERE TODAY, GONE TOMORROW?

Most people [1] *eat / are eating* three meals a day, at least in the USA and northern Europe: breakfast, lunch and dinner. But mealtimes [2] *constantly change / are constantly changing*. In some parts of Asia, Europe and Latin America, people [3] *have / are having* five meals a day, adding a mid-morning snack and a late supper to the list. Our eating habits in the past [4] *would be / used to be* quite different. Let's start with breakfast. Health experts are big fans of breakfast and [5] *are always telling / were always telling* us that it's the most important meal of the day. However, breakfast is in fact a relatively new concept. The ancient Romans, who [6] *are constantly worrying / were constantly worrying* about their health, [7] *were never having / never used to have* breakfast. They [8] *would think / used to think* that one meal a day was sufficient, while three was greedy. It wasn't until the 18th century, when people started working in factories, and did not break for lunch, that they [9] *would have / were having* a big breakfast before going to work. Habits [10] *still change / are still changing*. People may not [11] *feel / feeling* hungry first thing, or they are in a rush, and more and more of us [12] *would miss / are missing* breakfast. Perhaps, after a few hundred years of popularity, breakfast is gradually starting to disappear.

3 Correct the mistake in each sentence.

1 I use to play this game with my friends.
2 Nowadays, always we are looking at our phones when we should be asleep.
3 I used to go to bed late while I was on holiday last week.
4 I was always sleeping well when I was a kid, but I don't now.
5 I start school at 8 am, so I used to go to bed early.

4 Write a sentence for each situation. Use the grammar from Exercise 1.

0 something that really annoys you
My best friend is always using my phone!
1 something that you do every day
2 a habit from when you were younger
3 something you do that annoys others
4 something you're doing temporarily
5 a fact about you that was true ten years ago, but not any longer

VOCABULARY Expressing frequency

1 Complete the lists with the words and phrases in the box.

~~all the time~~ constantly from time to time most days/weeks/months occasionally (every) once in a while rarely regularly seldom

always	*all the time*	________	
often	________	________	
sometimes	________	________	________
almost never	________	________	

2 Read the rules about expressions of frequency. Then answer the questions using the expressions.

Single adverbs usually go before the main verb:
*You're **constantly** sleeping.*
Phrases go at the beginning or end of a clause.
*I sleep badly **every once in a while**.*
***From time to time**, I stay up all night.*

How often do you
1 watch documentaries?
2 argue with people?
3 sleep later than 11 am?
4 complain about things?
5 play games on your phone?
6 enter competitions?

3 Tell your partner six things about yourself, three true and three false. Use an adverb or phrase expressing frequency. Can your partner guess which are false?

I'm constantly losing my mobile!

Every once in a while, I get up in the middle of the night and watch a film.

WRITING An article (1)

1 **Discuss the questions.**

1. What articles have you read recently, in magazines or online?
2. Can you remember any of the titles?
3. What do you think makes an article interesting?

2 **Read the task and answer the questions.**

You see this notice in an international English-language magazine for students.

> **Articles wanted!**
>
> Write an article about a hobby or leisure activity that you used to enjoy but don't do now. What did you do? Why did you enjoy doing it? What made you give it up? What do you do now?
>
> Send us your article and see your name in print!

Write your **article**.

1. Where is the article going to appear?
2. Who is going to read it?
3. What is the topic?
4. Do you think the article should be serious or chatty in tone?

3 **Read the *Prepare to write* box. Then read the article and choose the best title.**

a Why I love my hobby
b A hobby I used to have
c Tips for finding a new hobby

PREPARE TO WRITE | Writing articles

In an article

- choose an interesting title.
- organise your ideas into paragraphs.
- include a topic sentence for each paragraph, which tells the reader what the paragraph is about.
- use a lively, chatty style.
- use interesting, descriptive language.
- address the reader directly, for example by asking questions.

4 **Underline the topic sentences in paragraphs A–C. Write a topic sentence for paragraph D.**

5 **Read the article again. How does the writer address the reader directly? What descriptive language is used?**

____

A I used to ride my bike a lot when I was a kid. My older brother gave me his bike when he got a new one, and I loved having my own way of getting around! From then on, I would cycle everywhere I went.

B Cycling gives you a great sense of freedom. You can go where you want and at any time you want, can't you? When I was nine, I joined an after-school cycling club and soon I was regularly taking part in races against my friends. It was great fun!

C When I went to high school, I stopped going to the club. I rarely won races because I wasn't that fast, and I had a lot more homework to do. I have great memories of my time there, though.

D ________ It's skateboarding! I can do it at any time, so it fits in better with school. In fact, I do it most days. It's just as much fun as cycling, but I'm much better at skateboarding. They're building a new skate park in my town, which I can't wait to try out. If you aren't already a skateboarder, you should try it!

PREPARE FOR THE EXAM

Writing Part 2 (An article)

6 **Read the task in Exercise 2 again. Write your article.**

- Use the tips in the *Prepare to write* box.
- Check your grammar and spelling.
- Write 140–190 words.

6 TOTALLY EMOTIONAL

ABOUT YOU

Which of these emotions have you experienced recently? Why did you feel this way?

anger *fear* *happiness* *satisfaction* *worry*

VOCABULARY Expressing emotions

1 Match the questions to the photos.

EP
1 Do you go to school in the morning feeling **cheerful about** the day ahead?
2 Do you generally feel **optimistic** or **pessimistic about** things?
3 Have you ever been **scared of** anything, like giving a class presentation?
4 Have you ever felt **furious with** someone, but not said anything?
5 What environmental problems are you most **concerned about**?

A

B

C

D

E

2 Complete the table with the adjectives with prepositions in Exercise 1.

Fear	
Anger	
Worry	
Happiness	*cheerful about, …*
Unhappiness	

3 Ask and answer the questions in Exercise 1.

23
4 Listen to Claudia, Ben, Jade and Olly. How are they feeling? Choose the correct options and complete the sentences.

1 Claudia's **fed up with** / **anxious about** …
2 Ben's **bad-tempered about** / **anxious about** …
3 Jade's **relieved about** / **over the moon about** …
4 Olly's getting **depressed about** / **irritated by** …
5 Jade's **down about** / **content with** not …
6 Olly's **petrified of** / **fed up with** some kind of …

5 Add the phrases in Exercise 4 to the table in Exercise 2. Use a dictionary to help you.

6 Discuss when you last felt …

- relieved about something
- over the moon about something
- fed up with someone
- irritated by something
- anxious about something

READING

1 Read the introduction to the article, ignoring the gaps. Which fears are mentioned?

PREPARE FOR THE EXAM

Reading and Use of English Part 1

2 Read the introduction again and decide which answer (A, B, C or D) best fits each gap.

	A	B	C	D
0	A beginning	(B) birth	C start	D origin
1	A predictable	B common	C shared	D usual
2	A phases	B stages	C times	D points
3	A progress	B arrive	C reach	D gain
4	A unexpected	B uncertain	C unlikely	D unsure
5	A emerge	B uncover	C expose	D reveal
6	A take	B fix	C make	D keep
7	A impression	B outcome	C reaction	D impact
8	A up	B over	C into	D on

3 Look at the names of three phobias. What do you think they mean? Read case studies 1, 2 and 3 and check your answers.

autophobia nyctophobia scolionophobia

4 Read the case studies again. Write the correct names.

1 Who was abandoned in a public place?
2 Whose family almost got into trouble with the law because of a phobia?
3 Whose phobia has made them more sociable?
4 Who recently had a bad experience at a friend's house?
5 Who has been accepted for further education?
6 Whose parents thought his fear was normal?

5 Match the highlighted words in the article to the meanings.

1 having your attention taken away from something
2 making you very worried or upset
3 the use of medicine, exercises, etc. to cure a person of an illness or injury
4 silly or stupid
5 likely to cause death

WHEN FEAR BECOMES PHOBIA ...

Fear is something we all experience from **(0)** *birth* and for good reason: without it, we would find it difficult to survive. It is thought to be the earliest emotion, evolving millions of years ago.

24

Some fears, such as a fear of heights, are **(1)** ________ to almost all mammals. Other fears, like a fear of mice, are specific to humans and, in this case, possibly result from **(2)** ________ when these rodents carried deadly diseases.

As we **(3)** ________ to adulthood, our fears change. Under the age of seven, fears frequently include imagined monsters or the dark. By ten, children fear events that are real, though extremely **(4)** ________ to happen, like murder or war. When we are teenagers, social fears begin to **(5)** ________, such as looking foolish in front of friends.

The vast majority of us are able to **(6)** ________ our fears under control. However, for others, a fear can get out of control and have a significant **(7)** ________ on their lives. When this happens, a fear has turned **(8)** ________ a phobia. Psychologists recognise over 500 phobias, from ablutophobia (fear of washing) to zoophobia (fear of animals).

CASE STUDY 1
NYCTOPHOBIA

As a child, Mustafa Aksoy used to be terrified of the dark. Until the age of eight, he spent most nights in his parents' room and insisted on leaving a light on. His parents never suspected a problem – after all, such fears are common among young kids. But Mustafa has never got used to sleeping in the dark and he's now 16. He still sleeps with a light on, which is fine, of course. However, Mustafa's nyctophobia can occasionally make everyday life difficult.

'I was at a birthday party last week. Someone turned the lights out while the candles on the cake were being lit,' Mustafa says. 'Even though I knew there was no real danger, I was still petrified of the dark!'

Mustafa can't explain the reasons behind his phobia. However, many phobias result from a distressing experience in childhood.

CASE STUDY 2
AUTOPHOBIA

Seventeen-year-old Poppy Scofield believes that her autophobia – the fear of being alone – comes from an incident when she was ten. She and her mum were shopping in a department store. Suddenly her mum got an urgent phone call from work and became distracted. She left the shop quickly and simply forgot her daughter was with her. Obviously Poppy was in tears until her mum returned, and she's suffered from autophobia ever since.

Although Poppy hasn't entirely got over her fear, she's now used to her autophobia and has several strategies she uses to cope with it. 'Reading or listening to music definitely helps. Plus I deliberately make lots of friends so I'm almost always with someone.'

Both nyctophobia and autophobia are common. But other phobias are quite unusual and, in some cases, possibly difficult to believe.

CASE STUDY 3
SCOLIONOPHOBIA

Scolionophobia has been recognised since the 1960s. Children who suffer from this will feel extreme anxiety about going to school, with symptoms such as headaches and feeling physically sick. For over three years, Noah Jenkins experienced just this. At one point, the school threatened to take Noah's parents to court for keeping their child at home. When his parents proved that Noah was studying at home, the school eventually agreed to help. Now, after a period of psychological treatment, Noah is a typical 18-year-old and is about to leave home for university.

'One of the worst things about that time was the fact that my school didn't believe me,' says Noah. 'They thought I was trying to get out of studying when, in fact, I've always enjoyed learning.'

TALKING POINTS

Why do you think some people suffer from phobias such as scolionophobia?

Do you think fear can be a useful emotion? Why?

GRAMMAR *be / get used to*

1 **Read the examples and the rules. What kinds of words can follow *be/get used to*?**

1 Although Poppy hasn't entirely got over her fear, she**'s** now **used to her autophobia**.
2 Mustafa has never **got used to sleeping** in the dark.

a We use *be/get used to* to talk about how familiar something is for someone.
b If you *are used to* something, you are familiar with it. You have experienced it often enough for it to seem normal to you and it is no longer strange.
c If you *get used to* something, you become familiar with it.

» **GRAMMAR REFERENCE AND PRACTICE PAGE 153**

2 **Choose the correct verbs.**

1 I feel exhausted. I*'m not / don't get* used to staying up so late.
2 We have to speak English in class all the time. At first, we found it hard, but now *we're / we get* used to it.
3 I can't *be / get* used to the school website now they've redesigned it. It's so confusing!
4 It took me several days to *be / get* used to the time change when we went to the USA.
5 Our school starts at 7.30, so I've always *been / got* used to getting up early.
6 I'm *being / getting* used to our new teacher, but I still miss our old one.

3 **Imagine a friend from abroad is coming to live in your country. What will they have to get used to? Write four sentences. Use the ideas in the box and your own ideas.**

daily routine	food	people	weather

You might find it difficult to get used to our sense of humour.

4 **Read the examples. Which one describes a past habit or state?**

1 She**'s used to being** alone now.
2 I **used to be** terrified of spiders.

5 **Complete the second sentence so that it means the same as the first sentence. Use between two and five words, including *used*.**

1 In the past, I was petrified of dogs.
I ________ petrified of dogs.
2 My new school no longer feels strange to me.
I ________ my new school.
3 Vicki is no longer worried about sleeping in the dark.
Vicki ________ in the dark now.
4 As a child, I was afraid of heights.
I ________ afraid of heights.
5 Did Samuel become accustomed to the cold weather in Norway?
Did Samuel ________ the cold weather in Norway?

6 **Correct the mistake in each sentence.**

1 I've got use to my new school now.
2 Jody can't get use to sharing a room with her sister.
3 You used to your new school timetable?
4 I swam in the lake every weekend as a child, so I was used to deep water quickly.
5 I'm used to my school – I hope that soon it'll feel like I've always been here.
6 I'd prefer to have a smaller car because I got used to them now.

VOCABULARY Adverbs: type and position

1 **Match the examples to the types of adverb.**

1 Fears **frequently** include imagined monsters or the dark.
2 Our cat spends most nights **outside**.
3 I was at a birthday party **last week**.
4 Mustafa can't explain the reasons behind his phobia. **However**, many phobias …
5 She left the shop **quickly**.
6 Reading or listening to music **definitely** help.

a adverbs of time
b frequency adverbs
c adverbs of certainty
d adverbs of manner
e adverbs of place
f connecting adverbs (which link to a previous sentence)

2 **Where in a sentence (beginning, middle or end) are the types of adverb (a–f) in Exercise 1 usually used?**

3 **Write the sentences with the adverbs in the correct positions. More than one answer is sometimes possible.**

1 He can sing. (beautifully)
2 I have been scared of insects. (never)
3 I'll get used to it. (probably)
4 I had an upset stomach. I had difficulty sleeping. (as a result)
5 I get anxious about homework. (usually)
6 I've been getting bad-tempered. (lately)
7 If we leave now, we'll be home. (by nine)
8 She left home. (a few minutes ago, definitely)
9 We have lunch in summer. (outdoors)
10 They were laughing. (loudly)

4 **Ask and answer the questions with a partner.**

1 How are you feeling today?
2 What makes you feel bad-tempered?
3 What's the last thing you felt relieved about?
4 Who makes you feel irritated?
5 Do you ever get anxious about things? What?

LISTENING

PREPARE FOR THE EXAM

Listening Part 1

1 **You will hear people talking in eight different situations. Read the questions. Underline the key words that might help you get the correct answers.**

1 You hear a student talking about her degree in psychology. What does she think about it?
- **A** It's more enjoyable than she thought it would be.
- **B** It will be very useful for her future career.
- **C** She finds the research fascinating.

2 You hear a boy telling his friend about losing his phone. How does the boy feel about losing his phone?
- **A** worried that people can access information on it
- **B** frustrated that he doesn't know where he left it
- **C** concerned that he won't be able to use it immediately

3 You hear a girl leaving a voicemail for her friend about a history test. Why is she calling?
- **A** to find out what it will cover
- **B** to suggest doing some revision for it together
- **C** to check some facts before doing it

4 You overhear two friends talking about a school project. What does the boy say about his project?
- **A** He's feeling optimistic about its progress.
- **B** He's worried that he won't finish it in time.
- **C** He's finding it difficult to understand what to do.

5 You hear a father talking to his daughter on the phone. How is he feeling now?
- **A** annoyed that his daughter hasn't been in touch before now
- **B** concerned about how his daughter will get home
- **C** relieved that his daughter is OK

6 You hear a boy telling a friend about learning to ride a motorbike. What is the boy's attitude towards his motorbike lessons?
- **A** pleased with what he has learned so far
- **B** worried that he isn't advancing quickly enough
- **C** satisfied that he has achieved an ambition

7 You hear a psychologist talking about being optimistic and pessimistic. What does she say about this?
- **A** People should make more effort to be optimistic.
- **B** It is difficult to balance optimism and pessimism.
- **C** Pessimism can be useful to people.

8 You hear two friends talking about a programme they have seen about phobias. What do they agree about it?
- **A** how sympathetic the presenter was
- **B** how difficult its advice will be to follow
- **C** how unusual some of the phobias mentioned were

2 (25) **Listen. For questions 1–8, choose the best answer (A, B or C). Then listen again and check your answers.**

» PREPARE FOR THE EXAM PAGE 131

SPEAKING Generalising

(26) **1** **Listen to Harry and Elif talking about their best and worst days of the week. Which person is more like you?**

(26) **2** **Who says these phrases? Listen again and write *H* (Harry) or *E* (Elif).**

1 What normally happens is …
2 Virtually every Monday …
3 As a rule, I …
4 Nine times out of ten, …
5 with the exception of …

(27) **3** **Listen to Steffi and Antonio. Complete the sentences.**

1 Two of Steffi's favourite subjects are ________ .
2 Steffi gets on really well with the ________ .
3 Antonio rarely does his homework on ________ .
4 Antonio has a bit of a phobia of ________ .

(27) **4** **Read the *Prepare to speak* box. Then listen again. Which phrases do Steffi and Antonio use?**

PREPARE TO SPEAK | Generalising

Generalising

Ninety percent of the time …
What normally happens is …
Nine times out of ten, …
Generally speaking, …
On the whole, …
As a rule, …
For the most part, …
Virtually every Monday, …

Exceptions

One exception is …
… with the exception of …

5 **Work in pairs. Interview each other. Use phrases from the *Prepare to speak* box.**

1 Which is your best/worst day of the week? Why? What normally happens on that day?
2 Which is your best/worst time of the year? Why? What generally happens then?
3 What's your favourite lesson at school? Why?
4 Describe a typical weekend for you.

CULTURE

COLOURS AROUND THE WORLD

1 **Ask and answer the questions with a partner.**

1. Think about your bedroom, your clothes and your possessions. What colours do you like the most? What colours do you like the least?
2. Do you have a favourite or special colour? What does it mean or represent for you?

2 **What emotions do you associate with the following colours?**

black blue brown green grey
orange purple red white yellow

3 **Read the article on page 41 quickly and compare what it says with your own ideas.**

4 **Read the article again. Discuss these situations with your partner using information from the article.**

1. You want to open a restaurant that serves organic and ecological food. Which colours would you use to decorate it?
2. Your class want to make signs in English to place around your school. Which colours would be effective and eye-catching?
3. You are creating a luxury fashion label. Which colours would you use to advertise your brand?
4. You are making a poster about the importance of a good night's sleep for your health. What colours would you use in the poster?

5 **Match the highlighted words in the article to the meanings.**

1. strong and energetic
2. type or degree of a colour
3. are immediately noticeable
4. the feeling of wanting something that someone else has
5. not clear, bright or shiny

28 **6** **Listen to four people being interviewed about the significance of colours in their cultures. In the table write the country each person is from and the colour or colours they mention.**

Speaker	Country	Colour(s)	Meaning / Use
1			
2			
3			
4			

28 **7** **Listen to the interviews again and complete the last column of the table. Makes notes on the meaning of the colours and how they are used.**

8 **Read the sentences. Look at the underlined phrase in the first sentence. Then choose the correct option in the second.**

USEFUL LANGUAGE

Expressions with colours

1. Sam saw red when I told him. He was really *happy / angry*.
2. He was green with envy when he saw my new phone. It's the *latest / oldest* model.
3. You look like you're feeling a bit blue. *Have you been away? / What's wrong?*
4. The rules are there in black and white. They *could / couldn't* be clearer.
5. Last week, out of the blue, I got a call from Daniel. I was really *miserable / surprised*.
6. He was caught red-handed as he left the museum. It was *obvious / unclear* that he had stolen the painting!

29

What COLOURS really mean

COOL

BLUE is considered to be a relaxing, calm colour, and it's often associated with peace. A pale blue is the typical colour of clear skies and water. It's perhaps for these reasons that blue is the world's most popular colour. On the negative side, blue suggests cold temperatures, as well as low energy. In English, for example, people who are sad or depressed say they 'feel blue'.

GREEN is the colour of plants, so it's often associated with life, nature and growth. In Ireland, people think it brings good fortune, and in Japan, it represents eternal life. However, green also has negative associations in English. It's the colour of envy – 'green with envy' – and people's faces 'turn green' when they feel sick.

PURPLE is a fairly unusual colour in nature. Some minerals are purple and there are plants with purple flowers, but they aren't common. In Europe, purple has been the colour of royalty since ancient times, when purple dye for clothing was rare and very expensive. Purple is often seen as a vibrant and bold colour choice.

WARM

RED is the colour of blood, so it's often associated with life, energy and strong feelings. For example, many people's faces turn red when they are feeling nervous, embarrassed or excited. In English, people also say they 'see red' when they are angry! A splash of red catches our attention, and red objects jump out at us because they appear to be closer than they really are.

YELLOW is the colour of sunlight, so it's often associated with warmth and happiness. It's also the most intense colour, which means a bright shade of yellow can be irritating – imagine a house painted in bright yellow! Yellow things are admired in China, where this colour also represents the Chinese element of earth. In India, yellow is associated with business and financial wealth.

ORANGE is a combination of lively red and cheerful yellow, making it a bright colour that catches our attention. It's also the colour of healthy foods, like oranges, carrots and pumpkins. Because of its high visibility, orange is often used for signs and for emergency equipment, like lifejackets.

NEUTRAL

BLACK is neutral because it absorbs all the colours of light. It's associated with darkness and night, as well as mystery and the unknown. In many countries, black is a serious colour, associated with death and sadness, but also with elegance and authority.

BROWN is the colour of earth, wood and autumn leaves, which makes it a neutral, calming colour. It's also the colour of many foods, such as bread, nuts and chocolate. However, lots of people consider brown dull and boring, especially for clothes.

WHITE is the colour of fresh snow, so it's often associated with cleanliness and purity. In many countries, it's the typical colour of wedding dresses. However, white also suggests emptiness, and in some countries, like Japan, it's linked to death.

GREY is the colour of foggy days, when we can't see clearly. Grey is between black and white, making it the most neutral colour. In English, the phrase 'grey area' is used to describe things that are unclear.

PROJECT

Colours in English-speaking countries

Work in groups of three or four to find out about colours in different cultures and countries. Use these steps to help you.

1 In your group, agree on one of the following countries to research:
Australia, Canada, Ireland, New Zealand, the UK, the USA

2 Search online for any special colour associations or traditions.
- Does the country have a national colour or colours?
- What are the colours of the country's flag? What do they mean?
- What is the significance of the nine colours mentioned in the article on this page?
- Are any colours considered to be lucky or unlucky?

Make a poster of your findings and present it to the class.

04 NOW WATCH THE CULTURE VIDEO

7 TELLING STORIES

ABOUT YOU

05 **Watch the video and answer the questions.**

What genres of story do you like?

What makes a good story, do you think?

Do you prefer reading books or watching films?

VOCABULARY Verbs of movement and sounds

1 **Match the sentences to the pictures. Then write the infinitives of the verbs.**

EP

1 Jade leant forward and tapped Megan on the shoulder.

2 Ewan rushed down the street to get his dog, which was trembling with fear.

3 Ollie was kneeling down when his sister slapped him on the back.

4 The door swung open and Butch wandered in.

A

B

C

D

30 **2** **Listen and decide which verb describes the sounds the people make.**

mumble sigh whisper whistle

3 **Match the sentence halves.**

1 She leant over and whispered
2 He sighed
3 The presenter mumbled his
4 José began to whistle

a introduction to the talk.
b a tune he'd heard on the radio.
c when he realised he'd forgotten his homework.
d her idea in his ear.

READING

1 **Look at the title of the story and the picture. Who do you think the people are? What genre do you think the story is? Read the extract quickly and check your answers.**

PREPARE FOR THE EXAM

Reading and Use of English Part 5

2 **You are going to read an extract from a novel about a detective called Sherlock Holmes and his friend Watson. For questions 1–6, choose the answer (A, B, C or D) which you think fits best according to the text.**

1 What do we learn about Holmes in the first paragraph?
A He would like more time to spend on his interests.
B He does not want to share his free time with others.
C He blames those around him when things go wrong.
D He feels annoyed when he cannot do what he wants.

> **Tip:** Read paragraph 1. Underline the words which give you the answer.

2 The word 'sneak' in line 24 is used to mean 'move
A noisily and aggressively'.
B quietly and secretively'.
C surprisingly quickly'.
D extremely slowly'.

> **Tip:** Read the sentences before and after the word carefully to work out the answer.

3 When Watson mentions the thefts in London, Holmes complains because
A he thinks Watson has got the facts wrong.
B all of the cases have already been solved.
C he believes his skills are wasted on such crimes.
D the weather has caused a big increase in theft.

> **Tip:** Read the conversation between Holmes and Watson about criminals.

4 What does 'it' refer to in line 36?
A a murder
B a reason
C a meeting
D an appointment

> **Tip:** Underline words A–D in the text. Which one does 'it' refer to?

5 Holmes suggests that his brother Mycroft is someone who
A uses the railway to get to work.
B is predictable in his routine.
C spends most of his time outdoors.
D is dedicated to his family.

> **Tip:** Read this part of the text carefully to work out the answer.

THE BRUCE-PARTINGTON PLANS

SIR ARTHUR CONAN DOYLE

31

It was the third week of November and a thick yellow fog had settled over London. From the Monday to the Thursday, it had rarely been possible from our windows in Baker Street to see even the houses across the street. The first three of these days Holmes had been patiently studying a subject which had been his hobby for some time – the music of the Middle Ages. But when, for the fourth time, we pushed back our chairs from breakfast and saw the heavy brown mist outside the windows, my friend's impatient and active nature could no longer take this dull existence. He wandered restlessly around our sitting room; he bit his nails; he tapped the furniture nervously; and he complained about the inactivity.

'Nothing of interest in the paper, Watson?' he said. I realised that by anything of interest, Holmes was asking about anything of *criminal* interest. There was the news of a revolution, of a possible war and of a likely change of government. However, these were of little interest to my companion. The only criminal reports I could find were very ordinary. Holmes sighed impatiently and continued to wander around the room.

'The London criminal is certainly a dull person,' he said, sounding like a hunter who can find nothing to shoot. 'Look out of this window, Watson. See how people suddenly appear, are briefly seen and then quickly disappear once more into
line 24 the mist. On a day like this, a thief or a murderer could **sneak** round London like a tiger in the jungle. No one would see him until he made his move.'

'There have,' I said, 'been a large number of small thefts.'

Holmes muttered something rude and then turned towards me. 'My abilities demand something far more worthy than that,' he said. 'It is fortunate for this community that I am not a criminal.'

'It certainly is!' I agreed enthusiastically.

'Imagine that I had a good reason to want to kill someone,' continued Holmes. 'How easy it would be on a day like this! I could suggest a meeting, I could make up an appointment
line 36 and **it** would all be over. It is just as well they don't have days of fog in countries where murder is common.'

There was the sound of someone knocking.

'At last!' cried Holmes. 'Here comes something to bring some excitement into our lives.'

He rushed over to open the door. It was the postman with a telegram. Holmes tore it open and before long burst out laughing.

'Well, well! I don't believe it!' he said. 'My brother Mycroft is coming round.'

'And so …?' I asked.

'And so …?' said Holmes. 'It is like coming across a train in the middle of the road. Mycroft has his rails, like a train, and he stays on them. His home in Pall Mall, his club, his office in Whitehall – that is where you find him. Once, and only once, has he been here. What disaster can have knocked him off his rails?'

'Doesn't he explain?' I asked.

Holmes handed me his brother's telegram. 'Must see you about Cadogan West. Coming at once. Mycroft.'

'Cadogan West?' I said. I had heard that name.

'It means nothing to me,' said Holmes. 'But it is extraordinary that Mycroft should do something so uncharacteristic. The moon might as well stop going round the Earth.'

from Cambridge Experience Readers, *Holmes: Three Adventures*, adapted by Richard MacAndrew

6 What is implied about Holmes' character in the story extract?

A He believes himself to be more intelligent than Watson.

B He thinks other people are less important than he is.

C He needs to keep his mind occupied.

D He has some doubts about his talents.

Tip: Read the whole text before choosing the answer.

> PREPARE FOR THE EXAM PAGE 124

TALKING POINTS

Which books have you read that have been made into films? What is the difference between stories told in books compared with films?

GRAMMAR Narrative tenses

1 **Look at the underlined verbs in the text on page 43. What tenses are they?**

2 **Complete the rules with the verb forms in the box.**

past continuous	past perfect	past simple

We use narrative verb forms in stories to describe events and actions. We use the

a ....
- to describe the main events of a story, in the order they happened.
- to describe a short action that interrupts an action in the past continuous.

b ....
- to describe an action in progress at a particular time in the past.
- to describe a continuing action interrupted by an action in the past simple.

c ....
- to describe a completed action that happened before a particular point in the past.
- with sequencing expressions (*when*, *after*, *by the time*, *as soon as*) when one event happened before another event.

» GRAMMAR REFERENCE AND PRACTICE PAGE 154

3 **Read six extracts from later in the story about Sherlock Holmes. Choose the correct options.**

1 The man *travelled* / *was travelling* back to Woolwich when he was killed and thrown out of the train.
2 Mycroft Holmes took off his overcoat and *sat down* / *had sat down* heavily in an armchair.
3 At nine o'clock, we *were all sitting* / *had all sat* in the study, waiting patiently for our man.
4 We *just reached* / *had just reached* the dark shadows at the back of the house when we heard footsteps.
5 We were walking past his office when suddenly the man *rushed off* / *was rushing off* into the fog.
6 Lestrade and Mycroft met us outside Gloucester Road Station in the morning. We *left* / *had left* the back door of Oberstein's house open the night before.

4 **Read another extract from later in the story and notice the verb form. Complete the rules.**

Inspector Lestrade suddenly spoke. He **had been listening** to the conversation with some impatience.

a We use the past perfect continuous instead of the past perfect when we want to talk about a longer action that continued until another past action.
b We form the past perfect continuous with .... + ... + *-ing*.

5 **Complete the sentences with the past perfect simple or continuous form of the verbs in the box.**

call	cry	leave	play	rush	shout

1 The man .... for almost an hour before anyone heard him.
2 By the time the game ended, we .... for over three hours.
3 I could tell from her eyes that she ....
4 Josefina was exhausted. She .... around all morning.
5 The noises outside stopped a few minutes after we .... the police.
6 I couldn't get into the concert because I .... my ticket at home.

6 **Choose the correct options.**

1 I *feel* / *felt* relieved when I passed my driving test.
2 Jo *read* / *was reading* her book when she heard a loud noise outside.
3 Aba *went* / *was going* to his friend's house last night and watched TV.
4 I told my brother that I *changed* / *had changed* my mind about going to the party on Saturday.
5 Karl *whistled* / *has whistled* a tune while he waited for the doctor to see him.

VOCABULARY Time phrases

1 **Complete the sentences with the words in the box.**

EP

before (x2)	for (x2)	in	on

1 Holmes tore open the envelope and .... **long**, he burst out laughing.
2 I only joined the school in March, but I made lots of new friends .... **no time**.
3 He was disappointed not to do better because he'd been studying .... **weeks on end**.
4 Callum slapped me on the back happily because we hadn't seen each other .... **some time**.
5 I used to catch the bus to school, but **the week** .... **last**, I started cycling instead.
6 We waited there **for hours** .... **end**.

2 **Choose the correct options.**

1 Don't worry, you'll find a holiday job *before long* / *for some time*.
2 I can play computer games *in no time* / *for hours on end*. I never get bored!
3 Thandie practised for her flute exam *for weeks on end* / *before long*.
4 Billy waited *for some time* / *in no time* before a bus finally turned up.
5 Aiden and Finlay went to see the new Spielberg movie *for hours on end* / *the week before last*.
6 The roads were clear and we arrived home *in no time* / *for some time*.

3 » **Work in pairs. Turn to page 138.**

WRITING A story

1 **Read the task and look at the photo below. What do you think might happen in the story?**

You have seen this announcement on your school website.

> **Stories wanted**
>
> We are looking for stories for our website. Your story **must** begin with this sentence:
>
> *Adam wished he hadn't offered to look after Blanca while his cousin was on holiday.*
>
> Your story must include:
>
> - bad weather
> - a search

Write your **story**.

2 **Read the story. Does it contain any of your ideas? Does the story include the ideas mentioned in the task?**

A Adam wished he hadn't offered to look after Blanca while his cousin was on holiday. It had been raining heavily all day, but the dog needed some exercise. Adam sighed and gently stroked the animal's head.

B [1] ...., the front door of the house burst open. Adam's brother ran in and ran straight upstairs. Before Adam could move, Blanca had disappeared out of the open front door. 'Stevie!' Adam shouted. 'Blanca's escaped!' In no time the brothers were chasing after her. She was heading towards the park. Adam whistled loudly, but the dog ignored him. [2] ...., Blanca reached the park and disappeared.

C The brothers searched for the dog for hours on end without success. When they finally got on the bus to go home, they were shaking with cold. [3] .... ten minutes, Stevie spoke. 'Look. We're going past Suzy's,' he said. Adam looked over at his cousin's house. Through the pouring rain, he could just see a dog on the doorstep. It was Blanca!

D [4] .... that evening their cousin called and asked about her dog. 'Blanca's been fine,' said Adam happily. 'We took her out for a really long walk today!'

3 **Read the *Prepare to write* box, then read the story again. Match paragraphs A–D to the functions in the box.**

background information | developing the story | ending | opening events

PREPARE TO WRITE Stories

A good story should

- include all the ideas mentioned in the task.
- be organised into paragraphs.
- have a clear beginning, middle and end.
- use suitable time expressions and different tenses to make it clear when actions happened in relation to other actions.
- use a range of vocabulary to make the story interesting or exciting.

4 **Complete the story with the time expressions.**

After | Before long | Just then | Later

5 **Explain why the writer uses these verb forms in the story.**

had been raining | had disappeared | were shaking

6 **Replace the highlighted words in the story with the words in the box.**

cheerfully | glanced | make out | rushed | vanished | yelled

PREPARE FOR THE EXAM

Writing Part 2 (A story)

7 **Read the task. Discuss what might happen in the story.**

You have seen this advertisement in a magazine.

> **Stories wanted**
>
> We are looking for stories for our magazine. Your story must **begin** with this sentence:
>
> *Gina hurried over to Ted's house as soon as she heard the news.*
>
> Your story must include:
>
> - a meal
> - an accident

Write your **story**.

8 **Write your story.**

- Use the tips in the *Prepare to write* box.
- Check your grammar and spelling.
- Write 140–190 words.

» PREPARE FOR THE EXAM PAGE 130

8 A GREAT PLACE TO LIVE

ABOUT YOU

06 **Watch the video and answer the questions.**

Where do you live and what do you like about it?

What do you think that young people can gain from studying abroad?

VOCABULARY Community

1 **Match the sentence halves. Are the adjectives used for people, places or both?**

EP

WHERE WOULD YOU LIKE TO LIVE?

When I leave home, I'd like to live …

1 somewhere quiet with a **relaxed**
2 somewhere busy and **urban**, with
3 in a place that's **remote** and **rural**, in
4 in a community which
5 somewhere friendly, with a **close** community, where
6 near an **industrial**
7 in a city that's culturally **diverse**, with shops

a the middle of nowhere.
b is **welcoming** and easygoing.
c atmosphere, like a **residential** suburb.
d estate, or in an **inner-city** neighbourhood.
e masses of **affordable** entertainment and leisure facilities.
f and **trendy** restaurants from around the world.
g everyone knows everyone else.

2 **Which kind of place would you like to live in? Discuss the sentences in Exercise 1.**

32 **3** **Listen to David, a British student, asking for advice about a place to study. Answer the questions.**

1 What is he going to do next year? Where?
2 Which adjectives from Exercise 1 describe his home town?
3 Which adjectives describe the city of Bristol?
4 Which adjectives describe the kind of place where he'd like to study?

READING

1 **Read the university recommendations written by five people (A–E). Match two of the recommendations to the photos on page 47.**

2 **Read the question and choose from the five people (A–E). Follow instructions 1–3.**

Which person recommends studying the local language?

1 Look at the underlined key words.
2 Find paragraphs that mention anything related to the underlined words.
3 Read these paragraphs and the question again carefully. Then choose the correct answer.

PREPARE FOR THE EXAM

Reading and Use of English Part 7

3 **Read the recommendations again. For questions 1–10, choose from the five people (A–E). The people may be chosen more than once.**

Which person

1 recommends a particular cold weather activity?
2 understands why one city's inhabitants have a particular approach to life?
3 mentions the quality of education at a recommended place of study?
4 is familiar with a city they do not study in themselves?
5 is impressed by the architecture of the city they recommend?
6 mentions a positive opinion of a programme of study by someone they know?
7 advises keeping an open mind about fellow students?
8 describes one place in a city that they enjoy visiting on a regular basis?
9 says they became relaxed when they went to view the university?
10 mentions one disadvantage for them of the university they attend?

4 **Find words or phrases in the recommendations to match the meanings.**

1 very interesting (A)
2 university buildings and the land that surrounds them (B)
3 in, from or to other countries (C)
4 start living somewhere you are going to live for a long time (D)
5 the size or level of something (E)

UNIVERSITY RECOMMENDATIONS

Five young people recommend their favourite cities to study in

A MARTA

It sounds as if you'd love Barcelona. The main university dates from the 1450s, and there's a huge student population in the city, making it very culturally diverse. The inner-city neighbourhoods are full of fascinating streets, and there are squares with trendy cafés. The city isn't all old, though. There are Gaudí's crazy, nature-inspired houses and his extraordinary Sagrada Familia cathedral, as well as incredible contemporary buildings like The Forum on the outskirts. La Rambla is always busy with people walking up and down looking at the stalls, but my favourite spot is Parc de la Ciutadella, near the Old Town. There's always a performance or something going on. I spend a great deal of time there and it's somewhere I return to frequently. It's beautiful in every season. I'll probably go after lectures tomorrow.

B AYAZ

How about Turkey? I'm about to start at Koç University, 30 km from Istanbul city centre. It has an excellent reputation for its teaching, and international students are welcome. It would make a difference if you learned some Turkish before coming, but don't worry about the classes – all of the university's undergraduate degrees are taught in English. When I visited, the campus seemed quite a close community, which made me feel at home, and it's set in woodland, so it feels as if you're in the middle of nowhere, even though the city isn't far away. Istanbul itself is exciting because it's where the East meets the West and the old part of the city is a United Nations World Heritage Site.

C THOMAS

It would make sense to go to an Australian university – they cater for overseas students of all nationalities and languages. I'm at Macquarie University in Sydney and I love it. The campus is surrounded by parkland, so it actually feels as if it's quite rural. There's a friendly atmosphere and for me, the only drawback is the location. I live quite a distance away and there's only one bus an hour. There isn't much to do near the university, so most students meet up in a place called Surry Hills. There's always something going on there – I don't go very often myself, but there's an event there tomorrow I'm going to. The city has a fantastic outdoors lifestyle, and at the weekends you can check out the city's world-famous beaches – when the weather's warm enough, that is! Sydney really is an impressive city – no wonder everyone living here is so optimistic.

D VALERIO

You should consider Milan. Lots of places offer undergraduate degrees in architecture, often in English. I know Milan quite well because we visit relatives there every New Year. It's a lively university city, so you'll have a great social life. It's a major cultural centre too, with everything from theatre and opera to festivals and pop concerts. After you've spent a few weeks there, you'll never want to leave. I've already decided I'm going to settle there when I'm older. Milan is the centre of the Italian fashion industry, so it's great for window-shopping. You may find yourself sitting next to some very stylish classmates, but don't be put off – underneath, people are welcoming and down-to-earth.

E ABRIL

I study geography at the Tecnológico de Monterrey university, where all the classes are in English rather than Spanish. A friend on the architecture course highly recommends it. Mexico City is a massive urban centre with millions of things to do – you'll certainly never be bored. There are restaurants from every continent and lots of surprises – you should definitely make use of the ski slopes of Popocatépetl volcano at the weekends. And you can easily make your way out to the Aztec pyramids in the ancient city of Teotihuacán. If you're into archaeology, you'll definitely be impressed by the scale of the ruins. I'm a real fan and I'm going again next weekend.

TALKING POINTS

Which of the universities recommended would you like to study at? Why?

Do you think every young person should go to university? Why? / Why not?

GRAMMAR Future (1): review

1 **Read the examples. Then complete the rules with the verb forms.**

1 I'**m about to** start at Koç University …
2 It's a lively city, so you'**ll have** a great social life.
3 I've already decided I'**m going to settle** there when I'm older.
4 You **may** find yourself sitting next to some very stylish classmates.
5 It's beautiful in every season. I'**ll** probably **go** after lectures tomorrow.
6 There's always something going on there – there'**s** an event there tomorrow.
7 I'm a real fan and I'**m going** again next weekend.

be about to	*be going to*	*may*
~~present continuous~~	present simple	*will* (x2)

We use
a *present continuous* for plans and arrangements.
b ………… for regular, timetabled events.
c ………… for decisions you've just made.
d ………… for plans and intentions.
e *be going to* and ………… to make predictions.
f ………… / *might* / *could* for things that are possible in the future.
g ………… for events that are going to happen very soon.

» GRAMMAR REFERENCE AND PRACTICE PAGE 155

2 **Read the examples and complete the rules. Do you use the same verb forms in your language?**

1 After you'**ve spent** a few weeks there, you'll never want to leave.
2 I'm going to settle there when I'**m** older.

After time conjunctions (e.g. *when*, *after*), we use ………… simple or ………… perfect to talk about the future.

3 **Read the text and choose the correct options.**

We've been talking about what we [1] *do / 're going to do* after we [2] *will leave / leave* school. I [3] *won't start / 'm not starting* university immediately because I've decided to have a year out, but I [4] *'ll definitely do / 'm definitely going to do* a course the year after. I haven't chosen a subject yet. I'm fascinated by human behaviour, so I [5] *'m studying / might study* anthropology or social sciences, but I [6] *'ll make / am making* a decision later. I [7] *'m talking / 'm about to talk* to a careers adviser. After I [8] *will speak / have spoken* to her, I'll have a clearer idea.

4 **Correct the mistake in each sentence.**

1 Have you decided what you going to do at uni?
2 I think I call my friend Anna to see how she is.
3 We could to visit the market in town.
4 The train will leaves at exactly 8 am every morning.
5 I go to the shop and get some more chocolate.

5 **Complete the sentences about you. Then compare your answers.**

1 When I'm older, …
2 I … university.
3 After I've done my homework, I …
4 This weekend, I …
5 I'm about to …

VOCABULARY *as if / as though*

1 **Choose the correct meaning for each example.**

EP 1 *It feels* ***as if*** */* ***as though*** *it's going to rain.*
a It's definitely going to rain.
b I think it's going to rain.

2 *It sounds* ***as if*** */* ***as though*** *we won't have enough money.*
a I don't think we will have enough money.
b We may have enough money.

3 *He was behaving* ***as if*** */* ***as though*** *he'd received some bad news.*
a He may have received some bad news.
b He might receive some bad news.

4 *It looks* ***as if*** */* ***as though*** *the train's going to be late.*
a The train might not be late.
b The train will probably be late.

2 **Read the examples again and complete the rules.**

1 We use *as if* and *as though* to talk about situations that *seem to be true / are definitely true*.
2 *As if* and *as though* have *the same meaning / different meanings*.

3 **Make sentences about the people in the picture. Use *look* + *as if / as though*.**

buy a paper	cross the road
get some crisps	like keeping fit
need a new umbrella	~~see something annoying~~
shout to a friend	walk into the lamppost

1 *She looks as though she's seen something annoying.*

LISTENING

1 **You will hear a teenager called Anna Asher talking about a new skate park. Read the sentences and predict what you might hear.**

A NEW SKATE PARK

Anna says that the leader of the action group is a **(1)** .... who works locally.

Anna was pleased that the group leader was able to help them apply for a **(2)** ....

Anna and her friends raised money by arranging a **(3)** .... and doing different jobs.

After six months, the group had almost reached their target of **(4)** £ ....

A local resident became involved in **(5)** .... the project.

Anna was impressed by the **(6)** .... on one company's website.

A **(7)** .... was held at a community meeting to agree who would design the skate park.

Anna says that **(8)** .... is the main material used in a jump for BMX riders called the 'whale tail'.

Anna liked the **(9)** .... which the main designer gave the group to look at.

The skate park was built on land where a **(10)** .... once stood.

PREPARE FOR THE EXAM

Listening Part 2

2 34 **Listen. For questions 1–10, complete the sentences with a word or short phrase.**

3 34 **Compare your answers with your partner's. Then listen again and check.**

» PREPARE FOR THE EXAM PAGE 132

SPEAKING Comparing photographs (1)

1 **You are going to compare two photographs. Look at the photographs below. They show two different kinds of village. Then read points 1–3 and make notes. Think about:**

1 similarities and differences between the two photographs
2 advantages and disadvantages of living in each village
3 how your home town differs from these villages

35 **2** **Listen to Thalía and Oleg comparing the photographs in an exam. Answer the questions.**

1 What similarities and differences between the photographs does Thalía mention?
2 How many comparisons does Oleg make between St Petersburg and the villages in the photographs?
3 How many of your ideas do they mention?

36 **3** **Read the *Prepare to speak* box. Then listen to Thalía and Oleg using the phrases.**

PREPARE TO SPEAK Comparing and contrasting

The main difference is …
Both of these places are …
Neither place looks as though …
It looks …, whereas the other village is …
While the village in the first photograph has …, the village in the second photograph has …
On the other hand, I assume that …

PREPARE FOR THE EXAM

Speaking Part 2

4 **Work in pairs.**

Student A: Compare the two photographs. Say what advantages and disadvantages the people living in these villages may have. Use phrases from the *Prepare to speak* box.

Student B: Which of these two villages would you prefer to live in? Why?

5 » **Turn to page 138 and complete the task.**

» PREPARE FOR THE EXAM PAGE 134

LIFE SKILLS CREATIVITY AND INNOVATION

CREATIVE WRITING

1 **Ask and answer the questions with a partner.**

1. How easy do you find it to express your thoughts and feelings? Can you give an example?
2. When was the last time you wrote a piece of creative writing using just your imagination? What was it? How did you feel?

2 **In pairs, think of some tips and ideas for writing creatively. Then read the text on the opposite page quickly and see if any of your ideas are mentioned.**

3 **Read the text again and complete the sentences with one or two words in each gap.**

1. Poetry, storytelling and sharing experiences are a form of .... for many people.
2. Start by writing about .... and .... that you know personally.
3. Besides writing as much as you can, you should also be doing lots of ....
4. As far as possible, aim to .... things clearly and in detail.
5. Looking forward to people reading your writing can give you a feeling of ....

4 **Match the highlighted words in the text to the meanings.**

1. something that is silly or stupid
2. attract and keep someone's attention
3. showing your personality, emotions or ideas, especially through art, music or acting
4. to a great degree
5. at the beginning of something

LIFE SKILLS

Creative writing

Creativity means using our imagination to create something new or unusual. Creative writing is an excellent way to explore our own creativity. Learning creative writing skills can help us to express our thoughts and feelings more clearly. It can also build confidence and help us become better readers and writers.

37 **5** **Listen to a radio interview with Zack, a creative writing expert. What do the creative writing exercises all have in common?**

37 **6** **Listen again and match the creative writing exercises (1–4) to the writing area that each one develops (a–e). There is one extra writing area that you don't need.**

Creative writing exercises	Writing areas
1 Round Robin	a point of view
2 Who on Earth is it?	b creative descriptions
3 What's in a list?	c plot development
4 Guess the celebrity!	d elements of a story
	e character development

7 **Complete the sentences with the words in the box.**

background collaborate imagination interests provoke

USEFUL LANGUAGE

Talking about creative writing

1. We need to use our ....
2. It's a good idea to write a description of the character's ....
3. The opening lines should .... a reaction in the readers.
4. We can express our personal .... in our creative writing.
5. Try to connect and .... with other writers.

CREATIVE WRITING 101

Why 101, I hear you ask? Well, 101 is the number often used to describe an introductory course in something, one where students don't need any previous knowledge of the subject. So if you have no, or very little, experience of creative writing, then you're reading the right article!

Creative writing is an art – the art of painting with words. It's not academic or technical, but something freer – a form of self-expression. Creative writing entertains an audience through storytelling or poetry and sharing common human experiences like fear, love, hope or joy. It can also be found in many different places, such as on stage, on the big screen, or in a speech delivered to a room full of people. And of course, in a novel or short story.

When you begin your creative writing journey, write about places and characters that you are familiar with and use language that you already know. Your personal background and experience are a great place to start! Later, be brave and use your imagination to write about things that you're not familiar with: places, periods in history or even a whole new world! There are those who think that creative writing is nonsense because it's not about real people and situations. In fact, that's exactly the beauty of it.

It's important that you write what you really want to write first, focusing completely on telling the story you want to tell. Then, when you re-read your writing, you can make changes so that it sounds as if you are *speaking* to your audience. In addition to writing as often as you can, you also need to be reading, and reading a lot! Surround yourself with literary works and become absorbed in each unique world.

Aim to hook your readers from the very first moment. The opening sentences should provoke a reaction in your reader, like making them laugh, or curious to know what happens next. Make your reader feel some kind of emotion. Try to use detailed descriptions – using sensations such as smells, sounds and feelings – in your writing whenever possible, ones that will create clear images in the reader's mind. Finally, allow your characters to tell the story through what they themselves do and say.

Last, but definitely not least, make sure that you enjoy the writing process. And when it comes around, finishing your first story will be a hugely satisfying moment. The excitement of looking forward to it being published and read by others will really make you feel like a writer!

PROJECT

Creative writing in groups

Work in groups of three or four to practise your creative writing. Use these steps to help you.

1. Choose one of the group creative writing exercises from the radio interview.
2. Complete the exercise together and take turns to share your writing with the class.
3. Discuss your reaction to each group's writing and agree on some feedback to help them improve their story.

REVIEW 2 UNITS 5–8

VOCABULARY

1 **Match the words to the meanings.**

ancestor century citizen
decade myth tribe

1 a group of people who have a traditional way of life
2 a period of ten years
3 someone who lives in a particular town or city
4 an ancient story that may explain an event in history
5 a period of 100 years, especially used in giving dates
6 a relative who lived a long time ago

2 **Complete the sentences by adding an adverb from the box in the best place.**

constantly occasionally regularly

1 He goes to the swimming pool, most often on a Saturday.
2 She's so careless! She's breaking things.
3 He apologises to people, but very rarely.

alternatively definitely outside

4 She's been ill for weeks now, so she needs to see a doctor.
5 It's lovely and sunny. Why don't we have lunch?
6 You may use the computers in the library. You can use the laptops in room 23.

3 **Match the sentence halves.**

1	I don't get anxious	a	of heights.
2	I'm so fed up	b	with this awful weather!
3	I'm petrified	c	about exam results.
4	He's furious	d	with second best.
5	I was a bit irritated	e	about what you said.
6	I'm never content	f	by all their questions.

4 **Complete the conversation with suitable adjectives.**

Adrian: Has your family always lived in Moscow?
Olga: No. In fact, my grandparents grew up in a really [0] *remote* area called Altai.
Adrian: That's in the middle of nowhere!
Olga: Yes, but they loved it. The [1] r________ way of life at that time was much more [2] r________ than the motorways and [3] i________ estates of modern [4] u________ life. It's a beautiful area, and their village was a [5] c________ community where everyone knew everyone else. The people were much more friendly and [6] w________ than in a city.

GRAMMAR

1 **Complete the sentences with the correct forms for present and past habits.**

1 When I was younger, I ________ into trouble. (constantly / get)
2 We ________ in the sea every day as children. (swim)
3 You ________ reasons not to visit these days! (always / find)
4 I'm lucky because I ________ my friends most weekends. (see)
5 He ________ of headaches. He should see a doctor. (constantly / complain)
6 My cousin and I ________ games for hours when we were children. (play)

2 **Complete the sentences with the correct future form of the verbs in brackets.**

1 When you ________ (finish) your exams, you'll be able to relax.
2 'Have you chosen a university course yet?' 'Yes, I ________ (study) Italian.'
3 The bus ________ (leave) in 20 minutes.
4 I think I ________ (buy) some new headphones with the money my grandma's given me.
5 Jed's still here, but he ________ (about to / leave), so you'll have to be quick if you want to talk to him.
6 I'm stuck in traffic, so I ________ (arrive) a bit late. I'm not sure what time yet.
7 The food all looks lovely. I think I ________ (have) a piece of that cake.
8 I ________ (meet) Jen on Saturday morning. Why don't you come too?

3 **Complete the sentences with the correct form of *be/get used to*.**

1 I had never driven a car before, but I ________ it quite quickly once I started.
2 I ________ washing up; I do it all the time.
3 The course was hard at first because I ________ still ________ studying for eight hours a day.
4 When we were living in Madrid, I ________ watching films in Spanish.

4 **Correct the mistake in each sentence. There may be more than one way to correct the mistake.**

1 Every night, we were going to the cinema and it was fantastic.
2 My mother told me that the old lady who was telling us stories died.
3 I've been disappointed many times in my life, so I have used it.
4 He saw a woman he never met before.
5 Try drinking more water and you are going to see a difference in how awake you feel!

PREPARE FOR THE EXAM

Reading and Use of English Part 1

1 **For questions 1–8, read the text below and decide which answer (A, B, C or D) best fits each gap.**

The new novelist

Amanda Wright, aged 17, has surprised everyone she knows by writing for weeks **(0)** *on* end to produce a full-length science-fiction novel. She frequently worked right through the night to complete the 375-page story, *Parallel Decades*.

Amanda's teachers and family began to get **(1)** ________ about her when she stopped being her usual cheerful self. She **(2)** ________ her appetite, fell asleep during classes and would wander around **(3)** ________ quietly to herself about imaginary characters and faraway civilisations.

No one had a clue what was going on, until a teacher asked her to talk about the most important thing she'd **(4)** ________ in her life. 'I've written a novel,' she said. The class fell silent with astonishment. Back at home, her parents learned what Amanda had been doing and were immensely proud of her. When it turned **(5)** ________ that this was the reason for her moods, they **(6)** ________ with relief. Finally, Amanda's odd behaviour made sense.

Does Amanda plan to write a **(7)** ________ of books? She is quite decisive about it. 'No, I won't! I just don't have the **(8)** ________. I'm exhausted!' she laughs.

	A	B	C	D
0	**A** in	**B** to	**(C)** on	**D** at
1	**A** pessimistic	**B** concerned	**C** furious	**D** irritated
2	**A** overlooked	**B** forgot	**C** missed	**D** lost
3	**A** muttering	**B** whistling	**C** yelling	**D** cheering
4	**A** earned	**B** realised	**C** achieved	**D** reached
5	**A** round	**B** up	**C** over	**D** out
6	**A** sighed	**B** whispered	**C** said	**D** mumbled
7	**A** version	**B** chain	**C** series	**D** course
8	**A** power	**B** push	**C** force	**D** drive

Reading and Use of English Part 2

2 **For questions 1–8, read the text below and think of the word which best fits each gap. Use only one word in each gap. There is an example at the beginning (0).**

Funny PHOBIA?

Every **(0)** *once* in a while, my old phobia reappears. It happens **(1)** ________ I see eggs on someone's plate. I never liked them as a child, and I've never **(2)** ________ used to their unpleasant texture and horrible taste. It's an irrational fear – it isn't as **(3)** ________ I think that the eggs **(4)** ________ actually going to do me any harm – but it isn't quite as unusual, or as funny, as you might think. The phobia even has a name: ovaphobia.

From time **(5)** ________ time, when my sister and I were really young, and Mum told us it was eggs on toast for lunch, I **(6)** ________ start to feel anxious about it. My sister laughed and held up bits of egg on her fork in front of my face. It was a joke to her, but **(7)** ________ a result, I became even more worried about having to eat them. Eventually, my mum realised how serious my phobia was, and she **(8)** ________ never cooked them since!

Reading and Use of English Part 3

3 **For questions 1–8, read the text below. Use the word given in capitals to form a word that fits in the gap. There is an example at the beginning (0).**

THE HAPPIEST PLACE ON EARTH

Norwegians are officially the most **(0)** *cheerful* (CHEER) people on Earth, according to a recent survey. The survey asked around 1,000 people a simple question: 'Where, on a ladder of ten steps, do you stand: at the bottom or at the top?' According to the findings, the people of Norway **(1)** ________ (APPEAR) stand above the rest of us, with a score of 7.54 out of ten!

Scandinavian countries often come out ahead of other places when it comes to **(2)** ________ (ENJOY) of life, and they certainly seem to hold the **(3)** ________ (BELIEVE) that their lives are pretty good. So what makes Scandinavians so **(4)** ________ (OPTIMIST)? Is it living in a pleasant **(5)** ________ (RESIDENT) neighbourhood? Is it having access to nice shops and **(6)** ________ (TREND) restaurants? Is it living in rural rather than more industrial locations?

While Scandinavians do have a better standard of **(7)** ________ (LIFE) than other countries and express less **(8)** ________ (SATISFY) with their lives, they pay higher taxes, too. The difference in happiness levels may be due to the fact that these taxes pay for better facilities in the community.

9 A BRIGHT FUTURE

ABOUT YOU

Do you feel positive or negative about the future? Are you generally an optimistic or pessimistic person?

VOCABULARY Collocations

1 **Complete the quiz with the verbs in the box.**

EP

achieve	go	have (x2)	looks	
make (x2)	making	put	see	take

OPTIMISTIC? PESSIMISTIC? REALISTIC?

Are you an optimist, a pessimist or a realist? Read the statements and decide on your scores from 1 (= strongly disagree) to 5 (= strongly agree).

1. I'm good at ________ **the best of** a bad situation.
2. I think the future of mankind ________ **bright**. For instance, one day, science will ________ **an end to** major diseases.
3. I'm always willing to ________ **a go** at something new. I always ________ **opportunities** that come my way and I ________ **the most of** them.
4. I rarely think it's my fault when things ________ **wrong**.
5. I ________ more **strengths** than **weaknesses**.
6. I really think I'll be able to ________ **a difference** to the world one day.
7. I hope I will ________ all my **goals** in life.
8. I often ________ **the best** in people, rather than **the worst**.

2 **Match the phrases in Exercise 1 to the meanings.**

a make something stop happening *put an end to*
b attempt to do something
c try to be positive about a bad situation
d improve a situation
e notice the most positive/negative qualities
f seems likely to be good or successful
g succeed in your aims
h use occasions to do or say something
i have good/bad qualities
j develop problems
k take full advantage of something because it may not last long

39 **3** **Listen to the conversation. Write Joseph's scores for each quiz question.**

4 **Read the quiz again and decide on your scores. Work in pairs and give reasons for your answers.**

5 **Add up your scores for each question, then turn to page 138.**

1. What does the quiz say about Joseph?
2. What does it say about you / your partner? Do you agree?

READING

1 **Read the article quickly and answer the questions.**

1. What is the text about?
2. Is each expert optimistic or pessimistic about future technologies?
3. Can you think of any themes that link the inventions?

2 **Read the article again. Correct these sentences.**

1. By the middle of this century, travelling to Mars will be a common event for us all.
2. Driverless cars will probably be similar in appearance to today's cars.
3. The main application for exoskeleton suits will be in manufacturing.
4. New forms of clothing will help athletes improve their physical abilities.
5. People in the future will use smartphones to communicate and go online.
6. Students will use VR technology in combination with printed textbooks.

3 **Match the highlighted words in the article to the meanings.**

1. happening often, so not considered special or unusual
2. areas of work or study
3. see something happen
4. taxis (informal)
5. giving the ability to

2050: A glimpse into the future

Have you ever wondered what we'll be doing in 2050? By the middle of this century, new technology will have changed the way we live our lives beyond recognition. Experts from the fields of transport, health and education share some interesting predictions about what lies ahead.

Missions to Mars

The idea of astronauts travelling to Mars may seem like something out of a science fiction movie, but humans may set foot on the red planet sooner than you think. According to experts, by 2050, we will already have been travelling to Mars for some years, with the first trips by astronauts expected as early as 2025. Some companies are even planning to establish a permanent settlement on our neighbouring planet, where trained crews will be able to live and work to further our understanding of the solar system. While missions to Mars will still likely only be for professional astronauts in 2050, it's expected that space tourism around the Earth and Moon will be relatively commonplace.

The death of the smartphone

You probably can't image life without your smartphone, but, according to technology experts, it's likely that these devices will have disappeared by 2050. But don't worry, you'll still be able to keep in touch with your friends or surf the web when you're out and about, thanks to advances in 'augmented reality', or AR, a technology which lays computer-generated images onto a user's view of the real world. Rather than walking around chatting on smartphones, people will instead be wearing small items of jewellery, such as bracelets, that can create a virtual screen that they can use to access and control all the apps they need.

Driverless taxis

If space travel isn't your thing, what about self-driving vehicles? Next year, a US company will be starting a trial of a driverless taxi service in Arizona, and experts think that in as little as ten years' time, we'll all be ordering driverless vehicles instead of traditional cabs to carry us from A to B. These driverless vehicles are likely to look more like a steel box rather than a recognisable car shape, but whatever form they take, there are so many companies in competition to bring us this new form of transport that the next generation won't even need to learn to drive!

Bionic bodies

Fancy being a real-life superhero? The car manufacturer Hyundai has developed an exoskeleton suit, which is a kind of mobile machine that can be worn in factories to make it easier to do jobs such as lifting heavy objects. But in the future, the main applications of this technology are expected to be outside the workplace. Exoskeleton suits have the potential to be hugely beneficial for people with back and leg injuries who currently have to use a wheelchair, enabling them to walk again. Other kinds of bionic clothing may give us superhuman properties, such as 'Spider-Man' suits. These are a softer version of the exoskeleton suit without all the machinery, that give the wearer extra strength or make them run faster. These could be useful for the police and firefighters to help protect them in dangerous situations and allow them to reach people more rapidly in an emergency.

Virtual reality classrooms

Virtual reality (VR) technology is already pretty advanced, and experts believe it could become commonplace in classrooms in the next 10 to 20 years. So, perhaps instead of opening your books at the beginning of a lesson, you'll put on a VR headset! Instead of studying from printed textbooks, apps will allow students to 'travel' via VR to places like the Great Barrier Reef in Australia, where they can observe underwater life and witness the environmental effects of tourism and climate change. This will be a valuable way for students to learn about the world from the comfort of their own classrooms.

TALKING POINTS

Why do you think it's important for technology to keep developing?

What technologies do you think there will be in 50 years' time?

GRAMMAR Future (2): continuous and perfect

1 **Read the examples. How do we form the future continuous, future perfect and future perfect continuous?**

1 Next year, a US company **will be starting** a trial of a driverless taxi service in Arizona.
2 **Will** driverless cars **be driving** us around in as little as ten years' time?
3 It's likely that smartphones **will have disappeared** by 2050.
4 By 2050, we **will** already **have been travelling** to Mars for some years.

2 **Complete the rules with *continuous*, *perfect* or *perfect continuous*.**

We use the
a future ________ for an action that will be in progress in the future or an action that is planned for the future.
b future ________ for an action that will be complete at a future time.
c future ________ to say how long an action has been in progress at a future time.

» GRAMMAR REFERENCE AND PRACTICE PAGE 156

3 **Complete the predictions about life in 50 years' time using the future continuous or future perfect. Which predictions do you agree with?**

1 Technology ________ (put) an end to our energy problems and people ________ (generate) most of their electricity from the sun.
2 We still ________ (not find) life on other planets by then, but some of us ________ (live) on them.
3 I definitely ________ (not work) because I ________ (earn) enough money to retire!
4 Many people will live until they are 150, as scientists ________ (discover) a cure for all diseases.

4 **Choose the correct verb forms.**

1 This time next week, we *'ll sit* / *'ll be sitting* on the beach in Spain!
2 I *'m waiting* / *'ll be waiting* for you at ten outside the space museum.
3 People's homes *will change* / *will be changing* a lot in the near future.
4 Will you *be visiting* / *have visited* anywhere interesting when you go to Africa?

5 **Make sentences about your future in three years' time. Use the future continuous, future perfect or future perfect continuous. Compare your sentences with your partner's.**

1 study at university – Yes/No?
2 travel abroad without your parents – Yes/No?
3 learn English – How long?
4 live with your parents – Yes/No?
5 learn to drive – Yes/No?
6 do an interesting job – Yes/No?

VOCABULARY Adjective and noun suffixes

1 **Look at the adjectives from the article on page 55. What are the noun forms of the words? What suffix has been added in each case?**

1 Missions to Mars will still likely only be for **professional** astronauts in 2050.
2 These could be **useful** for the police and firefighters …
3 … to help protect them in **dangerous** situations.

2 **We use suffixes to change word classes, for example from a verb to a noun or adjective. Find the correct forms of the words in the article on page 55.** (EP)

1 *settle* (verb) → ________ (noun)
2 *driver* (noun) → ________ (adjective)
3 *recognise* (verb) → ________ (adjective)
4 *compete* (verb) → ________ (noun)
5 *value* (noun) → ________ (adjective)

PREPARE FOR THE EXAM

Reading and Use of English Part 3

3 **Read the text and decide which kinds of word are needed in each gap. How do you know?**

HAPPINESS AND HEALTH
Dutch teenagers have it all!

Scientists have often linked **(0)** *emotional* **(EMOTION)** problems, such as depression, to illness, but, until recently, there has been little research into how happiness can be **(1)** ________ **(BENEFIT)** to your health. However, a new study has indicated a close **(2)** ________ **(RELATION)** between them. Conversely, a lack of **(3)** ________ **(ENJOY)** of daily activities and a pessimistic **(4)** ________ **(PERSONAL)** are closely associated with illness. The link between happiness and health is good news for teenagers, as a second report has found that 16- to 17-year-olds express higher levels of **(5)** ________ **(SATISFY)** with their lives than any other age group.

Furthermore, the **(6)** ________ **(MAJOR)** of teenagers also say they are optimistic about the future. And one study has shown that the happiest and healthiest teenagers of all are Dutch. So, what's different about Dutch teenagers? We're often told that having an **(7)** ________ **(ACT)** lifestyle makes us feel better. Dutch teenagers report spending more time than average watching TV and doing little exercise, yet a **(8)** ________ **(REMARK)** 95% of them still say they are content with their lives! Perhaps it is doing what you enjoy that matters most!

4 **Complete the text in Exercise 3. Use the word given in capitals to form a word that fits in the gap.**

» PREPARE FOR THE EXAM PAGE 122

5 » **Work in pairs. Turn to page 139.**

WRITING An essay (2)

1 Look at the two photos. Discuss the questions.

1 When do you think these photos were taken?
2 How are the lives of the people in each photo different?

2 Read the task. Add more information and your own idea to the notes.

> **'Life is better for young people now than it was 50 years ago.' Do you agree?**
>
> **Notes**
> Write about:
> 1 keeping in touch with friends and family
> 2 hobbies
> 3 .... (your own idea)

3 Read the essay and answer the questions.

1 Did the writer mention any of your ideas from Exercise 2?
2 What subjects other than hobbies or keeping in touch with friends and family did the writer mention?

It is common to hear adults talk about how things were different when they were young. Some believe life has improved dramatically for young people, whereas others feel life was simpler when they were young.

On the one hand, in comparison with 50 years ago, teenagers' lives are full of opportunities. Technology has made it easy for us to learn about anything and make friends with people who share similar interests. Moreover, we can easily stay in touch with friends and family, wherever they are in the world.

On the other hand, life was more straightforward half a century ago. While young people today are obsessed with their computers and phones, these things didn't exist when our grandparents were young. Furthermore, unlike now, parents weren't constantly anxious about their children's safety. As a result, young people would spend more time playing sport outside, or being sociable with their friends.

In my view, compared to now, life was definitely less complicated for young people 50 years ago. On balance, however, I believe life today is more interesting and enjoyable, as long as we make the most of our lives and the opportunities we receive.

4 The highlighted words and phrases in the essay are used to organise ideas. Write the words next to the functions.

1 Adding a new point: ...., ...
2 Introducing a personal opinion: ....
3 Showing a logical consequence: ....
4 Summing up: ....

5 Read the *Prepare to write* box and find the expressions in the essay. Then choose the correct options below.

PREPARE TO WRITE | Comparing and contrasting

These expressions are used to compare and contrast ideas:
in comparison with/to
compared to/with
unlike
while/whereas
on the one hand / on the other hand

1 *While / Unlike* my brother, I'm an optimist.
2 *In comparison with / Compared* my friends, I get to go out a lot.
3 My best friend wants to get a job after he leaves school, *whereas / compared to* I want to do a degree.
4 *Compared to / On the one hand* many young people, I have an easy life.
5 In ten years, I'll have my own place, which will be great, but *whereas / on the other hand* I'll be paying for everything myself!

PREPARE FOR THE EXAM

Writing Part 1

6 Read the task. Add more information and your own idea to the notes.

> **'In 25 years, young people's lives will be very different to how they are now.' Do you agree?**
>
> **Notes**
> Write about:
> 1 studies
> 2 entertainment
> 3 .... (your own idea)

7 Write your essay. Use all the notes and give reasons for your point of view.

- Organise your essay into paragraphs.
- Use phrases from the *Prepare to write* box to compare and contrast the present and the future.
- Use expressions from Exercise 4 to organise your ideas.
- Check your grammar and spelling.
- Write 140–190 words.

10 SURPRISE!

ABOUT YOU

07 **Watch the video and answer the questions.**

What's the biggest surprise you've ever had?

Do you like surprises? Why? / Why not?

VOCABULARY Phrases with *in*, *out of*, *at*, *by*

41 **1 Listen and match the speakers (1–5) to the topics (a–f). There is one extra topic.**

a an unexpected extra
b a surprise invitation
c an unexpected visit
d a surprise party
e a surprise wedding
f a shock result

41 **2 Complete the sentences with the words in the box. Listen again and check.**

EP

at fault at risk by accident ~~by chance~~ in advance in all in detail in secret out of character out of nowhere

0 It was only *by chance* that I glanced through the door.
1 The whole concert lasted over two hours ________.
2 Unfortunately, he found out about it ________.
3 I'd left an email open ________.
4 He burst into my room ________.
5 It's not exactly ________ for my brother to turn up like that.
6 United are now ________ of finishing the season without any trophies.
7 United's goalkeeper was partly ________ for the goal.
8 She refused to speak ________ about the ceremony, but said that it had taken place ________ a couple of weeks ago.

3 Match the phrases in Exercise 2 to the meanings.

a before a particular time
b including all the information about something
c altogether
d without telling other people
e unusual in terms of someone's personality
f suddenly and unexpectedly
g without intending to do something, not on purpose
h when something happens because of luck
i responsible for something bad that has happened
j in a situation where something bad is likely to happen

4 Discuss the questions with your partner.

1 Has anyone you know acted in a way that was out of character? What did they do?
2 Would you ever have an argument with someone even if you knew you were at fault?
3 Do you tend to plan your free time in advance?
4 Have you ever broken anything by accident?
5 Do you think it's mean to talk about friends in secret?

READING

1 Read the article quickly and choose the best alternative title (A–C).

A Why we should ban flash mobs
B The world's best flash mobs
C The evolution of flash mobs

PREPARE FOR THE EXAM

Reading and Use of English Part 6

2 Six sentences have been removed from the article. Read sentences A–G and notice the underlined words.

A <u>As a result</u> of such unwelcome incidents, some cities have <u>banned</u> flash mobs.
B They began organising flash mobs <u>all over the world</u>, often through <u>social media and text messaging</u>.
C <u>Despite this</u>, they kept a close eye on the participants.
D Over the next three months, <u>he</u> organised <u>seven successful flash mobs</u> in shops, hotels, parks and stations all around New York.
E They have realised the <u>potential</u> of <u>promoting their products</u> by creating <u>unexpected events in public</u>.
F Recently, over a million people took part in <u>one</u>, at different times on the same day, in over 25 cities <u>around the world</u>.
G One afternoon, <u>he</u> emailed 60 friends, inviting <u>them</u> to meet at a small local shop at exactly 7.24 pm.

3 Choose from the sentences A–G the one which fits each gap (1–6). Use the underlined words to help you decide. There is one extra sentence which you do not need to use.

4 Replace the bold phrases with the correct form of the highlighted phrasal verbs in the article.

1 I've got used to Sam **arriving** late.
2 They're **doing** tests to see if the building is safe.
3 Jem has **thought of** an idea for the end-of-term party.
4 When we got back, Nate had already **tidied up** after the party.
5 I didn't enjoy that book, but don't let that **discourage** you.

FLASH MOB FUN

Imagine it's Saturday at a busy shopping centre. People are doing all the things you'd normally expect – chatting on phones, looking in shop windows and so on. Then suddenly, the people in front of you stop moving. They're completely still, frozen in the middle of whatever they were doing. You look around. There are more of these people – perhaps a hundred or so. Other shoppers look just as confused as you are. Several minutes go by and the frozen people remain in exactly the same positions. Then, as suddenly as they stopped, they begin moving again, as if nothing had happened. You've just experienced a flash mob!

The definition of a flash mob is 'a group of people who meet suddenly in a public place, perform an unusual act for a brief time, then quickly leave'. A US man, Bill Wasik, came up with the idea. [1] ________ They shouldn't say anything to the assistants or each other, he told them. They didn't need to buy anything. They just had to browse for precisely seven minutes and then leave. It would have been the world's first flash mob. However, someone had warned the police, and when Bill and his friends arrived, the police were waiting, and the flash mob couldn't go ahead.

Bill wasn't put off by this failure, however, and started planning the next event. [2] ________ Each time, Bill's friends received their invitations by email. They met at an exact time, carried out their instructions, such as forming a queue or just clapping, and then they left.

Before long, stories and videos of these funny and often bizarre events appeared online. Wasik's idea instantly captured the attention of creative people everywhere. [3] ________ These methods of communication helped spread the message far and wide. Flash mobs quickly became part of modern urban culture and the phrase was even added to the Oxford English Dictionary.

One of the most popular events has been the annual international flash mob pillow fight. [4] ________ However, the event in San Francisco left a park covered in thousands of feathers! It was estimated that it would cost thousands of dollars to clear up the mess. The organisers posted a message online. 'We shouldn't have left such a mess,' they wrote. 'We're sorry.'

Flash mobs are not only potentially costly, though. There is also a danger that they can get out of control. When a 'silent disco' was advertised at a London station, the instructions to anyone who saw it were to bring music, wear headphones and dance. The organiser needn't have worried whether anyone would come: 12,000 people turned up! After 45 minutes, the station was closed, trains were delayed and thousands of passengers were furious. [5] ________

Since the early days of flash mobs, the events have developed into commercial opportunities for companies. [6] ________ In one mobile phone advertisement, for example, a crowd of 500 singers and dancers flooded into Heathrow Airport's arrivals hall to greet people who had just got off flights. The performers had rehearsed in secret for months before the day, and the company was terrified it would go wrong. However, the resulting advert more than lived up to everyone's expectations and has been seen by millions.

TALKING POINTS

Do you think people find flash mobs fun or annoying? Why?

Are flash mobs just entertainment, or can they have a more serious purpose?

GRAMMAR Modals (2): modals in the past

1 **Read the examples. What type of word follows *would have*, *should(n't) have* and *needn't have*?**

1 It **would have been** the world's first flash mob.
2 We **shouldn't have left** such a mess.
3 I **should have sent** the invitation to more people.
4 The organiser **needn't have worried**.
5 They **didn't need to buy** anything.

2 **Complete the rules with some of the modal verbs from Exercise 1.**

We use
a *would have* + past participle to imagine something in the past that didn't happen.
b ________ or *shouldn't have* + past participle to criticise or express a regret about the past.
c ________ + past participle to talk about something which happened but wasn't necessary.
d ________ + infinitive to talk about something which didn't happen because it wasn't necessary.

» GRAMMAR REFERENCE AND PRACTICE PAGE 157

3 **Choose the correct modal verbs.**

1 He *wouldn't* / *shouldn't* have driven when he was so tired. He put all our lives at risk.
2 You *needn't* / *wouldn't* have bought me a present.
3 We left at eight because we *didn't need to be* / *needn't have been* there until nine.
4 I'm glad I didn't see that spider. I *should* / *would* have been petrified!
5 I *needn't* / *shouldn't* have watched that film. I'm going to have difficulty sleeping tonight.
6 You *should* / *would* have told us you were going to be late. We were really concerned.

PREPARE FOR THE EXAM

Reading and Use of English Part 4

4 **Complete the second sentence so that it has a similar meaning to the first sentence, using the word given. Do not change the word given. You must use between two and five words.**

1 It was wrong of you to use my phone without my permission. **SHOULD**
You ________ before you used my phone.
2 It wasn't necessary for you to panic. **HAVE**
You ________ in a panic.
3 It was unfortunate that he went without checking the train times in advance. **SHOULD**
Before going out, ________ the train times.
4 It was a bad idea for me to walk home on my own. **NOT**
I ________ home on my own.
5 Why didn't you tell me you were going out? **SHOULD**
You ________ me know you were going out.
6 We had no homework last night. **NEED**
We ________ do any homework last night.

5 **Correct the mistake in each sentence.**

1 We needn't have gone shopping so we stayed at home and watched TV.
2 You would have seen the doctor about your cough. It sounded awful.
3 I should have gone skating with you yesterday. Why didn't you ask me?
4 You didn't have cooked, but I'm glad you did!
5 My brother wouldn't have told Mum and Dad about the surprise I'd planned for them. It was annoying!

6 **Complete the sentences about you. Then compare them with your partner. Ask more questions to find out details.**

1 Yesterday, I would have … , but …
2 Last weekend, I shouldn't have …
3 This morning, I didn't need to …
4 Last week, I needn't have …
5 Last year, I should have …

VOCABULARY Extended meanings of words

1 **Read the examples. What do *frozen* and *flooded* mean here? What is their literal meaning?**

1 They're completely still, **frozen** in the middle of whatever they were doing.
2 A crowd of 500 singers and dancers **flooded** into Heathrow Airport's arrivals hall.

2 EP **Complete the sentences with the correct form of the words in the box.**

boil bright flood freeze hit weigh

1 You're an excellent student with a ________ future.
2 The students have been ________ by the news that their favourite teacher is leaving.
3 Mind if I leave the door open? It's ________ in here.
4 Having ________ up the pros and cons, he's decided to go to university.
5 She ________ when she saw the spider.
6 I opened the curtains and light ________ into the room.

3 EP **What do you think the words mean in these sentences?**

1 Simon is hardly an **angel**.
2 My memory is **foggy**.
3 The police **grilled** the suspect.
4 The good news **lifted** everyone's mood.
5 Josie **sailed through** her exams.
6 Molly and her sister have a **stormy** relationship.

4 » **Work in pairs. Turn to page 139.**

LISTENING

1 Has anyone ever thrown you a surprise party? Have you ever been to a surprise party for someone else? What happened?

PREPARE FOR THE EXAM

Listening Part 4

2 Listen to part of a radio interview and answer these questions.

43

1. Was it normal for Amanda and her friend to go to this café?
2. Whose idea was it to go to the cinema?
3. What does Amanda say about her actual birthday?

3 Listen again and choose the best answer to question 1.

43

1 Why didn't Amanda suspect her friends were organising something on Saturday?
- **A** They often went to a café before seeing a film.
- **B** She had invited her friends to go to the cinema.
- **C** Saturday wasn't actually her birthday.

4 You will now hear the complete radio interview. For questions 2–7, choose the best answer (A, B or C).

44

2 When Amanda's uncle arrived at the restaurant, Amanda thought he
- **A** seemed uncomfortable.
- **B** was in a hurry.
- **C** would prefer to be alone.

3 What did Amanda think about Jenny's suggestion to go downstairs?
- **A** It was strange because they weren't going to eat.
- **B** It wasn't worth moving because they had to leave soon.
- **C** It was a good idea because it might be quieter there.

4 When Amanda first saw the party, she
- **A** was surprised to see certain people there.
- **B** felt unhappy about being filmed.
- **C** became emotional and cried.

5 What does Amanda say about her parents?
- **A** They stayed longer than she would have liked them to.
- **B** Her dad gave a special performance for her.
- **C** Her mum seemed concerned about making a speech.

6 What has happened as a result of Amanda's party?
- **A** She has recognised how positive her relationships with friends are.
- **B** She has made more effort to spend time with people she likes.
- **C** She has become more confident about receiving attention.

7 What did Amanda's parents think about the idea of a surprise party?
- **A** They were concerned about the cost.
- **B** They didn't think Amanda would enjoy it.
- **C** They were worried it would be too much work.

» PREPARE FOR THE EXAM PAGE 133

SPEAKING Expressing surprise

45 **1** Listen to the conversation. What is Jared surprised about?

45 **2** Listen again and complete the extracts

1. Did she? That's ....!
2. I'd never have .... Lisa was a good writer.

46 **3** Listen to another conversation. What are both Michael and Jared surprised about?

46 **4** Read the *Prepare to speak* box. Then listen to Michael and Jared again. Which expressions do you hear?

PREPARE TO SPEAK Expressing surprise

I'd never have guessed.
It was the last thing I expected.
You're kidding!
That's amazing!
No way!
Really?
Was he?, Did she? (echo questions)

5 Write three pieces of surprising news about yourself. Use the ideas in the box or your own ideas.

an accident | a birthday present
moving house | someone you met
something you bought
something you read online

6 Work in groups.

- Tell each other your news and react.
- Use phrases from the *Prepare to speak* box.

I got a scooter for my birthday!

Did you? You're so lucky!

CULTURE

PERCEPTIONS OF TIME

1 **Ask and answer the questions with a partner.**

1. Do you think more about your past or your future? Why?
2. Do you ever feel that sometimes time goes more slowly or quickly than usual? In what situations?

2 **Read the title and the first paragraph of the article on page 63. How do you think that the language a person speaks can affect the way they perceive time? Read the article quickly and check if any of your ideas are mentioned.**

3 **Read the article again and answer the questions.**

1. How do English and German speakers talk about future events differently?
2. What effect might this difference have on the way that English and German speakers manage their money?
3. How do English and Spanish speakers talk about periods of time differently?
4. Who might think about their future being 'below' them. Why?

4 **Match the highlighted words and phrases in the article to the meanings.**

1. notice or understand the difference between two things
2. feeling that you must do something quickly
3. is in the future
4. form a picture of someone or something in your mind
5. passes very quickly

47 **5** **Listen to three people talking about time and culture. Match the summaries (A–C) to the speakers (1–3).**

A The way in which people think about time individually can be classified into two different groups, each with different perspectives or habits related to time.
B Generally, there are two different ways that cultures view time. The first way is as a sequence or line. The second is to see time as a cycle and something that doesn't start or end.
C The academic study of time uses two different groups to help us understand how time relates to culture and non-verbal communication.

47 **6** **Listen again. Are the sentences true (*T*) or false (*F*)?**

1. People in future-orientated cultures have a relaxed view of time.
2. Western cultures usually see time as a sequence of events or a line.
3. Meeting deadlines is very important in cyclical time cultures.
4. The main priority for people who like multi-tasking is reaching goals and getting results.
5. Time is very valuable in places like Japan.
6. In polychronic cultures, people pay more attention to other people's needs rather than deadlines.

7 **Read the sentences 1–6. Match the phrases in bold to the meanings a–f.**

a certain to happen, but you do not know when
b at the last minute and before it was too late
c not having more time available
d for the moment / temporarily
e the result will be known or seen in the future
f find and dedicate time to doing something

USEFUL LANGUAGE

Expressions with *time*

1. Just stay there **for the time being** and I'll call you in a while.
2. You got here **just in time**. I was about to leave!
3. It's really important to **make time** for yourself and your family.
4. I'm not sure if I made the right decision, but **time will tell**.
5. Well, that's it for today. I'm afraid we're **out of time**.
6. Your parents will find out! It's only **a matter of time**.

CAN THE **LANGUAGE YOU SPEAK** CHANGE HOW YOU VIEW **TIME**?

Time always moves forward at exactly the same rate, but our experience of it can change dramatically. Think about how slowly time seems to pass when you're bored, waiting for something or doing something you don't want to do … But time flies when you're having fun or feeling rushed! Well, new research suggests that the language we speak can affect how we perceive time, and even how we manage our money!

A group of Australian economists has suggested that the way a language 'talks' about the future can affect the way its speakers save their money. Many languages have clearly defined tenses or structures that they use to talk about the future. For example, when making plans, an English speaker might say 'I'll buy a new car next year' or 'I'm going to buy a new car next year'. They wouldn't say 'I buy a car next year'. It has been suggested that speakers of such languages are less likely to save for the future because they see future events as being more distant and less connected to the present. So what about speakers of languages that don't distinguish the future from the present grammatically? They view the future as closer and more real, and so are more likely to save money for it. Speakers of German and Mandarin Chinese, for example, typically talk about the future using a present simple construction: *I buy a car next year*. However, critics of this theory claim that these are just generalisations and many other, more important factors determine people's spending and saving habits.

A different study suggests that the language we use to talk about the duration of an event affects how we think about time. For example, speakers of languages that use mostly 'distance' words to describe time perceive time differently from speakers of languages that use mostly 'volume' words. English and Swedish are examples of languages that generally use distance words to describe time, for example, asking how *long* a film lasts, talking about the *length* of a holiday, or taking a *short* break. Languages like Spanish and Greek, on the other hand, mainly use words of size and volume, for example, asking how *much* time a lesson will last, or taking a *small* break. The study suggests that these differences can affect the speakers' ability to accurately estimate periods of time in different situations.

But it's not just the way we *talk* about language that affects the way we perceive time. Linguists say that the way we read and write our native language also affects the way we visualise time. For example, most languages, including English, are written horizontally from left to right. Speakers of these languages imagine time as a horizontal line with the past behind them, while their future lies ahead of them. However, Mandarin is traditionally written vertically, and therefore its speakers visualise time vertically, from top to bottom. They see the past as being above them and the future below them.

It's fascinating when you start to consider how language affects not only our sense of time, but also the way we think in general and our perception of the world. Take some time to think about it!

PROJECT *Investigating attitudes to time*

Work in groups of three or four to investigate the attitudes towards time amongst people you know. Use these steps to help you.

1 Create a questionnaire about people's views on the following areas:
- punctuality
- saving money
- meeting deadlines
- prioritising tasks

2 Ask people you know, such as friends and family members, to fill in the questionnaire.

Present the results of your questionnaire to the class.

08 NOW WATCH THE CULTURE VIDEO

11 WE ARE FAMILY

ABOUT YOU

09 **Watch the video and answer the questions.**

Who do you get on with best in your family? Why?

Do you think it's important to know about your family history?

What do you think makes a happy family?

VOCABULARY Phrasal verbs: relationships

1 Match the pairs of sentences.

EP
1 Sarah really **looks up to** her father.
2 My eldest sister **looks down on** me.
3 Luke **takes after** his father.
4 My family always **stick together**.
5 I don't want to **fall out** with you.
6 My brother's **gone off** his girlfriend.
7 Lisa has just **finished with** her boyfriend.
8 I didn't **hit it off** with Jake.
9 I can always **count on** my parents.
10 Anna won't **let** you **down**.

a He's 1.92 m tall, the same as his dad.
b She makes me feel completely unimportant.
c I found him very difficult to talk to.
d I think they're going to split up.
e We never fall out and we're very close.
f I hate getting into arguments.
g They'll always help me if I need them to.
h He's a very good role model for her.
i She's single again now.
j If she says she'll help, she will help.

49 **2 Listen to the conversations and answer the questions you are asked.**

3 Ask and answer the questions about your family or friends with a partner.

1 Have you ever met someone and hit it off with them immediately?
2 Have you ever let anyone down? How?
3 Who can you really count on?
4 Who do you look up to? Why?
5 Who do you take after?
6 Have you ever felt that someone looks down on you? Who?
7 Does your family stick together?
8 Have you ever gone off someone? Why?
9 Have you ever finished with a girlfriend or boyfriend?
10 How often do you fall out with friends?

READING

PREPARE FOR THE EXAM

Reading and Use of English Part 2

1 Read the example answer (0) in the first paragraph of the text. What type of word is given in the gap?

2 For questions 1–8, read the first two paragraphs of the text and think of the word which best fits each gap. Use only one word in each gap.

3 Read the rest of the text. Match the sections (A–C) to the headings (1–5). There are two extra headings.

1 Long-distance love
2 Opposites attract
3 Family nightmares
4 Wrong number
5 Staying local

4 Answer the questions.

1 What 'mistake' did Attis make?
2 Why did the Palestino fans take pity on Nobu?
3 Why didn't Rachana like Amir at first?

HOW WE MET ...

No one says that **(0)** *being* part of a family is easy, but families do generally provide us with the love, comfort and security we need. **(1)** ________ is partly because of a shared history, which is often recorded in photos. What many families enjoy doing **(2)** ________ looking back at the people and events in their lives through these photos. And it's always fun to see which of our ancestors we take **(3)** ________.

Family members also like to share things they remember, **(4)** ________ as fond memories of their relatives, or amusing stories of **(5)** ________ grown-ups did when they were small. Perhaps most of **(6)** ________, we enjoy hearing about how our parents and grandparents first got to know each other. The more unusual or romantic the story, the more we enjoy hearing **(7)** ________. The same stories are often told over and over again without losing their impact, and bring families closer together **(8)** ________ time they hear them.

Here are some family stories of how people met.

50

A MARKOS FAFOUTAKIS
Athens, Greece ________

It was love at first sight for Markos's grandparents, despite the fact that they had fallen out before they met face to face. It all started when his grandfather, Attis Fafoutakis, called a friend. Marie Wouters, who had just moved to Greece from Belgium, answered the phone. When she explained that she didn't know the friend Attis was looking for, Attis got a little annoyed. But when Marie repeated her number slowly, Attis realised his mistake. He was in a hurry, so he simply hung up. Later, Attis couldn't stop thinking about the woman he had spoken to. There had been something in her voice which had really appealed to him and so he decided to start all over again. Attis redialled the number that he had called by accident and used all his charms to apologise to Marie. She forgave him and they ended up chatting for ages. In fact, they got on so well that they arranged to meet, and the rest is history.

B PANCHO YAMAMOTO
Talcahuano, Chile ________

Pancho Yamamoto's parents didn't exactly hit it off the first time they met. The Yamamotos moved from Japan to Chile to work in the mines around 1915. Pancho's father, Nobu, was a big fan of Huachipato, a football team from his home town of Talcahuano. Nobu took pride in going to every Huachipato match and one winter, he travelled 500 km to Santiago de Chile, where Huachipato was going to play against Palestino. At the match, he was surprised to find that he was the only Huachipato fan in the stadium. The Palestino fans laughed and whistled at lonely Nobu throughout the game. Then, when the game ended, some of them took pity on him, invited him for dinner and they soon forgot all about their teams' rivalry. One Palestino fan, Carolina Fernández, had been laughing at Nobu all along, like the others. But she knew it was wrong, so she made an effort to get to know him during dinner. Despite living at different ends of the country, they started writing letters to each other – in all about 200 passed between them before they got married.

C LUCINDA SHAH
Marrakesh, Morocco ________

Lucinda Shah tells us about how her parents almost didn't get together ...

Lucinda's mother, Rachana, who is Indian, grew up in Mumbai and ended up working as an actress in London. Lucinda's father, Amir, a film producer whose work is mainly in the UK, was born in India to an Afghan father and a Scottish mother. Amir Shah met Rachana in 1999 through a mutual friend, Carrie. 'She thought we'd get on well, and invited us both to a dinner party,' says Rachana. Unfortunately, it wasn't love at first sight. 'I thought he was rude and arrogant!' she continues. 'I'm very confident and chatty, whereas he hardly spoke and just kept staring at me.' When Amir had left the party, Rachana shared her doubts with her friend. 'Carrie told me that Amir was shy and that the more he liked someone, the quieter he was. She said it was a good sign!' Rachana decided to give Amir another chance, and the pair met up for coffee. 'This time,' says Rachana, 'I asked Amir lots of questions about his work, and we chatted for the rest of the afternoon and we really hit it off!'

TALKING POINTS

How do family relationships differ from friendships?

Do you think friends can be more important than family in certain situations?

GRAMMAR Relative clauses

1 **Read the examples and underline the relative clauses. Are they defining (D) or non-defining (ND)?**

1 Marie Wouters, who had just moved to Greece from Belgium, answered the phone.
2 Attis couldn't stop thinking about the woman he had spoken **to**.
3 Attis redialled the number that he had called by accident.
4 There had been something in her voice which had really appealed to him.
5 Lucinda's father, whose work is mainly in the UK, was born in India.
6 Nobu travelled to Santiago de Chile, where Huachipato was going to play against Palestino.

2 **Read the rules and check your answers.**

a A defining relative clause gives essential information about a noun. We:
- can leave out the relative pronoun if it is the object of the clause.
- cannot leave out the relative pronoun if it is the subject of the clause.

b A non-defining relative clause adds extra information about a noun. We:
- cannot leave out the relative pronoun.
- do not use *that* for people or things.
- always use commas before and after the relative clause.

» GRAMMAR REFERENCE AND PRACTICE PAGE 158

3 **Read the examples in Exercise 1 again. Where is the bold preposition in example 2?**

4 **Read the text. Add a relative pronoun before each relative clause. Put the relative pronoun in brackets if you can leave it out. Add commas where necessary.**

We went to the island of Rhodes, which is where my ancestors used to live.

I'll never forget our family holiday in Greece. We went to the island of Rhodes is where my ancestors used to live. It's an area has a fascinating history, and my parents wanted to find the village they used to live in. We couldn't find any records could help us, but eventually we found a village just like the one in the old photos we had been given. We asked in a café and we were introduced to an old man great-grandparents had lived next to our old family home. The house had been knocked down, but it was nice to make a connection with someone knew a bit about our family history.

5 **Rewrite the sentences using relative clauses.**

0 I have a cousin the same age as me. She is really good fun.
I have a cousin the same age as me, who is really good fun.
1 That's Shelly. She wants to buy my bike.
2 Our apartment has views across the whole city. It was built five years ago.
3 My uncle is now a teacher at our school. He always played with us as children.
4 Here's the money. I owe you it for the concert ticket.
5 This is a photo of my grandparents. They got married in 1967.

6 **Correct the mistake in each sentence.**

1 I went with my wife and son is two years old.
2 The area, wich has lots of farms, is great for walking.
3 At the café, we met a girl which my friend Saif knows.
4 The beach, who is really long and wide, is perfect for playing ball games.
5 There are 30 students will attend the class.

VOCABULARY Compound adjectives

1 EP **Complete the compound adjectives. Use the past participle form of the words in the box.**

age	balance	behave
~~build~~	organise	pay

0 Sam is tall and weighs 86 kg. He's fairly well-*built*.
1 The holiday was well-______, thanks to my mum.
2 My dad's 45, so I guess he's middle-______.
3 I try to eat a well-______ diet.
4 My aunt has a very well-______ job.
5 I can't stand badly ______ pets! My dog's so good!

2 EP **Complete the sentences. Combine one word from each box to form compound adjectives.**

grown	high	last	~~long~~	self	short

confident	~~distance~~	minute
tech	term	up

0 We make a lot of *long*-*distance* phone calls.
1 Mark is really ______-______. He doesn't mind performing in front of huge audiences.
2 My uncle's living with us at the moment, but it's only a ______-______ arrangement. He's moving out to his own place soon.
3 I've got two ______-______ cousins who are a lot older than me. They have their own homes and families now.
4 There's always a lot of ______-______ equipment in our house because my mum's a software developer.
5 We didn't book the football tickets until the day before the match. It was a ______-______ decision, so we were lucky to get seats.

3 » **Work in pairs. Turn to page 139.**

WRITING An article (2)

1 **Read the article. In what way has Sebastian's brother influenced him?**

Someone I admire

by Sebastian Duchamps

Can you think of someone who you really look up to? Is there anyone who you can rely on, no matter what? For me that person is my older brother, Louis.

When I was 13, he had a big impact on my life. I was having problems with a gang at school who used to bully me all the time. Talking to my parents didn't help because they don't understand teenage stuff, but I did talk to my brother about it. Discussing the issues with him made a huge difference to me. The thing I admired most about him was his patience. I must have talked about the same problem 100 times, yet he always listened as if it was the first time. I think that makes him a pretty grown-up person.

Louis has been a really important influence on me ever since. What I've learned more than anything is the importance of being thoughtful. Instead of sounding sympathetic and then forgetting all about friends' problems, I listen properly now.

What about you? Who has been a big influence in your life?

2 **Read the task, then read Sebastian's article again. Answer the questions.**

You see this notice in an English-language magazine for teenagers.

> **Articles needed!**
> Do you have a friend or family member that you look up to?
> What makes this person special?
> What have you learned from him or her?
> The best articles will be published in our magazine.

Write your **article**.

1. Can you think of a more interesting title for Sebastian's article?
2. Does Sebastian answer the three questions in the task?
3. How does he organise his answers?
4. How does Sebastian get the reader's attention?

3 **Read the *Prepare to write* box. Match the sentence structures in the *Prepare to write* box to the highlighted parts of the article.**

PREPARE TO WRITE | Varying sentence structure

You can make your writing more interesting by varying your sentence structure. Try using

- questions.
- *-ing* forms as subjects.
- structures which add emphasis.

4 **Complete the second sentence so that it means the same as the first. Use ideas from the *Prepare to write* box to help you.**

1. I met Adam and that changed my life.
   ________ Adam changed my life.
2. I admire her kindness the most.
   What I ________ is her kindness.
3. I love my uncle, especially his sense of humour.
   The thing ________ about my uncle is his sense of humour.
4. I spent time with my aunt, and that helped me become more confident.
   ________ with my aunt helped me become more confident.
5. I find his determination really amazing.
   ________ amazing is his determination.
6. I really like his positive attitude to life.
   The thing ________ his positive attitude to life.

PREPARE FOR THE EXAM

Writing Part 2 (An article)

5 **Read the task in Exercise 2 again and plan your own article.**

- Think of a family member or friend.
- Make notes. Think of examples which will help you to answer the questions and develop your ideas.
- Put your ideas in order.
- Think of a topic sentence to begin each paragraph.
- Think of an interesting title.

6 **Write your article.**

- Try to vary your sentence structure.
- Remember to address your reader to get their attention.
- Check your grammar and spelling.
- Write 140–190 words.

12 MAKING A DIFFERENCE

ABOUT YOU

Which of the photos below do you like best? Why? Do you think seeing these things can make a difference to how people feel?

VOCABULARY Verbs of communication

1 **How many of the photos can you match with each sentence?**

EP

1. This was done to cheer people up.
2. This is probably intended to amuse people.
3. This is intended to highlight a cause or problem.
4. This is to congratulate someone.
5. I think this is there to stimulate people to think.
6. Whoever did this wanted to speak out about an issue.
7. Things like this reassure people that things will work out well.
8. I think it is there to spread happiness.
9. This one's obviously there to promote a business.

51 **2** **Listen to James and Rosie discussing photos A–D. Which verb(s) do they associate with each photo?**

3 **Discuss three things that …**

- cheer you up.
- you'd like to speak out about.
- amuse you.

READING

1 **Read the text quickly. What is a random act of kindness? Give two examples.**

PREPARE FOR THE EXAM

Reading and Use of English Part 5

2 **Read the text again. For questions 1–6, choose the answer (A, B, C or D) which you think fits best according to the text.**

1 When Sarah was at the supermarket, she says that she felt
- **A** content about having spent time with her friends.
- **B** pleased by the success of her earlier shopping trip.
- **C** worried about being able to fulfill her father's request.
- **D** concerned about the motives of someone who approached her.

2 What reason does Alison give for helping others?
- **A** She is keen to give something back to people who have helped her.
- **B** She enjoys seeing people's delight at receiving an offer of help.
- **C** She likes the way doing things for other people makes her feel.
- **D** She finds it interesting to try out helpful new activities.

3 What is suggested about Alison in the fourth paragraph?
- **A** She was impressed by how rapidly random acts of kindness became popular.
- **B** She was enthusiastic about the idea of improving her mood through physical contact.
- **C** She was motivated to think of some random acts of kindness to carry out herself.
- **D** She was encouraged to do something in return for the person who helped her.

4 What does 'merely' mean in line 49?
A easily **B** barely **C** simply **D** slightly

5 What was Sarah's attitude when she first heard about *caffè sospeso*?
- **A** She thought it was unfair to customers who had to pay for their coffee.
- **B** She realised that it was something she'd like to do.
- **C** She believed it could be confusing for customers.
- **D** She found it a highly unusual concept.

6 In the final paragraph, we understand that Sarah feels
- **A** disappointed so few people want to help others.
- **B** hopeful for a future where people are nicer to one another.
- **C** optimistic that she would benefit from others' kindness one day.
- **D** keen to appear as generous as the people she had recently come across.

RANDOM ACTS OF KINDNESS

By Sarah Longman

Have you experienced a 'random act of kindness'? Imagine the scene: you've been out shopping all day with friends. You're loaded with bags and heading home. Then your dad calls and asks if you can pick up a few things at the supermarket on the way back. You do the shopping, then, standing outside the supermarket, wonder how you're going to get everything home. Another customer approaches you. 'Need a hand?' she asks. What should you say?

As a matter of fact, when this happened to me, I was a little suspicious. Why would someone want to help me carry my bags all the way home? 'It's just a random act of kindness!' the woman said. She reassured me it was no problem, and I accepted her offer with relief.

As we were walking along, the woman introduced herself as Alison and told me that many people had been kind to her in the past. Now she wanted to do something for someone else. She explained that random acts of kindness are doing favours for someone you have never met before, and for no special reason. The whole idea is simply to cheer strangers up. I was amused by the idea myself, and asked whether she did this all the time. 'I like to do a few random acts every once in a while. It makes me happy that I've done something to benefit others,' explained Alison. 'It could be any number of things, from picking up litter in a stranger's garden to swapping places with the person behind you in a queue. As far as I'm concerned, by far the best part is watching people's reactions. Some people are comfortable with it immediately, others are doubtful initially, and a few don't want to be helped at all.'

Alison's interest in helping others began when she was hugged by a complete stranger at a bus stop on a trip to the United States. An old lady was standing there with a sign that said *Free Hugs*. When Alison asked her what it meant, the woman just hugged her. 'It made a difference to my day,' she said. While Alison was waiting, the woman hugged several other people – young and old, men and women. A few days later, Alison came across the video for *All the Same* by the band Sick Puppies, which shows the first Free Hugs group hugging shoppers in Sydney. 'The video went viral and incredibly got millions of views!' she said. As a result of this, the idea spread quickly and there are now Free Hugs campaigns in most countries. Millions of people have been inspired by the idea, which has gone beyond **merely** giving hugs to include other random acts of kindness like the one I experienced from Alison.

A few weeks later, I went into a café to get a takeaway coffee. While I was being served, a man walked in behind me and asked, 'Are there any free coffees?' I could hardly believe my ears, especially when the barista said, 'Yes.' The customer got the barista to give him a coffee – for nothing. Then the barista crossed off a mark on the blackboard. When the man had left, I asked the barista what was going on. '*Caffè sospeso,*' he explained. 'It's an old tradition from Naples, in Italy. It means 'suspended coffee' in Italian, and it's when someone who's had good luck or who is feeling generous orders two coffees, one to drink and one a *sospeso*, for a future customer who needs a coffee but can't afford one. We take the payment and add a mark here on the board. Then people can come in and ask if we have any *sospesos* – any free coffees. We don't promote it, but our regulars know we do it.'

In a world where we are often let down by people's behaviour, I felt glad to witness such generosity of the human spirit. Wondering whether charity and kindness could become the philosophy of the modern age, I ordered a cappuccino 'to go' – and one *caffè sospeso*.

3 **Match the highlighted words and phrases in the text to the meanings.**

1. people who often go to a particular shop, restaurant, etc.
2. done or chosen without any plan or system
3. not trusting someone
4. became very popular very quickly on social media
5. small pieces of rubbish that are left in public places

TALKING POINTS

Which of the random acts of kindness in the text appeals to you the most? Why?

How do you think you would react if someone offered you a random act of kindness? Why?

GRAMMAR The passive (1): review

1 Read the passive examples. What tenses are they?

1 She **was hugged** by a complete stranger.
2 While I **was being served**, a man walked in behind me and asked …

2 Read the rules. Why is the passive used in each sentence in Exercise 1?

We use the passive
a when who or what does something is unknown, unimportant or obvious.
b to emphasise the person who receives an action, rather than the person who does the action.
We use *by* if it is important to add who or what does something.

» GRAMMAR REFERENCE AND PRACTICE PAGE 159

3 Complete the text with the passive form of the verbs in brackets.

Free hugs STOP the city

Members of the Free Hugs Campaign [0] *have been asked* (ask) to go home early after their annual meeting caused chaos this evening. Although thousands of members [1] .... (invite), organisers only expected a few hundred to turn up. They were wrong, and huge numbers of people arrived. Roads around the city centre [2] .... (block) by the enormous crowds for three hours earlier today, and even now drivers [3] .... (advise) to avoid the area until midnight. Police are warning that public transport [4] .... (might / affect) until later tonight as well. 'Throughout the day, we [5] .... (impress) by the organisers,' said a police spokesperson. And 'I [6] .... (never / hug) by so many people in one day!' he added.

4 Correct the mistake in each sentence.

1 The food was really tasty. It makes by my dad.
2 This game can be play online.
3 The pool was closed because it has been repaired.
4 This is the most powerful book that was written in the last decade.

Causative *have/get*

5 Read the examples and answer the questions.

1 I needed to **have** my bags **carried**.
Who did the writer think should carry her bags?
2 I was pleased to **get** my shopping **delivered**.
Who was delivering the writer's shopping?
3 The customer **got** the barista **to give** him a coffee – for nothing.
Who gave the customer a coffee? Did the customer pay?

» GRAMMAR REFERENCE AND PRACTICE PAGE 159

6 Write sentences using the verbs in the box and the causative.

cut	redeliver	repair	~~replace~~	wash

0 Your dad's watch stops.
He could have/get the batteries replaced.
1 Your sister's hair is too long.
2 Your mum's car was dirty.
3 The screen on your phone has cracked.
4 They tried to deliver a parcel while I was out.

VOCABULARY *both, either, neither*

1 Read the examples. Then match the words to the meanings.

You've **both** got heavy shopping bags to carry.
Both (**of** my) bags are full of shopping.
Is **either of** you tired?
I'll carry **either** this bag **or** that one.
Neither of you has any energy left.
Neither you **nor** your friend has any energy left.

1 both — a one or the other
2 either (… or) — b one and the other
3 neither (… nor) — c not one or the other

2 Choose the correct options.

1 Both of them *is / are* mine.
2 Either George or Sam *is / are* lying.
3 Neither Sam nor Jo *was / were* willing to help.

3 Write one or two words in each gap.

1 You can go along .... Park Street or Market Street – .... ways are fairly quick.
2 A police officer and a taxi driver were offered hugs, but .... them accepted.
3 Two students asked me if I'd like a free hug, so I had hugs from .... them!

4 » **Work in pairs. Turn to page 139.**

LISTENING

53 **1** **You will hear a woman called Amy Linton talking about something she heard recently. What was it?**

PREPARE FOR THE EXAM

Listening Part 2

2 53 **Read the sentences below carefully. Try to work out what kinds of answer are needed. Then listen again and, for questions 1–10, complete the sentences with a word or short phrase.**

MUSIC IN THE CITY

Amy works as a **(1)** ………… in London.
Amy first heard violin music when she was in the **(2)** ………… at the station.
Amy uses the word '**(3)** …………' to describe how well the woman was playing the violin.
Amy was amused to see that, unlike her, the violinist was wearing **(4)** ………… .
The violinist had put a **(5)** ………… on the ground for people to put money in.
When a little boy stopped to listen, the violinist **(6)** ………… briefly.
Amy realised that she knew the piece of music from a **(7)** ………… she'd listened to.
When the music stopped, Amy felt **(8)** ………… by what she had heard.
Amy realised that she'd seen the violinist once before at a **(9)** ………… .
The violinist said she liked to play in **(10)** ………… because the sound was always interesting.

SPEAKING Discussing options

54 **1** **Listen to Alexandra and Johann talking as part of a speaking exam. They are talking about giving help to disabled children in the local community.**

1 Tick (✓) the five things that they talk about.
2 What do they both agree they would help with?

access to school computer gaming
going out at the weekend going shopping
homework reading and writing
sports tidying up

55 **2** **Read the** ***Prepare to speak*** **box. Then listen to part of the conversation again. Which expressions do you hear?**

PREPARE TO SPEAK Keeping talking

Starting to talk
Let's start with …

Asking for clarification
What exactly do you mean?
Are you referring to … ?

Keeping talking
Again, as with … , we could …
What else? / Anything else?
I was just going to say that …
Do you want to add anything?

PREPARE FOR THE EXAM

Speaking Part 3 and Part 4

3 56 **Work in pairs. Listen to the instruction and look at the task for one minute. Then complete the task. Use phrases from the** ***Prepare to speak*** **box.**

Is it a good idea for students to spend time helping elderly people in their local community?

- having time for schoolwork
- spending free time with friends
- learning from older people
- getting practical skills
- understanding other people's lives

4 **Ask and answer the questions with a partner.**

1 What are the most common ways in which people help others?
2 How important is it to help other people?
3 Do you think it can be difficult for people to ask for help? Why?
4 Why do you think some people do not want to be helped?
5 If you don't offer help, you won't receive it. Do you think this is true?
6 'People only help others when they want something in return.' Do you agree?

» PREPARE FOR THE EXAM PAGES 136–7

LIFE SKILLS COLLABORATION

VOLUNTEERING

1 Ask and answer the questions with a partner.

1 Have you ever volunteered? What for?
2 Do you know anyone who volunteers? What do they do?

2 In pairs, make a list of things you could do as a volunteer and organisations you could help. Then read the text on the opposite page quickly and see if any of your ideas are mentioned.

3 Read the text again and answer the questions.

1 What can you learn about if you volunteer locally?
2 Why will volunteering look good on future university or job applications?
3 What key question should you ask yourself to find the right volunteer role for you?
4 Who could you contact if you're interested in the arts?
5 Why is it better to begin by dedicating less time and then increase your involvement slowly?

4 Match the highlighted words and phrases in the text to the meanings.

1 a safe place to live and be protected
2 happening without most people knowing about it
3 collecting money for a cause or charity
4 responsibilities which are part of your role
5 the set of characteristics that make a good leader

LIFE SKILLS

Volunteering

There are many ways that you can volunteer. You may want to support a cause that is important to you, or volunteer for an activity which allows you to explore your interests. Volunteering is a great way to gain new skills and new experiences, and to show how responsible you can be.

57 **5 Listen to a talk about summer volunteer programmes abroad. Put the topics mentioned in the correct order.**

A Financial considerations and suggestions ____
B Benefits of participating in a volunteer programme ____
C Types of volunteer programmes abroad _1_
D Planning a summer volunteering experience ____
E Final preparations ____

57 **6 Listen again and complete the sentences with between one and three words in each gap.**

1 If you enjoy spending time with children, you might want to try teaching ____________.
2 Volunteering can help increase ____________ and improve your ability to adapt.
3 Asking organisers ____________ can help you feel fully informed about volunteering.
4 Travel and accommodation are examples of the ____________ you will probably need to pay.
5 You'll need to organise your travel ____________ and write a ____________ list.

7 Complete the sentences with the words in the box.

budget	build	host	intercultural
reviews	sustainable		

USEFUL LANGUAGE

Choosing and planning a summer volunteer opportunity

1 Volunteering will help you to ____________ relationships.
2 You'll develop your ____________ understanding.
3 Is the project ____________?
4 Find ____________ online from previous participants.
5 Working out your ____________ will be key.
6 Research the ____________ country carefully.

CAN YOU SPARE SOME TIME?

58

So you're thinking of volunteering and wondering how to find out more about it? Whatever the reasons for wanting to volunteer, there are many benefits. Firstly, through helping others locally, you'll become more aware of the social issues which are facing your community. Obviously, you'll also end up meeting new people and that will help you to develop a sense of empathy and better understand the needs of others.

Apart from the satisfaction you'll feel from knowing that you're making a difference to your community, volunteer work will also look great on future applications for university or a job! That's because, while you're volunteering, you'll develop a range of transferable skills such as time management, organisation, leadership and conflict resolution. These skills, and many more, will be very useful to you both now and in the future!

Volunteering is basically like having a job (but an unpaid one!) and you'll need to take it seriously. Finding the right area to work in is very important when looking for a volunteering opportunity, and the best way to do this is to sit down and think about it carefully first. Do you feel passionate about any particular social or environmental issues? Would you prefer to be working with members of the public or working behind the scenes? Realistically, how much time will you have to offer? But probably the most important question of all is: what are you interested in?

If you're interested in music, could you help out at a local music festival? Or if you're keen on becoming a vet or a zoologist, why not approach a local animal shelter and ask if they need help caring for the animals? Maybe you're into sports? Well, talk to a local sports league or the organisers of a local fundraising event, like a run, and ask how you could play a part.

Perhaps you'd just like to be with others and help people. How about supporting people with special needs, or lending a hand at your neighbourhood food bank? Or maybe the arts are more your thing? Local museums are always looking for volunteers to lead visitor tours of their galleries and exhibits. If you're not a big fan of museums and prefer the outdoors, try contacting an environmental organisation and see what initiatives they're involved in locally.

Your duties as a volunteer will depend on the exact role you choose. However, there are a few things to consider which are relevant to all volunteering opportunities. Firstly, think carefully about how much time you can dedicate. It's much better to start off with a smaller time commitment and gradually increase your participation as you become more involved. You don't want your volunteering to interfere with your study time. You'll also need to think about how to get to the place where you'll be volunteering. Are there buses or trains, or will someone give you a lift? And lastly, remember that you might need to do some basic training before you can begin, and there could be a minimum age requirement for the volunteer role that you're interested in.

Ready to expand your horizons? Get out there and start looking – there's a volunteer opportunity waiting just for you!

PROJECT

Choosing a volunteer programme

Work in groups of three or four to choose and research a summer volunteer programme. Use these steps to help you.

1. Search for summer volunteer programmes online and decide on one which everyone would like to do.
2. Research your chosen programme or project. Find information about what it involves and how to apply for it.
3. Search for images and videos of people participating in the programme. Find some reviews from previous participants.
4. Create a short presentation about your chosen programme and take turns to share your individual reasons for wanting to do it.

Present your work to the class.

REVIEW 3 UNITS 9–12

VOCABULARY

1 **Match the two parts of the phrases.**

1 make the	**a** goals
2 put an	**b** best of something
3 have a	**c** go at something
4 achieve your	**d** best in people
5 see the	**e** end to something

2 **Complete the meanings with the words in the box and a preposition.**

accident advance character fault secret

1 When you do something before it's needed, you do it ________.
2 When you do something you wouldn't normally do, you act out ________.
3 When you do something and hide it from others, you do it ________.
4 When you're responsible for something that's going wrong, you're ________.
5 When you do something you didn't mean to do, you do it ________.

3 **Complete the conversations with a compound adjective that means the opposite of the underlined words. Use the words in the box.**

badly last self short well

1 **A:** Is Martin the tall <u>slim</u> boy?
B: No, he's the ________-built one.
2 **A:** Did you plan your holiday well <u>in advance</u>?
B: No, it was a ________-minute decision.
3 **A:** Were the students <u>good</u>?
B: There were a few ________ behaved boys, but nothing serious.
4 **A:** Is your brother's job abroad <u>permanent</u>?
B: No, it's only a ________-term contract.
5 **A:** Is Louise still as <u>shy</u> as she used to be?
B: No, she's much more ________-confident now.

4 **Rewrite the underlined phrases using the phrasal verbs in the box. Make any other changes necessary.**

fall out go off let down look down on
stick together take after

1 I feel terrible about <u>disappointing Tom</u>, but I'm just too tired to go out tonight.
2 We always <u>support each other</u> in my family.
3 My brother <u>is a lot like</u> our dad.
4 I've <u>stopped enjoying</u> chocolate.
5 My sister and I are constantly <u>having arguments</u>, but we always make up again.
6 It always feels as if Susanna is <u>thinking that I'm less important than her</u>.

GRAMMAR

1 **Choose the correct options.**

1 By the end of the year, we'll *be finishing / have finished* this book.
2 Maybe we could borrow my dad's car. He won't *be using / have used* it today.
3 I might be tired on Saturday evening, as I'll *have revised / have been revising* all day.
4 I will have been learning Spanish *by the time we go to Madrid. / for a year soon.*
5 I can give Mike the key. I'll *be seeing / have seen* him later.
6 Emily's going to university next year. She'll *have finished / have been finishing* school then.

2 **Choose the correct options.**

1 I *shouldn't / wouldn't* have done the shopping if I'd known we were going out.
2 Sally made all the arrangements in advance, so we *didn't need to do / shouldn't have done* anything.
3 You *shouldn't / wouldn't* have let John down yesterday. He needed your help.
4 I'm glad I didn't wear my jacket. I *shouldn't / wouldn't* have been comfortable.
5 I *should / would* have persuaded Josie to come and see that film. She'd have loved it.
6 It was an easy history test. I spent ages learning dates, but I *needn't / wouldn't* have.

3 **Complete the sentences with *who*, *that*, *which*, *whose*, *where*, *when* or *why*. Write the word in brackets if you can leave it out.**

1 This is the hospital ________ Sam's dad works.
2 We waited for Marcus, ________ eventually turned up 30 minutes late.
3 Sam's the girl ________ mum you met.
4 Can I borrow the book ________ you were reading?
5 Do you know the date ________ we have to hand in our essay?
6 I don't know the reason ________ he left.

4 **Correct the mistake in each sentence.**

1 You mentioned that you have to leave by 4.50 pm. That's not a problem, we will have been finished by then.
2 The time that the show should start was 19.30, but it started 45 minutes later.
3 Your group has been booked into the Palace Hotel, which address you will find in the leaflet.
4 That time we spent together was great, because I made some good new friends, which are some of my closest.
5 I inspired to read the book after I had watched the film.

PREPARE FOR THE EXAM

Reading and Use of English Part 2

1 For questions **1–8**, read the text below and think of the word which best fits each gap. Use only **one** word in each gap.

WHY PEOPLE LIKE SURPRISES

I hate surprises, and I wouldn't **(0)** *have* believed anyone who said they really liked them. That is until I read about a fascinating experiment that **(1)** ________ carried out by neuroscientists in America, **(2)** ________ wanted to find out why some people appear to like surprises and others don't. During the experiment, the scientists poured either water **(3)** ________ juice into the mouths of those who had agreed to be involved. Sometimes the subjects knew which one they were going to **(4)** ________ given, and sometimes they didn't.

(5) ________ some of the subjects had previously stated that they didn't like surprises, their brains told a different story. As the water or juice was put into their mouths, the subjects' brain activity was recorded **(6)** ________ machines. Images showed that their brains responded more strongly to the unexpected pleasures than the subjects might have thought. This surprised the scientists, **(7)** ________ expectation was that the brain **(8)** ________ respond to any pleasurable substance.

Reading and Use of English Part 3

2 For questions **1–8**, read the text below. Use the word given in capitals to form a word that fits in the gap.

90 ACTS OF KINDNESS

'I had a great **(0)** *friendship* (**FRIEND**) with my grandfather,' says 17-year-old Josie Taylor. 'He was kind, and made a big **(1)** ________ (**DIFFERENT**) to those around him, simply by being friendly. When he passed away at the age of 90, I decided to do 90 acts of kindness in his memory. I'm a **(2)** ________ (**PRACTICE**) person, so I thought I'd use my main **(3)** ________ (**STRONG**) – cooking – to make others happier.

With **(4)** ________ (**ENCOURAGE**) from my grandmother, I baked a cake for a neighbour. He was thrilled! That was when I realised how **(5)** ________ (**EFFECT**) one small act can be.

I learned a **(6)** ________ (**VALUE**) lesson from my acts: I noticed that even a kind word or smile can be **(7)** ________ (**BENEFIT**) in terms of well-being – for both the person who receives it and the one who gives it. With all my schoolwork, finding time to do 90 acts of kindness was an **(8)** ________ (**REAL**) goal and I couldn't reach it. But I did make time to say hello to neighbours and help people when they needed it!'

Reading and Use of English Part 4

3 For questions **1–6**, complete the second sentence so that it has a similar meaning to the first sentence, using the word given. **Do not change the word given.** You must use between **two** and **five** words, including the word given.

0 Oh, no – you don't have any chocolate left and I don't have any either! **US**
Oh, no – *neither of us* has any chocolate left!

1 Because we did well, the teacher gave everyone in the class a certificate. **WAS**
Everyone in the class ________ doing well.

2 This suitcase of mine is heavy and so is that one! **MY**
Both ________ heavy.

3 Next December, I'm going to swim across the lake. **HAVE**
By the end of December, I ________ across the lake.

4 Is Simon persuading you not to go to the cinema? **PERSUADED**
Are you ________ Simon not to go to the cinema?

5 It would have been a good idea to invite Alex to my party, but I didn't. **SHOULD**
I ________ Alex to my party, but I didn't.

6 I could see my classmates laughing while the teacher was telling me off. **BEING**
While ________ off by the teacher, I could see my classmates laughing.

13 LEADING THE WAY

ABOUT YOU

What do you think are the qualities of a good leader? Which of these qualities do you think you have?

VOCABULARY Leadership and achievement

EP **1** **Read the quiz. Check the meaning of the words and phrases.**

Team player? Team leader?

1. I rarely doubt my ability, as I'm confident and have high self-esteem. ☐
2. I include everyone in activities and treat people fairly. ☐
3. I'm conscientious and always take a lot of care with my work. ☐
4. I'm motivated and can get a lot done when I put my mind to it. ☐
5. People think of me as a sympathetic person who is always ready to listen. ☐
6. I react negatively to bossy people and don't enjoy being told what to do. ☐
7. I set myself targets and I have a lot of drive. ☐
8. I'm willing to be different and stand out from the crowd. ☐

2 **Read the quiz again and decide on your scores from 1–3 (1 = not true for me, 2 = sometimes true for me, 3 = always true for me).**

3 **Add up your scores for the quiz, then turn to page 140. What does the quiz say about you? Do you agree?**

59 **4** **Listen to four people. Which of them do you think would make a good leader? Why?**

59 **5** **Listen again. Complete the sentences with the correct names: *Phoebe*, *Mo*, *Nathan* or *Ruby*.**

1. .... doubts that he/she will ever be a leader.
2. .... has improved his/her self-esteem through doing an activity.
3. .... isn't very sympathetic towards people who lack drive and try to get out of doing things.
4. .... admits to being quite a bossy person.

READING

60 **1** **Listen to someone talking about the *Three Dot Dash* challenge. What do all the teenagers' ideas have in common?**

2 **Read the profiles of four teenagers taking part in *Three Dot Dash*. In pairs, decide which basic need each teenager is addressing.**

education food health shelter

PREPARE FOR THE EXAM

Reading and Use of English Part 7

3 **Read the profiles again. For questions 1–10, choose from the teenagers (A–D). The teenagers may be chosen more than once.**

Which teenager

1. has been recognised for their project in their own country?
2. has improved the lives of people in several countries through their idea?
3. is working locally on their project, but wishes to expand it to other locations?
4. has worked with the kinds of people their project helps for a long time?
5. has involved their relatives closely in their project?
6. was motivated when they suffered from a personal experience?
7. is initially aiming their project at primary school children?
8. did some research to find out the extent of a problem?
9. has helped individuals to get back in contact with each other?
10. combined different interests to create something students would enjoy?

Three Dot Dash Challenge

61

A HECTOR FERRONATO

Hector Ferronato has never had any doubt that he wants to make a difference in the world. So for his project, he took two of his favourite passions – computer programming and the environment – and did something with them. Hector knew that, in general, young children and teenagers appreciate being involved in their learning and would put their minds to work when they were involved. So he and two friends created 'The World of Piatã', a website about the adventures of a young Brazilian girl. Visitors are taught about environmental issues through fun and motivating games. The website is aimed at 7 to 11-year-olds to begin with, but Hector wants to expand it to older children and start a revolution in environmental education.

B YASH GUPTA

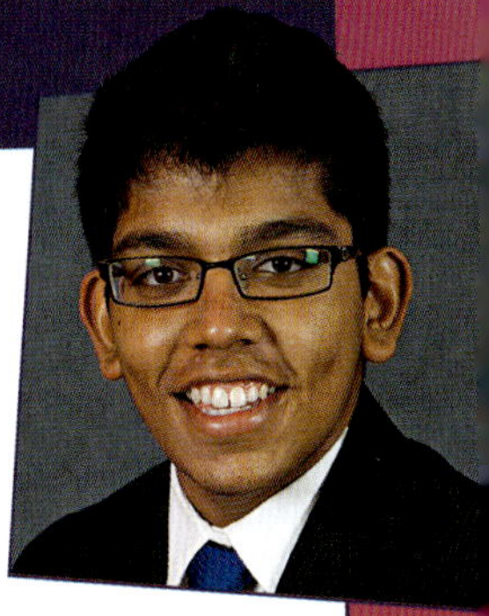

Yash Gupta's project was inspired by breaking his glasses! While he was waiting for a new pair, Yash had to go to school for a week without them. Unable to see clearly, Yash soon found keeping up in class difficult. Yash went online to do a bit of research into poor sight and discovered that around 130 million people worldwide depend on their glasses every day. Furthermore, he learned that an astonishing 300 million need glasses but can't afford them. In developing countries, around 10% of children at primary school, between 6 and 11, have poor vision and often struggle in class as a result. So sympathetic Yash set up *Sight Learning*, which distributes unwanted glasses to eye clinics to give children their vision back. The first clinic to be started was in Mexico and has already given thousands of young children the glasses they need. This initial success has led to further clinics overseas, and Yash has insisted on being involved in each of them.

C NATASHA SURI

For Natasha Suri, it all began when her older sister got a part-time job at a bakery. One evening, Natasha's sister turned up at home with a huge bag of bread and cakes that the bakery had been planning to throw away. Natasha was shocked at the amount of wasted food in the USA, where one in six people don't get enough to eat every day. She started thinking about how this food could be distributed to people who needed it. With the help of friends and family, and her own drive, Natasha began collecting food from two bakeries in her home town of Scarsdale, New York, and delivering it to homeless shelters and retirement homes. This led to the website *FoodSync*. Natasha had this built for her to give live reports on the availability of leftover food and those in need of it. In just a few months, she had delivered 500 kg of food that would have gone in rubbish bins. Natasha set up *FoodSync* in New York, but she's setting herself high targets and really wants her idea to be adopted all over the country.

D ANOOP VIRK

Anoop Virk, from Canada, has always been passionate about helping people and started volunteering at homeless shelters at a young age. Having been brought up by a single mother, Anoop is aware of the importance of both family and friends in our lives. She knew that there were many organisations providing essentials to the homeless, but wanted to do something different. Project HELLO (Helping Everyone Locate Loved Ones) was founded when Anoop was 16. It aims to put homeless residents in Vancouver, Canada, in touch with lost family and friends. In three years, Project HELLO has reconnected 300 people with their friends and family through letters, phone calls and even face-to-face meetings, increasing their happiness and self-esteem. In addition to her invitation to Three Dot Dash, Anoop was included in the '20 under 20' list, which celebrates the top 20 young people under the age of 20 in Canada who are brilliant innovators and who stand out from the crowd.

TALKING POINTS

Why do you think some people are motivated to try and help others?
What qualities do you think young people need to take on the Three Dot Dash challenge?

GRAMMAR The passive (2): other structures

1 **Read the examples and complete the rules with *be*, *to be* or *being*.**

1 Natasha **wants** her idea **to be adopted** all over the country.
2 **The first clinic to be started** was in Mexico.
3 Yash has insisted **on being involved** in each of them.
4 She started thinking about how this food **could be distributed** to people who needed it.
5 Hector knew that, in general, young children and teenagers **appreciate being involved** in their learning.

There are some special structures for the passive. We use
a ________ + past participle after some verbs (*appreciate*, *enjoy*, *feel like*, etc.).
b ________ + past participle after some verbs (*want*, *hope*, etc.).
c ________ + past participle after prepositions.
d ________ + past participle after *the first/second/last* + noun.
e ________ + past participle after modal verbs.

>> GRAMMAR REFERENCE AND PRACTICE PAGE 160

2 **Complete the second sentence so that it means the same as the first sentence. Use a passive form.**

0 They invited her first.
She was the first person *to be invited*.
1 He hates it when people criticise him.
He hates ________.
2 They blame me all the time and I am fed up with it.
I am fed up with ________.
3 Maybe we can sell the tickets online.
The tickets could ________.
4 We must treat everyone fairly.
Everyone must ________.
5 I hope they make me team captain soon.
I hope ________.
6 They told me last.
I was the last ________.

3 **Write the sentences in the passive form.**

0 I hate / tell / what to do.
I hate being told what to do.
1 Everyone expects / criticise / from time to time.
2 He insisted on / put / in charge.
3 The first student / award / a prize was from my class.
4 The singer appreciates / take / seriously as an actor.
5 You will / give / the results of your exam this week.

4 **Choose the correct sentence in each pair.**

1 **a** The shop was closed because it was be repaired.
b The shop was closed because it was being repaired.
2 **a** She wants to be recognised as one of the best rock climbers in the country.
b She wants being recognised as one of the best rock climbers in the country.
3 **a** We saw the guy being carried out to sea.
b We saw the guy be carried out to sea.
4 **a** Would you enjoy to be woken by the sound of waves?
b Would you enjoy being woken by the sound of waves?

5 **Work in pairs. Take turns to complete the sentences with a passive verb and your own ideas.**

1 I can't stand being …
2 I dream of being …
3 I prefer being … to being …
4 In a few years, I hope to be …

VOCABULARY Phrasal verbs with *up*

1 EP **Complete the sentences with the correct form of the phrasal verbs in the box. Check your answers in the profiles on page 77.**

keep up	set up	turn up

1 One evening, Natasha's sister ________ at home with a huge bag of bread and cakes.
2 Natasha ________ *FoodSync* in New York.
3 Unable to see clearly, Yash soon found ________ in class difficult.

2 **Match the phrasal verbs in Exercise 1 to the meanings.**

a start a company or organisation
b arrive or appear
c be able to understand what is happening

3 EP **Match the phrasal verbs to the meanings.**

1 If you want to be heard, you'll need to **speak up**.
2 I **made up** an excuse about being busy because I couldn't be bothered to go.
3 I was waiting outside the station when a young man **came up to** me.
4 The film didn't quite **live up to** my expectations.

a approach someone
b talk louder
c be as good as hoped
d invent something that isn't true

4 **Ask and answer the questions.**

1 Which of your friends always turns up last when you meet?
2 Do you find it easy to keep up with schoolwork?
3 Have you ever been to an event that didn't live up to your expectations?
4 Are you good at making up stories?
5 Have you ever set up a club or something similar?

WRITING A formal letter or email

1 **Tick (✓) the situations which require a formal letter or email.**

to make a complaint ☐
to enquire how a relative is ☐
to apply for a part-time job ☐
to request information about a college course ☐
to tell your news to a friend ☐

2 **Read the task and answer the questions.**

You have seen this advertisement for a holiday job in your town.

> **Children's holiday club leader wanted!**
> We're looking for a creative and confident leader for our children's holiday club.
> Why would you be suitable for the role? What do you enjoy about working with children? Are you available at weekends?
> If you're capable of inventing and running fun activities for 4 to 11-year-olds, we'd love to hear from you.

Write your **letter**.

1 What kind of person are they looking for?
2 What information do you need to include in your application?
3 Would *you* be suitable for this role? Why? / Why not?

3 **Read Bethany's application. Has she answered all the questions in the advert? Do you think she would be suitable for the role? Why?**

> Dear Sir/Madam,
>
> I have seen the advertisement for children's holiday club leader on your website and I would like to apply for the position.
>
> I believe that I would be suitable for the role because I already have some experience of working with children. Last summer, I volunteered at a local sports club, where I taught young children how to play tennis. I also have two younger brothers, and my parents often leave me in charge when they go shopping, for example. I often invent interesting games for them to play and I am responsible for their safety.
>
> I enjoy working with children because they are interested in everything and they're good fun, too. I like how they think about the world and how much energy they have. They enjoy life!
>
> I would be grateful if you would consider my application and I look forward to hearing from you.
>
> Yours faithfully,
>
> *Bethany Ward*

4 **Read the *Prepare to write* box, then read Bethany's application again. Find:**

a an opening expression
b five formal full forms
c three other formal phrases
d a closing expression

PREPARE TO WRITE Formal letters and emails

In formal letters and emails:

- use formal titles.
  Dear Mr Thompson / Ms García
  Dear Sir/Madam
- use a formal opening expression.
  I have seen your advertisement …
  I would like to apply for …
  I am writing to enquire/complain about …
- use full rather than contracted forms.
  do not *cannot* *would not*
- use formal language.
  I believe that … *I would be grateful if …*
  I would like to know … / Could you tell me …
- use a formal closing expression.
  emails: *Best regards* *Best wishes* *Yours*
  letters: *Yours sincerely* *Yours faithfully*

5 **Bethany hasn't answered the final question in the task. Choose the best sentence (a or b) to answer the question.**

a I won't be able to work at weekends because that's when I spend time with my friends, but I can do plenty of hours during the week.
b Unfortunately, I am not available at the weekends due to other commitments, but I am fully available during the week.

PREPARE FOR THE EXAM

Writing Part 2 (A formal letter or email)

6 **Read the task and plan your answer.**

You have seen this advertisement on the school notice board.

> **Take part in a science quiz show on TV!**
> We're looking for team members from around the country to take part in a science quiz show on TV.
> Write and tell us why you would like to take part. Tell us about your interest in science and why this would make you a good participant on the show.

Write your **email**.

7 **Write your email to apply for the science quiz show.**

- Answer all of the points in the advert.
- Use the tips in the *Prepare to write* box.
- Check your grammar and spelling.
- Write 140–190 words.

14 GETTING THERE

ABOUT YOU

10 **Watch the video and answer the questions.**

Describe the longest journey you've ever been on.

What's the best journey you've ever been on?

Which types of holiday do you think are best suited to young people?

VOCABULARY Phrasal verbs: transport

1 **Read the sentences and match them to the photos (A–L).**

EP

1 I was **held up** because there was an accident further down the road.
2 I **broke down** in the middle of nowhere.
3 Come on, **speed up** a bit – we're going to be late!
4 I put my foot on the brake, and the car **slowed down**.
5 The train **pulled into** the station exactly on time.
6 As I got to the platform, the train was **pulling out** of the station.
7 The taxi **pulled up** outside our house.
8 The police officer told the driver to **pull over** to the side of the road.
9 I found it really hard to **keep up with** her.
10 I **ran over** some glass and got a puncture.
11 The bus **drove off** without waiting.
12 I **ran into** the back of the car in front when it stopped suddenly.

62 **2** **Listen to eight situations and decide what is happening or has happened. Use the phrasal verbs in Exercise 1.**

1 Sophie's dad has driven off without her.

READING

1 **Look at the pictures opposite. What do you think they show? Read the first paragraph of the article and check your answers.**

2 **Read the article about the Hyperloop quickly. Choose the best alternative title (A–C).**

A International public transport
B Public transport of tomorrow
C Futuristic airplanes

3 **Read the article again and answer the questions.**

1 What will the Hyperloop system look like?
2 Which two systems gave Musk the idea for the Hyperloop?
3 Aside from passengers, what else will the Hyperloop be able to carry?
4 Why wasn't Musk impressed with California's high-speed rail project?
5 For what reasons will Hyperloop be better than other forms of transport?
6 What is Elon Musk's attitude to the plans he created?
7 How are plans progressing to make the Hyperloop a reality?

4 **Match the highlighted words and phrases in the article to the meanings.**

1 make the effort
2 using something to help you
3 for no particular reason
4 goods carried by trains, trucks, ships or aircraft
5 moving somewhere very quickly

THE HIGH-SPEED HYPERLOOP

Can you imagine whizzing through a tube from city to city at speeds of 1,200 kilometres an hour? Well, this could soon be a reality with the 'Hyperloop', a futuristic form of transport in which passengers will speed between cities in capsules travelling faster than the speed of sound. By as early as 2030, some of us could be zooming around in what will be not only the world's fastest form of transport, but the safest and most efficient, too.

So, where did the idea come from? Billionaire technology entrepreneur Elon Musk came up with the idea after being inspired by the tubes which are used to transport mail between offices in some buildings. In Hyperloop, with the aid of strong magnets, long capsules will float through airless tubes that are raised above the ground on columns. This will virtually eliminate friction, allowing the capsules to reach speeds higher than any other form of land transport. Musk compares the experience to that of an amusement park ride, saying it will be 'like getting a ride on Space Mountain at Disneyland'. He hopes that the Hyperloop capsules will transport passengers, as well as cars and freight. This will speed up people's journeys, avoid them being held up in traffic jams, and reduce the number of polluting vehicles on the roads.

Musk decided to work on a new and innovative form of transport after reading about California's high-speed rail project. While Musk agreed that it would be good if there were an alternative to having to drive or fly, he didn't think high-speed rail was the answer. Since it would be slower and more expensive than it would be to fly, this would mean few passengers would actually bother with the system.

Musk wasn't just being critical for the sake of it, but was considering ways in which a public-transport system could be made better. This, according to Musk, means making a system that is not only faster but safer, more convenient, weather-proof, sustainable and efficient – all the things that he believes the Hyperloop can do. 'You want the future to be better than the past,' he says.

Hyperloop is intended for cities which are less than 1,500 kilometres apart and which have high volumes of traffic travelling between them. The system would allow passengers to travel between, for example, Los Angeles and San Francisco, a distance of over 600 kilometres, in under 30 minutes. That's five hours less than it currently takes to drive in a car. What's more, Musk thinks there could be as many as 70 capsules operating at any one time, pulling into and out of 'stations' every 30 seconds!

Although Musk doesn't intend to be involved in building a full Hyperloop network himself, he published a design and invited feedback to see if people could find ways to improve it.

The idea is that other companies use the design to develop and test their own Hyperloop systems. And it may not be too far into the future that Musk's ideas come into being. 'I know there are various companies that are trying to create the Hyperloop,' he said. The first full-scale capsule has already been constructed and revealed at a special ceremony, and rival companies HyperloopTT and Hyperloop One are working hard to get projects off the ground in various places. HyperloopTT, for instance, already has plans to start building a Hyperloop track to replace Abu Dhabi's rail network.

However, with such high speeds and long distances involved, the process won't be straightforward, and some leading engineers have raised concerns about the safety of the technology. After a successful test by Hyperloop One at speeds of 110 km/h over a short distance in the Nevada Desert, Philippa Oldham, a senior engineer at the Institution of Mechanical Engineers, said that Hyperloop could only ever be used by the public if the right safety systems were put in place. She added, 'Whilst this was a successful first trial, the speeds were still relatively low, so it will be interesting to watch the development of this programme.'

So, who knows, with some amazing minds behind the Hyperloop, we may soon be travelling hundreds of kilometres in a matter of minutes.

TALKING POINTS

Would a Hyperloop transport system benefit your country? How?

Do you think there are any advantages to travelling more slowly?

GRAMMAR Reported speech

1 **Read the direct and reported speech. Why do the tenses sometimes not change? Read the rules and check.**

1 You want the future to be better than the past.

Musk says that you want the future to be better than the past.

2 It will be like getting a ride on Space Mountain at Disneyland.

Musk says it will be like getting a ride on Space Mountain at Disneyland.

3 Whilst this was a successful first trial, the speeds were still relatively low.

Oldham said that whilst this had been a successful first trial, the speeds had still been relatively low.

a When we report sentences we usually change the tense, e.g. present simple → past simple.
b We don't usually change the tense when we are talking about
- general truths and opinions.
- an event which is not in the past.

In these cases, we often use a reporting verb in the present simple or present perfect, e.g. *says*, *agrees*, *has said*, etc.

» GRAMMAR REFERENCE AND PRACTICE PAGE 161

2 **Choose the correct verb forms.**

1 'It's quicker to pull up at the back door than stop outside the main door.'
Tom says it *'s* / *was* quicker to pull up at the back door than stop outside the main door.
2 'You should learn to drive.'
He said I *should learn* / *should have learned* to drive.
3 'You must carry your passport with you at all times.'
The law says you *had to* / *must* carry your passport with you at all times.
4 'The holiday will be my first without my parents.'
Sarah points out that the holiday *will* / *would* be her first without her parents.
5 'We're going there tomorrow.'
Dad told me last week that they *were* / *'re* going there the next day.

3 **Tick (✓) the sentences which are right, and correct the mistakes in the other sentences.**

1 My parents told us that we will spend our holidays in the Netherlands that summer.
2 My dad said it was worth the long journey to see something so incredible.
3 I asked where my case was, and someone told me it was in the lost property office.
4 She wanted to know why I am slowing down.
5 Johanna told me that the bus has driven off without her.

4 **Complete the reported-speech sentences.**

1 'The hotel won't take guests under 18.'
The travel agent says ________
2 'I want to take a year off before university.'
My sister told my parents ________
3 'My mum's a better driver than my brother.'
Amy reckons ________
4 'I've been travelling through Europe in the holidays.'
Dylan said ________
5 'We've been waiting for over an hour!'
Amy claims ________

VOCABULARY Reporting verbs

1 **Read the sentences. <u>Underline</u> the reporting verbs and check their meaning.**

EP

a My sister agreed to slow down.
b My grandparents insisted that I went home early.
c Tom persuaded his friend to overtake the car in front.
d My parents forbade me from travelling home alone.
e The woman enquired whether the trains were on time.
f The police officer pointed out that his driver's licence wasn't valid.
g She recommended travelling after the rush hour.
h He confessed to driving above the speed limit.

64 **2** **Listen and match the speakers to the sentences in Exercise 1.**

PREPARE FOR THE EXAM

Reading and Use of English Part 4

3 **Complete the second sentence so that it has a similar meaning to the first sentence, using the word given. Do not change the word given. You must use between two and five words, including the word given.**

1 'It's best to leave your passports in the hotel safe,' the receptionist told them. **RECOMMENDED**
The ________ passports in the hotel safe.
2 'It was me who lost the tickets,' Jo said. **CONFESSED**
Jo ________ the tickets.
3 'I definitely locked the door before I left,' Sam said. **INSISTED**
Sam ________ the door before he left.
4 'Do you think I should pull over here?' Karen asked. **ENQUIRED**
Karen ________ pull over there.
5 'Going camping would be a brilliant idea. Let's go!' Mum said to me. **PERSUADED**
Mum ________ camping.
6 'Getting a family room will be cheaper,' the travel agent said. **POINTED**
The travel agent ________ a family room would be cheaper.

4 » **Work in pairs.** **Turn to page 140.**

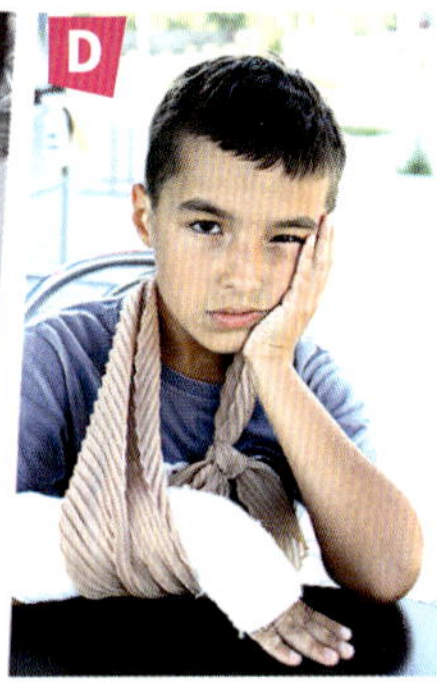

LISTENING

1 **Look at photos A–D. Can you explain the travel problem in each photo? Have you experienced any of these problems yourself?**

65 **2** **You will hear five people talking about bad travel experiences. Match the people to the photos. Which person's story doesn't match a photo?**

PREPARE FOR THE EXAM

Listening Part 3

3 65 **Listen again. For questions 1–5, choose from the list (A–H) what each speaker says. Use the letters only once. There are three extra letters which you do not need to use.**

A I was too young to understand why something went wrong.
B A joke I played ended in difficulty.
C The problem we had was our own fault.
D Illness prevented me from enjoying myself.
E An accident temporarily interrupted the trip.
F An unexpected event delayed our arrival.
G I blame someone else for what happened.
H Nobody could have predicted such a situation.

Speaker 1 ....
Speaker 2 ....
Speaker 3 ....
Speaker 4 ....
Speaker 5 ....

SPEAKING Linking ideas

66 **1** **Listen to Anita and Marco answering questions about travel and transport. Number the questions in the order they answer them. There is one extra question.**

a What's public transport like in your country?
b How often do you use public transport? (Which form of transport do you use most?)
c How do you spend your time when you're travelling on public transport or by car?
d Tell us about an interesting journey you've made recently.
e Do you like travelling by car? (What do you like about it?)
f What's the longest journey you've ever made? (Did you enjoy it?)
g Do you ever travel by bike? (What's good about doing that?)
h Have you ever been on holiday by plane? (Did you enjoy travelling by plane? Why? / Why not?)

66 **2** **Read the *Prepare to speak* box. Then listen again. Who uses each linking word or phrase? Write A (Anita) or M (Marco).**

PREPARE TO SPEAK | Linking ideas

Giving examples
like ... such as ...

Adding information
as well as ... besides that ...

Returning to an earlier point
as I was saying ... anyway ...

Showing contrast
but sometimes ... however ...

3 **In pairs, answer question b in Exercise 1.**

4 **Make notes on your answers to the other questions in Exercise 1. Think about how you can link your ideas together.**

PREPARE FOR THE EXAM

Speaking Part 1

5 **Ask and answer the questions with a partner.**

- Ask the questions from Exercise 1.
- Answer using words or phrases from the *Prepare to speak* box.

CULTURE

GAP YEARS

1 **What do you think a 'gap year' is? What kind of things do you think people do on one? Read the article quickly and check your ideas.**

2 **Read the descriptions of four people and choose the best gap year experience from the article for each one. Compare your ideas with your partner's.**

1 You like to feel useful and that you are helping others. You'd also like to go abroad and use your communicative skills.
2 You know exactly what you want to study at university, but it's a very difficult course to get a place on. Therefore, you want to use a gap year to make your CV more attractive.
3 You like getting to know new people and finding out about how they live. You are also looking for an experience that will help boost your confidence so you can do more things by yourself.
4 You love the idea of going backpacking, but you want to get some money in your wallet at the same time!

3 **Match the highlighted words and phrases in the article to the meanings.**

1 doesn't interest you
2 officially register for and be accepted on a course
3 showing good judgement
4 when someone learns a job and skills from an expert
5 travelling with all your possessions and clothes in one big bag

67 **4** **In pairs, make a list of pros and cons for taking a gap year. Then listen to a talk by a school careers advisor. Does he mention any of your ideas?**

67 **5** **Listen again and choose the correct answer for each of the questions.**

1 What warning does the speaker make at the beginning of his talk?
   A Thinking about the advantages and disadvantages of a gap year can take a long time.
   B Your parents might want to decide whether or not you can go on a gap year.
   C Taking a gap year isn't the right thing to do for all young people.

2 Why is it good to take a gap year between finishing school and starting university, rather than doing it later in life?
   A Young people feel refreshed and ready for new challenges at this age.
   B Young people have few commitments in life to deal with at this age.
   C Young people's parents can pay for their gap year.

3 When doing a gap year job, being young and inexperienced
   A can be a disadvantage.
   B can be an advantage.
   C has neither a positive nor negative impact.

4 For what type of people is a gap year **not** suitable?
   A People who are motivated and responsible.
   B People who are goal-orientated.
   C People who like to have deadlines.

5 What recommendation does the speaker give at the end of the talk?
   A Young people should be prepared to explain to other people why they want to do a gap year.
   B Young people should always follow their parents' advice.
   C Young people should talk to other people for advice about whether to do a gap year or not.

6 **Complete the sentences with the words in the box.**

candidate	consideration	distraction
financial	motivate	practice

USEFUL LANGUAGE

Talking about plans for life after school

1 You may need to take several things into ________.
2 This is exactly what makes you the perfect ________ for the job.
3 University is a major ________ investment.
4 You have to be able to ________ yourself.
5 You'll learn lots of things that you can put into ________ at university.
6 A year out could become a ________.

ARE YOU READY FOR A GAP YEAR ADVENTURE?

GAP YEAR FACT

Approximately 10% of students in the UK, Australia and New Zealand take a gap year before they enrol at university.

So, the end of life as you know it is in sight! What's next? Straight to university? Maybe the world of work is calling you? Or perhaps the next thing for you is an apprenticeship in a company? Whatever your next step may be, don't forget that there is another option: a gap year! Essentially, this is taking a year-long break between school and university to … well, this is the unbelievable bit: to do whatever you like!

Now, I don't mean sitting around and watching TV series all day or spending a year at the beach! I'm talking about something that will energise you after all those years of sitting down in a classroom. An experience to reward yourself for all your hard work and open new doors to the future. Interested? I thought you would be! I'm talking about taking a gap year. While they remain uncommon in many countries, gap years have long been popular in countries like the UK, Australia and New Zealand. Let's take a look at just a few of the amazing things you could get up to on yours.

68

TRAVEL

Pack your bags and go and explore the world! Yes, travel is always one of the most popular gap year choices. You'll discover new cultures, meet lots of people and become much more independent. How about backpacking across Asia, taking a train through Europe, or flying to Australia? The possibilities are endless. The world's a big place and the only limit is your wallet!

VOLUNTEERING

Does travelling appeal to you, but you're the type of person that needs to feel you're doing something constructive? In that case, taking part in a volunteer programme abroad may be the best gap year option for you. You can help other people while supporting a good cause and gaining valuable life skills. You could sign up to teach languages to children, participate in wildlife conservation, or help to build infrastructure in remote villages. And best of all, you'll be satisfying your desire to see somewhere new in the world at the same time.

PAID WORK

You may like the idea of spending a year travelling and keeping yourself busy, but you'd prefer to get paid for your time. Well, paid employment is definitely a gap year option, too. There are plenty of jobs around the world in agriculture or working in the tourism industry, like working in a hostel for backpackers. Of course, finding paid work near where you live is also an option if travelling isn't your thing.

WORK EXPERIENCE

Getting paid in a job that's easy to find might sound good. However, some people's priority is to get work experience that is relevant to the specific degree they want to study for in the future. This could take the form of a work placement or internship, and be over a period of several weeks to a year. However, if this is your gap-year choice, make sure you apply early. This type of work experience is popular, and competition for places is usually very high. Besides, many of these positions are unpaid, so if you need to make some money for university, this probably isn't an option for you.

In the past, I've heard people referring to gap years as a year *off*, but the reality is far from that. The most important thing is to spend the time wisely. Whichever of the ideas above sounds most interesting to you, it'll be a year full of new, exciting experiences and valuable life lessons!

PROJECT *Choosing and planning a gap year*

Prepare a presentation about your ideal gap year. Use these steps to help you.

1. Which of the gap year choices from the article would you most like to do?
2. Choose a specific destination, job, programme, etc. for your ideal gap year.
3. Find out more about your choice, including images and videos if possible.
4. Prepare a presentation to talk about your ideal gap year.

Present your research to the class.

11 NOW WATCH THE CULTURE VIDEO

15 THE BIGGER PICTURE

ABOUT YOU

12 Watch the video and answer the questions.

What national or global issues do you feel concerned about? Explain why you are concerned.

Do you think that young people should have a role in government? Why? / Why not?

VOCABULARY Global issues: nouns and verbs

1 Match the sentence halves. Check the meaning of the verbs.

EP

1 Aid agencies are cooperating
2 We've collected
3 Cars should be banned
4 The local council has been criticised
5 You seem to think I don't support
6 It's great that Ann's been elected

a for not dealing with litter in the city.
b your views on animal rights.
c £100 for an anti-poverty charity.
d with the state government.
e as leader of the school council.
f from busy city streets.

69 **2** Listen to six people using these nouns and verbs and check your answers to Exercise 1.

69 **3** Complete the sentences with the noun form of the verbs in Exercise 1. Listen again and check.

EP

ban collection cooperation
criticism election supporter

1 Unfortunately, ________ between the two organisations hasn't worked out.
2 Sometimes we organise a food ________ for a local homeless hostel.
3 A ________ on private cars would make a huge difference in the city centre.
4 There has been further ________ of the local council for closing down leisure facilities in the area.
5 I'm a great ________ of animal rights.
6 I'm so proud of her for winning the ________!

READING

1 Read the title of the text. What do you think *MYP* and *UKYP* could mean? Read the first two paragraphs of the text to find out.

PREPARE FOR THE EXAM

Reading and Use of English Part 1

2 Read the first two paragraphs of the text again and decide which answer (A, B, C or D) best fits each gap.

	A	B	C	D
0	**A** containing	**(B)** consisting	**C** involving	**D** forming
1	**A** act	**B** run	**C** set	**D** lay
2	**A** ensure	**B** reassure	**C** assure	**D** secure
3	**A** sense	**B** influence	**C** aspect	**D** theme
4	**A** demonstrate	**B** represent	**C** produce	**D** regard
5	**A** recently	**B** shortly	**C** freshly	**D** newly
6	**A** stay	**B** keep	**C** live	**D** hold
7	**A** presented	**B** provided	**C** supplied	**D** given
8	**A** consequence	**B** impression	**C** reaction	**D** impact

3 Read the whole interview. Choose the best summary of it (A–C).

A Charity talks about her personal experiences of being an MYP and gives a few examples of specific projects she has worked on.
B Charity mentions some of the things she achieved as an MYP and gives advice to readers who may wish to be elected as MYPs.
C Charity describes the range of people you are likely to meet as an MYP and how to handle them.

4 Complete the sentences with highlighted words and phrases from the text.

1 We need to strike a ________ between good service and price.
2 What ________ does Jon play in the organisation?
3 I'll help you tidy up ________ for help with this assignment.
4 Honesty is ________ when you want people's cooperation.
5 Suzy spends a ________ of her time supporting worthy causes.

70

MYPs @ UKYP

The UK Youth Parliament is a youth organisation in the United Kingdom, **(0)** *consisting* of elected members aged between 11 and 18. There are currently hundreds of MYPs who meet with MPs and local politicians, organise events, **(1)** ________ campaigns, make speeches, hold debates and **(2)** ________ the views of young people are listened to by decision-makers. A key **(3)** ________ of any MYP's job is making certain they **(4)** ________ the views of the young people in their area. We talked to Charity Mhende about the position she has **(5)** ________ taken up as an MYP.

Charity, your year as a Member of the Youth Parliament must have been a really interesting experience. Did it (6) ________ up to your expectations?
It was absolutely amazing! I have grown so much and have been **(7)** ________ so many incredible opportunities. I really believe now that you have to make the most of every opportunity that comes along, as it could be something that has a long-lasting **(8)** ________ on your life.

'YOU HAVE TO MAKE THE MOST OF EVERY OPPORTUNITY THAT COMES ALONG.'

It can't have been easy, though, doing this on top of your schoolwork and everything else that a normal 15-year-old likes to do! Did anything suffer?
For some people, being involved in the UKYP means they end up giving up their social lives, but it shouldn't be like that. It's all about getting a good work–life balance. At the same time, you always have to remember that you only get what you give. If you put in the work, you will get loads back in return.

And what did you focus on as an MYP?
I was elected as one of the Media Representatives for the West Midlands, where I live, so I was heavily involved in media work. And my year was when history was made – we were the first non-Members of Parliament to be allowed to debate in the House of Commons like real politicians. It was my role to make sure the press knew about it and that our work got recognised. My biggest achievement was being on the national TV news and on the radio.

You must be very proud of that. It sounds like the experience might have changed your approach to life. Has it?
Yes! I have definitely grown in confidence and I have learned the art of socialising and negotiating, because communication is key if you want to get something done. In this role, you can make links with decision-makers and people that could help you a great deal in the future. You just need to take the opportunities that come your way.

'DON'T BE AFRAID TO ASK QUESTIONS!'

Some situations must have been quite scary, in that they were completely new for you. What advice would you give other teenagers in that position?
Well, it's true that you might be put into unexpected situations, but you just need to be brave and do the best you can. And don't be afraid to ask questions! Youth workers, staff and other MYPs will all be happy to help you. You will meet so many people and have loads of new challenges, but it will all be worth it in the end.

TALKING POINTS
Do you think politicians represent the views of young people?
In what ways can young people help to improve their society?

GRAMMAR Modals (3): deduction

1 Read the examples. Is each sentence about the past, the present or the future?

1 You **must be** very proud of that.
2 You can make links with people that **could help** you a great deal in the future.
3 The experience **might have changed** your approach to life.
4 Some situations **must have been** quite scary.
5 It **can't have been** easy.

2 Complete the rules with the modal verbs in the box.

can't	could	couldn't	may
may not	might	might not	must

We use modal verb + infinitive to make guesses about the present and future.
We use modal verb + *have* + past participle to make guesses about the past.
We use
a .... for things we are certain are true.
b .... or .... for things we are certain are not true.
c ...., ... or .... for things that are possible.
d .... or .... for things that are unlikely.

» GRAMMAR REFERENCE AND PRACTICE PAGE 162

3 Choose the correct options.

1 Carla *couldn't have stuck* / *must have stuck* that poster here. She's trying to advertise her charity event.
2 There's someone at the door. It *must be* / *can't be* Dan; he's not around today.
3 Jacob often does collections for this group, so he *must be* / *couldn't be* a supporter of our ideas.
4 We're waiting for an important document. There was a postal strike last week, so that *must delay* / *might have delayed* it.
5 Kids from that school *couldn't damage* / *couldn't have damaged* the car. They are banned from entering the car park, and it's always locked.
6 Their friends are away, so they *mustn't have* / *might not have* anyone to talk to.
7 My brother usually keeps in touch, but we haven't heard from him for ages. I'm not sure, but there *can't be* / *may be* some sort of problem.
8 Tina has sent a few text messages of support, so she *could lose* / *can't have lost* her phone.

4 Correct the mistake in each sentence by replacing the bold words with one or two words.

1 You **could** not believe this, but it's true – Andy's passed his guitar exam at last!
2 Within a few years, many people in the country **can** be living in poverty.
3 Our holiday was OK. It could **be** much worse than it was.
4 It **could** have been Mandy who left the window open – there's no one else it could have been.
5 You **must** left the book at home if it isn't in your bag.

5 Look at the photos. In pairs, make guesses about the situations.

A

B

C

D

VOCABULARY Phrases with *in*

1 Charity Mhende used the phrase *in return*, meaning 'in exchange'. Match the phrases to the meanings.

EP

1	in the light of	a	happening or being done now
2	in general	b	one after another
3	in progress	c	considering the whole of something
4	in favour of	d	to emphasise what is true or give information
5	in actual fact	e	because of, considering
6	in turn	f	approving of a plan or idea

2 Complete the sentences with the phrases in Exercise 1.

1 People thought the politician had suggested a ban on advertising, but .... he'd said something quite different.
2 Josh and Liam are .... splitting up the band. They aren't getting on any more.
3 .... the bad weather, the match has been postponed until next weekend.
4 Let's speak to everyone .... and then report any criticism or positive comments back to the class.
5 Building work is ...., so the library will remain closed until Friday.
6 Apart from your studies, how are things going for you ....?

3 » Work in pairs. Turn to page 140.

WRITING An essay (3)

1 **Look at the diagram about employment. Choose two more topics and create a diagram for each.**

1 education
2 health
3 travel
4 the environment

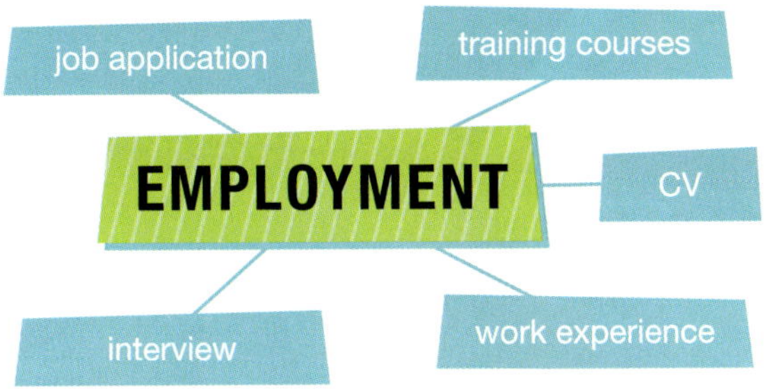

2 **Read the essay. Is it about employment, education or both?**

This is a complex question, and conditions vary greatly around the world. In my own country, there are no job opportunities, or very few. Once teenagers leave school aged 16–18, they often find it very hard to get work. Youth unemployment is 50% higher than it was ten years ago. Employers these days are happy to take on young people, provided they already have some experience, but it can be difficult for young people to get experience in the first place. That's why many young people accept unpaid jobs, just to learn more about the world of work.

On the other hand, the opportunities to learn are much greater than they used to be. It is possible to study a wider range of subjects today and it is much easier to get into university. My grandfather never had the chance to attend university, whereas a large percentage of today's generation will do so.

Young people today have a lot more opportunity to travel now that there are lots of low-cost airlines and you can plan trips online. They say that travel broadens the mind, and it has never been easier to gain experience of other cultures.

In conclusion, even though the job market is difficult at the moment, today's young people still have more opportunities than their parents and grandparents did.

3 **Choose the question that matches the essay in Exercise 2.**

a How has access to education and work changed over the past two generations?
b What life skills can young people acquire today that their grandparents couldn't?
c Does society offer more or fewer opportunities for young people today?

4 **Read the *Prepare to write* box and find the linking words in the essay.**

PREPARE TO WRITE Linking words (1)

We use linking words to join short sentences together to make complex sentences:
I've got a car. I can visit you more often.
→ *I can visit you more often* ***now*** *that I've got a car.*
You can use these linking words to join sentences:
even though, now (that), once, or, provided (that).

5 **Complete the sentences with the linking words and phrases in the box.**

even though now once or provided

1 The situation at school has been improving, ________ that's what we've been told.
2 Are you sure you want to leave? Remember that you can't criticise the group ________ you've left.
3 She's enjoying the position ________ that she's got more responsibility.
4 I'll lend you my camera, ________ you look after it properly.
5 She did really well, ________ she had had relatively little experience.

PREPARE FOR THE EXAM

Writing Part 1

6 **Read the task. Add more information and your own idea to the notes.**

'Existing environmental problems will continue to cause harm if we don't act to solve them.'
Do you agree?

Notes
Write about:
1 population growth
2 pollution
3 ________ (your own idea)

7 **Write your essay.**

- Write about all the ideas in the notes.
- Use linking words to make complex sentences.
- Check your grammar and spelling.
- Write 140–190 words.

16 NEW AND IMPROVED!

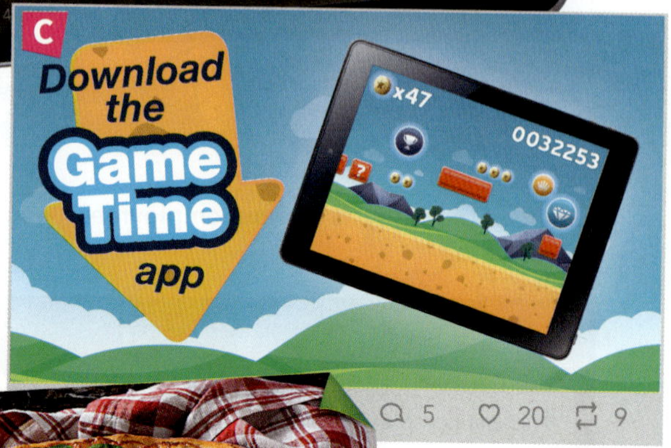

ABOUT YOU

Which current TV adverts do you love or hate? Why?
What do you think makes a good advert?

VOCABULARY Advertising: nouns and verbs

71 **1 Look at the adverts. Listen to Daniel and Jade talking and answer the questions.**

1 Which ad don't they talk about?
2 Which ads does Daniel actually like? Why?
3 Who do you think the products are aimed at? Why?
4 How does Daniel's attitude to advertising change during the conversation?

71 **2 Complete the sentences. Listen again and check.**

EP

ad breaks | aimed at | appeal to | consumer | launching | product placement | sample | sponsored

1 Jade enjoys the ________ on TV.
2 Jade said that the gaming app advert would ________ Daniel, but isn't ________ non-gamers like her.
3 Jade sometimes gets a free ________ of an advertised product in a magazine.
4 The car manufacturer they hear is ________ a new model.
5 Jade says Daniel is a ________ like everyone else.
6 Jade says Daniel is influenced by ________ in programmes.
7 The football team they're supporting is ________ by a bank.

3 Discuss the questions.

1 What do you think of the ad breaks on TV?
2 Who sponsors the biggest football clubs in your country?
3 Are you ever offered free samples of products?
4 Do you ever notice product placement in TV shows? Does it have an effect on you?

READING

1 Read the text quickly. What is the main idea?

A Most advertisers have started to use guerrilla marketing.
B Guerrilla marketing involves new and clever methods.
C Viral marketing is the latest trend in online advertising.
D Guerrilla marketing will take over from traditional advertising.

PREPARE FOR THE EXAM

Reading and Use of English Part 2

2 For questions 1–8, read the first two paragraphs of the text and think of the word which best fits each gap. Use only one word in each gap.

3 Answer the questions.

1 Why is body advertising an uncommon sight?
2 Why is viral marketing relatively cheap?
3 Why isn't viral marketing guaranteed to succeed?
4 Why do actors doing undercover marketing have to be unknown?
5 What is the risk associated with undercover marketing?
6 Why isn't reverse graffiti against the law?

GUERRILLA MARKETING

72

Wherever you are in the world, if you switch on the TV or open a magazine, you **(0)** *will* probably see an advert. Love it or hate it, publicity is a fact of modern life. For the keen consumer, ads can provide entertainment as well as **(1)** ________ informative. Attractive logos, witty slogans and beautifully designed ads are seen by some as a welcome addition **(2)** ________ their TV viewing. Others, however, who watch TV to relax, feel they live in a busy world in **(3)** ________ adverts are simply an annoying interruption. For them, adverts are a waste **(4)** ________ resources and their appearance is visual pollution. **(5)** ________ matter what your feelings are, ads are becoming more sophisticated every day. They have developed hand in hand **(6)** ________ technological advances. In the early days, they appeared **(7)** ________ simple printed messages, before being heard on the radio and seen on TV, and later popping up on computer or phone screens. Today, 'guerrilla' marketing **(8)** ________ using ever more innovative techniques – usually imaginative and sometimes irritating – to get ads seen.

BODY ADVERTISING

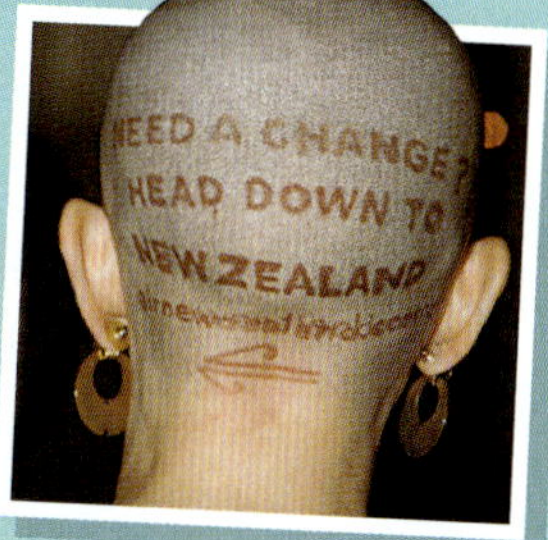

How would you like an advert painted on your body? It would have to be somewhere visible such as your forehead or even your eyelids! Body advertising looks striking, some might say offensive, but the ads can usually be washed off after a couple of days. Still, it's no wonder you don't see it very often. It is either used to advertise to a specific, local audience, who see the advert in person, or photos of the body advertising are intended to go viral.

VIRAL MARKETING

Imagine that you're a computer games developer and you're trying to launch a new BMX racing game on a limited budget. You need to promote the game cheaply if you have little money for publicity, so you commission a short film with talented but unknown BMX riders. The film is dramatic and fast-moving, following a crazy ride around an inner-city neighbourhood to a soundtrack of heavy rock music. The clip shows the riders arriving home exhausted, lying on the sofa and playing your game. It ends with your logo and a link to your website. A BMX magazine uploads the video to YouTube and you're very lucky: viewers love it. If the clip is shared and 'liked' enough, you could end up with millions of views. If the same clip had appeared as a TV ad, it would have cost millions to broadcast it. How many viral videos like this have you watched and shared and how many products have you helped to promote for free?

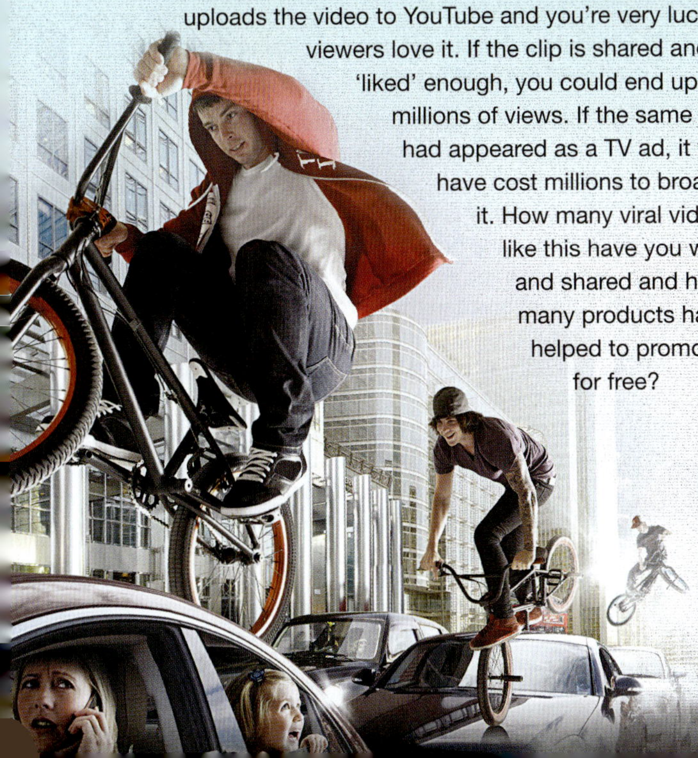

UNDERCOVER MARKETING

Actors are sometimes paid to raise awareness of products secretly. For example, a phone company might place an actor with their latest mobile in a city centre location. The actor approaches passing strangers, the type of person the phone is aimed at, and asks, 'Would you mind taking a photo of me on my phone?' While their photo is being taken, the actor chats with the potential customer about what an amazing phone it is. It's no good using well-known actors: undercover marketing only works if the actors' identities and motives remain secret. It would damage a company's reputation if consumers realised it was marketing. Undercover marketing is expensive, but effective, because an interaction with a real person is much more believable and memorable than any other kind of advertising.

REVERSE GRAFFITI

If you sprayed an image onto a wall, you'd probably get arrested – graffiti is illegal in many places. But reverse graffiti is clever, as there's no need to break the law. To create reverse graffiti, you cut words and shapes into a sheet of plastic. Then lay the plastic against a flat surface and spray water and cleaning products into each gap. The result is a clean, bright image surrounded by a dirty bit of wall or pavement. It is cheap and there are no laws against cleaning, which means it is popular with street artists who want to create beautiful images in unloved urban locations. Photos of the best reverse graffiti ads can be seen by millions globally if they go viral.

TALKING POINTS

Which guerrilla marketing techniques do you think are most likely to be effective? Why?

Do you think that guerrilla marketing will ever replace advertising on TV or online? Why? / Why not?

GRAMMAR Conditionals (1): review

1 Read the examples and answer the questions.

1 **If** you **switch** on the TV or open a magazine, you **will** probably **see** an advert.
Is it certain or possible you will see an ad?

2 **If** the same clip **had appeared** as a TV ad, it **would have cost** millions.
Did the ad appear on TV? Did it cost millions?

3 You **need** to promote the game cheaply **if** you **have** little money for publicity.
Is this a possibility or a true statement?

4 It **would damage** a company's reputation **if** consumers **realised** it was marketing.
Was the company's reputation damaged?

2 Read the examples again and complete the rules with the words in the box.

future	general	past	likely

We use the
a zero conditional to talk about ________ truths.
b first conditional for ________ events in the future.
c second conditional for impossible or unlikely situations in the ________.
d third conditional for imaginary results of ________ situations that never happened.

» GRAMMAR REFERENCE AND PRACTICE PAGE 163

3 Match the sentence halves.

1 If you take LongLife vitamins,
2 You wouldn't have been late
3 If I wasn't using my laptop,
4 If it's raining later,
5 This door makes a loud noise

a she'll probably get the bus.
b of course I'd lend it to you.
c you'll be healthy forever.
d unless you open it carefully.
e if you'd left home on time.

4 Correct the mistake in each sentence.

1 If the doorbell would ring, the dog barks loudly.
2 If that ad comes on again, I'd turn the TV off!
3 If I would see those guys again, I'd be able to identify them.
4 You would have had fun if you came to the party.
5 If I were you, I will get some snacks during the ads.

5 Complete the conditional questions. Then ask and answer with a partner.

1 If you ________ your phone, what would you do? (lose)
2 What ________ yesterday if your classes had been cancelled? (you / do)
3 What ________ when it's hot? (you / wear)
4 If you ________ your exams, will you go to university? (pass)
5 Where ________ if you had £1 million? (you / go)

VOCABULARY Adverb + adjective collocations

1 Complete the sentences with the adverbs in the box.

EP

ecologically	environmentally	financially
globally	incredibly	regularly
scientifically	well	

1 It's fast, it's cheap, it's ________ **friendly**. Travel by Metro!

2 Take VitX every day – ________ **proven** to give you extra energy. Remember – always take vitamins as part of a ________-**balanced** diet.

3 Get all the latest sports news using our ________ **updated** app.

4 This ________ **recognised** brand is a bestseller on every continent.

5 Don't you want to be ________ **independent**? Work part-time from home and earn extra cash now!

6 WEPRINT
Our printers use ________ **safe** inks and they're ________ **economical** to run.

2 Complete the second sentence using the correct form of the bold words.

0 This work is so **easy** it's **ridiculous**!
This work is *ridiculously easy*!
1 Your brother always **dresses** in **nice** clothes.
Your brother is always ________.
2 It's **amazing** how **tasty** this dish is.
This dish is ________.
3 I am **involved** in their project quite **actively**.
I am ________ in their project.
4 The railway is **located** at a **convenient** distance from the college.
There's a ________ railway station near the college.
5 My dad has a **natural talent** for telling jokes.
My dad is a ________ comedian.
6 The recipe says you have to **chop** the onions **finely**.
The recipe requires ________ onions.

3 » **Work in pairs. Turn to page 140.**

LISTENING

1 You will hear a girl called Sophia Spencer talking about an unusual advertising campaign. Underline key words in sentences 1–10 below and predict what you might hear.

PREPARE FOR THE EXAM

Listening Part 2

2 (73) Listen and, for questions 1–10, complete the sentences with a word or short phrase. Listen again and check.

AN UNUSUAL ADVERTISING CAMPAIGN

Sophia recently took up the role of **(1)** .... in her school.

Sophia originally thought that the parcel she received must be from a **(2)** ....

Sophia's favourite item in the box was a personalised **(3)** ....

The band called The Emissary aims to appeal to girls in the **(4)** .... age group.

Advertisers believe that a **(5)** .... is the best form of advertising for Sophia's age group.

Sophia uses the word '**(6)** ....' to describe what she thought of the advertiser's strategy.

Sophia was given tickets for a performance held in a local **(7)** ....

Sophia was contacted by a **(8)** .... who wanted to talk to her about a new campaign.

Sophia was asked to promote clothing through a strategy known as '**(9)** .... advertising'.

Sophia was excited to meet some well-known **(10)** .... at a launch event in London.

3 Discuss the questions.

1. What do you think of undercover advertising?
2. What would you do if you were Sophia?
3. How would you feel if an ad agency wanted to work with you?

SPEAKING Expressing opinions

1 How do you think companies make decisions on what kind of advertising to use?

2 (74) Look at the task below, then listen to the conversation. What form of advertising do Sun and Johann agree is the best value for companies?

3 (75) Read the *Prepare to speak* box. Then listen to Sun and Johann using the phrases. Which expressions do you hear?

PREPARE TO SPEAK | Expressing opinions

Expressing opinions

I assume/imagine/reckon (that) …
I get the feeling/impression that …
The good/bad thing about … is …
As I see it, …

Justifying opinions

It seems to me that …
On the one hand, … on the other hand, …
From the point of view of …
If you think about it, …

PREPARE FOR THE EXAM

Speaking Part 3 and Part 4

4 Work in pairs. Complete the task in Exercise 2. Use phrases from the *Prepare to speak* box.

5 Ask and answer the questions with a partner. Use phrases from the *Prepare to speak* box.

1. Do you think companies would sell less if they didn't advertise their products?
2. Do you think it's true that watching adverts always makes people want to buy things? (Why? / Why not?)
3. Some people think advertising can be harmful because it encourages people to buy things they can't afford. Do you agree? (Why? / Why not?)
4. Some people say it is wrong to show adverts for toys during children's shows. Do you agree? (Why? / Why not?)
5. Do you think it would be better if there were no adverts on TV? (Why? / Why not?)
6. Some people think that adverts can be more entertaining than the actual shows. What do you think?

LIFE SKILLS CRITICAL THINKING

ASSESSING ADVERTISING

LIFE SKILLS

Assessing advertising

Advertisers use many techniques and tricks to try to influence the way we think and feel, often on a subconscious level, in order to get us to buy or use their products and services. It's therefore important to be aware of advertising and have the necessary skills and tools to be able to assess ads properly and make well-informed decisions when it comes to spending our money.

1 Ask and answer the questions with a partner.

1 How many adverts do you think you see in a typical day?
   a 40 **b** 400 **c** 4,000
2 Do you have a favourite advert at the moment? Why do you like it?
3 How do you think adverts try to make us buy or consume things?

2 Read the first three paragraphs of the article on page 95 quickly. Which of these sentences is the best summary?

A We only look at the adverts we're really interested in, and their influence on us is limited.
B Adverts come in a surprising variety of forms and it's easy to see how they influence us.
C Most adverts today are found online and they aim to increase our desire for something.

3 Read the whole article and answer the questions.

1 Why might the number of 4,000 ads not be precise?
2 What do ads try to do after they have been successful in getting you to look?
3 Why do adverts include people who are similar to you?
4 Is it hard to identify examples of product placement? Why? / Why not?
5 How can assessing advertising critically make you feel more confident about your choices?

76 **4 Listen to a media studies teacher giving a talk to a group of students about common advertising techniques. Number the techniques in the order she mentions them.**

.... the bandwagon effect
.... association
.... fear and embarrassment
.... celebrity endorsements

76 **5 Listen again and choose the best answer (A, B or C).**

1 In her introduction, the teacher says that adverts are
   A simply images of and information about products.
   B designed to be eye-catching.
   C designed to influence us without us realising.
2 The association technique is when advertisers
   A try to make people feel happy and attractive.
   B use positive images in their ads.
   C try to sell their products to people in different countries.
3 The second technique mentioned might be used in an ad for
   A deodorant.
   B a smartphone.
   C washing-up liquid.
4 What does the teacher point out about celebrity endorsements?
   A Products promoted by celebrities tend to be more expensive.
   B Celebrities often don't really use the products they advertise.
   C Brands create products imitating the style of clothes that celebrities wear.
5 The bandwagon effect is when advertisers try to make us feel that
   A we're the first to try a product.
   B we're the only ones not using a product.
   C we don't have much time left to enjoy a product.

Do you REALLY want to buy it?

77

Some studies estimate that we're exposed to up to 4,000 adverts every day! That seems like a huge amount, so let's have a think about how that could add up. First of all, it depends on our definition of an ad. Many people believe that this includes seeing a logo or a product's packaging, as well as more obvious adverts in print, on TV and those popping up while we're watching our favourite series, playing games or streaming music online.

In fact, when we're on the internet or using apps, we're constantly being bombarded by ads. We're also exposed to a huge number of ads on the way to and from school or when we're out shopping. While the exact figure of 4,000 might be difficult to prove, what's very clear is that we see a massive number of adverts in our daily lives.

A large amount of the advertising we see is designed to make us want something. Now, you might think that you don't let adverts influence your opinion about things. But in reality, that's very difficult to demonstrate. Why is it that we really want one thing, but don't want another because we 'know' that it's not fashionable? More often than not, it depends to a large extent on the adverts we've seen. Ads usually aim to grab our attention, affect us emotionally and encourage us to buy something.

Persuasive advertising doesn't always send positive messages. Many adverts exploit our worries and make us feel less self-confident, more unattractive, or like we're not part of a group because we don't have the 'right' things. This is often done by using peer influence on social media, where people of a similar age to you are pictured with the product being advertised. From a psychological point of view, this works because it creates the idea that the brand or item will somehow 'make' you become 'better' than you are. We need to take a step back and look at adverts from an independent and critical perspective. Feeling confident and informed enables us to assess and control the influence adverts can have on us.

And it's not just the obvious adverts which we need to assess critically. Product placement – when companies use media like TV shows, films or games to promote their brands and new products – has become the norm in the world of advertising. Perhaps your favourite character is wearing a certain brand of clothing or enjoying a new drink. Or a singer you like has the latest mobile in her new music video. Product placement can come in many forms, but it's usually very difficult to spot the product because it is 'hidden'. However, you can be sure that your brain has 'seen' it on a subconscious level. Try spotting product placements and you'll be amazed at how widespread it is!

There are some key lessons to learn here. When you want to buy a specific product or brand, ask yourself a few questions before you make a decision: What does it 'mean' to you to have this thing? Is the product attractive because of how it looks, feels or sounds? Or do you perhaps find it attractive because it's associated with the celebrity, model or setting used to advertise it? Assessing advertising in this way will make you feel a lot more in control of your choices and spending decisions.

6 **Complete the sentences with the words and phrases in the box.**

associate	endorsements	missing out
subconscious	targets	

USEFUL LANGUAGE

Assessing an advert critically

1. Advertisers try to influence us on a ________ level.
2. Companies try to ________ positive images with their products.
3. This ad ________ people's fear of having bad skin.
4. Many brands use celebrity ________ to sell their products.
5. The aim of this advert is to make us feel like we're ________.

PROJECT

A critical assessment of an advert

Work in groups of three or four to critically assess an advert. Use these steps to help you.

1. Search for and choose a selection of adverts from print and digital sources.
2. Decide together on one advert that you'd like to work on.
3. Use the ideas from the article and the techniques from the talk to perform a critical analysis of the advert.
4. Create a presentation to share your assessment.

Present your work to the class.

REVIEW 4 UNITS 13–16

VOCABULARY

1 Complete the sentences with the words in the box.

conscientious doubt self-esteem sympathetic targets

1 Mike seems nice, but he isn't very ________ to other people's problems.
2 Arran's a very ________ boy and always hands his work in on time.
3 Suzanne's got pretty high ________. She has a lot of confidence in herself.
4 I'm always full of ________ about being able to do new things.
5 It's important to set realistic ________ so you can achieve them.

2 Complete the sentences with the correct form of the phrasal verbs. Use a word from A and a word from B.

A break keep live pull speak

B down out up up to up with

1 My scooter ________ all the time. It's really unreliable.
2 Can you ________ a bit? I can't hear you very well.
3 I got to the platform as the train was ________, so I missed it.
4 Did the party ________ your expectations?
5 It's hard to ________ Steph because she walks so fast.

3 Choose the correct options.

1 The world's leading phone brand has just *launched* / *aimed* a budget model for the first time.
2 It is aimed at *samples* / *consumers* who can't afford the £500+ products that have made the brand so successful.
3 The phone will *appeal* / *sponsor* to people who want a good-quality phone for a lower price.
4 The new product is being shown during TV *product placement* / *ad breaks* and is likely to be very successful.
5 A local store has agreed to *sponsor* / *launch* our football team, which means we don't have to close the club down!

4 Match the sentence halves.

1 It's an environmentally
2 I eat a fairly well-
3 I am financially
4 There are no scientifically
5 It's a globally

a friendly car.
b independent.
c proven benefits.
d recognised brand.
e balanced diet.

GRAMMAR

1 Choose the correct options.

1 Joe *must* / *can't* be on holiday because I saw him this morning.
2 The thief *might have* / *can't have* stolen your bag. It's locked in the car, remember!
3 Be careful! You *might* / *can* fall off the ladder.
4 Tina *might not have* / *can't have* wanted to go to the party. I thought she looked a bit tired.
5 That man *could not have* / *can't have* paid his bill. Look – the waiter's running after him!
6 You *must* / *can't* have been really pleased when you got a new phone for your birthday.

2 Complete the sentences with the passive form of the verbs in brackets.

1 I love ________ for dinner. (take out)
2 You won't be the last person ________ this question. (ask)
3 Were you pleased ________ a prize for your essay? (award)
4 Who else should ________ to the party next week? (invite)
5 Why does he always insist on ________ first? (serve)
6 No one likes ________ at. (laugh)

3 Complete the conditional sentences using the <u>underlined</u> words.

1 It's a pity you missed the barbecue last week. <u>you / love / it / if / you / go.</u>
2 Alex will be here in a few minutes. We've met him before, so I'm sure <u>we / recognise / him / when / he / arrive.</u>
3 Exercise is so important to me. <u>if / I / not / do / it / regularly, / I / feel / unhealthy.</u>
4 Imagine winning a £1,000 holiday! <u>if / you / win / one / who / you / take?</u>
5 I know you didn't go to university, but <u>what / you / study / if / you / go?</u>
6 You know about science, don't you? <u>if / you / heat / iron / what temperature / it / melt / at</u>?

4 Correct the mistake in each sentence.

1 How much do you expect to be pay in your holiday job?
2 These programmes must not watched by really young children.
3 David told by the security guard that photos were forbidden in the palace.
4 John said me he had some good news.
5 Now I can email on my tablet, I needn't to get annoyed about how slow my laptop is.
6 I died if the men that were fishing had not called the police.
7 I will offer you a 10% discount if you booked for 18 months.

PREPARE FOR THE EXAM

Reading and Use of English Part 1

1 **For questions 1–8, read the text below and decide which answer (A, B, C or D) best fits each gap.**

The Teamwork Challenge Award for Scouts

The Scouts is an organisation for 6- to 25-year-olds around the world, which **(0)** *supports* young people in developing important life skills, such as teamwork and leadership. Through a range of interesting and varied activities, which include everything from kayaking to looking after animals, Scouts **(1)** .... skills and character. This enables them to become **(2)** .... and not rely on others for support.

The Teamwork Challenge Award is incredibly useful, teaching team members to **(3)** .... with the group to set **(4)** .... and reach goals. To gain the award, Scouts must prove what role they have fulfilled within teams, take part in team-building exercises, and **(5)** .... up in Scout forums. While Scout meetings are in **(6)** ...., members are encouraged to express their opinions about items on the agenda.

Participating in such activities helps young people form strong relationships and **(7)** .... out from the crowd when it comes to finding employment. Many former Scouts go on to **(8)** .... up businesses, or become teachers and leaders, Olympic athletes and even astronauts!

	A	B	C	D
0	**A** influences	(**B**) supports	**C** persuades	**D** promotes
1	**A** build	**B** create	**C** produce	**D** raise
2	**A** independent	**B** individual	**C** available	**D** free
3	**A** cooperate	**B** help	**C** aid	**D** assist
4	**A** achievements	**B** ambitions	**C** targets	**D** plans
5	**A** chat	**B** talk	**C** discuss	**D** speak
6	**A** performance	**B** completion	**C** progress	**D** action
7	**A** step	**B** look	**C** stand	**D** hold
8	**A** do	**B** set	**C** make	**D** put

Reading and Use of English Part 2

2 **For questions 1–8, read the text below and think of the word which best fits each gap. Use only one word in each gap.**

NEW PUBLIC TRANSPORT

Interesting ways of keeping citizens moving are constantly **(0)** *being* employed around the world. In many cities, large numbers of people have already been persuaded **(1)** .... cycle or use electric scooters because they're quick and cheap. **(2)** .... you cycle, you'll often arrive before a car, bus or train. Some people use public hire systems. With their credit card or phone, they **(3)** .... release a bike or scooter from wherever it has been left in the street and ride it for as long as they like. Sometimes the first hour is free, and they then **(4)** .... to pay a small fee for subsequent periods.

The first large-scale cycle system to **(5)** .... introduced was the Vélib in Paris, **(6)** .... tens of thousands of bicycles are now ridden every day **(7)** .... people of all ages. Without the Vélib's enormous success, several hundred other cities around the world, including London, New York, Barcelona and Mexico City, might not have **(8)** .... able to fund their own bicycle-hire systems.

Reading and Use of English Part 4

3 **For questions 1–6, complete the second sentence so that it has a similar meaning to the first sentence, using the word given. Do not change the word given. You must use between two and five words, including the word given.**

0 'You should get a new phone,' Stevie said to Maria. **THAT**
Stevie told Maria *that she ought* to get a new phone.

1 Sara said, 'It was me who broke Dan's headphones.' **ADMITTED**
Sara .... who had broken Dan's headphones.

2 It would be good to get an invitation to Cheryl's wedding, but I'm not too bothered about it! **MIND**
I .... invited to Cheryl's wedding, but I'm not too bothered about it!

3 I'm sure João was at work yesterday because his car was in the car park. **BEEN**
João .... at work yesterday because his car was in the car park.

4 The advert was going to cost $1 million, but the film company never made it. **IF**
The ad would have cost $1 million .... made.

5 'I've had a recommendation from someone about this café,' Jan said. **RECOMMENDED**
Jan said that someone .... him.

6 Jules said to me, 'You always make such a mess!' **CRITICISED**
Jules .... such a mess.

17 MAKING HEADLINES

ABOUT YOU

13 Watch the video and answer the questions.

Where do you hear or read the news?

Who or what is in the news at the moment that you're particularly interested in? Why?

VOCABULARY The media

1 Read the quiz. Match the phrases in the quiz to the meanings below.

EP

What's the purpose *of the media?*

The media is there to …

1 help me **keep up to date** with the sports results ☐
2 **celebrate achievements** such as discoveries and firsts ☐
3 **gossip about** celebrities ☐
4 tell me what's **making headlines** around the world ☐
5 **make fun of** public figures ☐
6 **comment on current events** ☐
7 **keep** people **amused** ☐
8 **cover** interesting **stories** ☐

a give positive information about successes
b help someone feel interested and happy
c give opinions about the news
d deal with news items which people may want to know about
e talk about people's private lives
f be an important news story in the media
g make unkind jokes about someone
h have the latest information about the news, sport, etc.

78 **2 Listen to eight short recordings. What is happening in each one? Use the phrases in Exercise 1 in your answers.**

3 Read the quiz again and tick the statements you agree with. Compare your answers with your partner.

4 Think about recent news stories. Which statements in Exercise 1 do they match?

READING

1 Look at the photos and read the article quickly. What does it give advice about?

A how to write a realistic news story
B how to deal with a particular kind of journalism
C how to ignore news which may be harmful

PREPARE FOR THE EXAM

Reading and Use of English Part 3

2 Look at the example answer (0) in the first paragraph of the article. What type of word is it?

3 For questions 1–8, read the first three paragraphs of the article. Use the word given in capitals to form a word that fits in the gap.

4 Read the whole article and answer the questions.

1 Why can fake news be a problem?
2 How do fake news stories appear to be real?
3 What advice is given about checking whether a story is genuine or not?
4 Why are people tempted to read fake news stories?
5 What does the text say about quotes in news stories?
6 What is the advice given in the article's conclusion?

5 Match the highlighted words and phrases in the article to the meanings.

1 where something comes from
2 can be trusted
3 arranged
4 words someone else has said or written
5 make us notice something

FAKE NEWS:

WHAT IS IT AND HOW CAN YOU SPOT IT?

79

If you're on social media and like to keep up to date with the news, you'll almost **(0)** *certainly* (CERTAIN) have read at least one fake news story, if not dozens. So, what *is* fake news? Well, it's a story which is deliberately **(1)** ______ (MISLEAD). In other words, it's partially or entirely **(2)** ______ (TRUE).

While making up news is **(3)** ______ (DEFINITE) not a new phenomenon, social media is helping it to reach bigger audiences than ever.

Many stories are relatively **(4)** ______ (HARM) and cause no problems. Some, however, can actually be **(5)** ______ (DAMAGE) to people's reputations, especially for people in power, like **(6)** ______ (POLITICS).

There are several reasons why news is made up. One is to get people clicking onto a website which promotes companies' **(7)** ______ (ADVERT) campaigns and earns the site more money. Other reasons include attempting to influence readers' opinions or making fun of public figures. Some readers are unaware that these stories may not be **(8)** ______ (FACT).

How can we distinguish between what is fake news and what is a genuine news article? Many fake stories have the appearance of a real news item, and as a result of this, they're shared, reaching many millions of people worldwide. They are laid out like actual news stories, with a headline, photos of the people mentioned in the article, and often indicate who the news provider is. This makes it very difficult for readers to determine whether a story is real or fake.

One of the ways in which it is possible to find out whether a story is genuine is to do a search for the news provider. We are all familiar with the big news providers in our own countries, and we know that they're trustworthy. If the provider isn't one you've ever heard of, or something makes you suspect it isn't a recognised source, then it probably isn't. If you have any doubts about the story, you can verify it by looking on a well-known news site, such as the BBC. If it appears there, then you can safely assume it's real, since genuine providers check facts and make sure their stories are true. In addition to checking the provider and verifying the story, you can also look out for things like missing logos or the names of journalists being left out, which credible news stories always include.

The problem is that fake news headlines can be very convincing and cover what seem to be interesting events. This makes us want to read them and catch up on what's happening, especially if they appear to be gossiping about stars: 'Top Hollywood couple split up!' Or if they make absurd claims: 'Scientists say you can survive on chocolate!' Headlines like this are guaranteed to grab our attention and draw us in. And if you think that the presence of a quote makes a story more likely to be true, think again. These can also be made up, and this is where someone's reputation may be affected.

Here's your checklist for spotting fake news:

- Is the source reliable? Do you recognise the news provider and is their logo visible?
- Is the journalist's full name on the piece? You can look them up, too!
- Did someone you know and trust share the story with you?
- Can you find the same story on a reputable news site?
- Does the story *seem* fake? If so, it probably is!
- And finally, remember to be critical about what you read online – especially if you plan on including facts or quotes in school assignments.

MAYOR SAYS HE **HATES** OUR CITY

Miracle fruit makes you TALLER!

TALKING POINTS

What are the consequences for people of believing fake news?

Do you think social media sites should ban advertising? Why? / Why not?

GRAMMAR Conditionals (2): mixed

1 **Read the examples and answer the questions.**

1 If you **hadn't read** this article, you **wouldn't know** how to spot fake news.
Did you read this article?
Do you know how to spot fake news?

2 If I **weren't aware** of fake news, I **might have believed** that fake story.
Are you aware of fake news?
Did you believe the fake story?

2 **Match the examples in Exercise 1 to the rules.**

Mixed conditionals combine elements of the second and third conditional. We use them:

a to talk about an imaginary situation in the present that is affected by a past action: *if* + past perfect, *would/might/could* + infinitive.

b to talk about an imaginary situation in the past that is affected by a present situation or permanent conditions: *if* + past simple, *would/might/could* + *have* + past participle.

» GRAMMAR REFERENCE AND PRACTICE PAGE 164

3 **Complete the mixed-conditional sentences.**

0 We haven't got wi-fi because our router stopped working last night.
We *would have* wi-fi if our router *hadn't stopped working last night*.

1 We speak English, so we understood the report.
We ______ the report if we ______ English.

2 This is a safe area, so I didn't lock the back door.
If this ______ a safe area, I ______ the back door.

3 You're wet because you didn't bring an umbrella.
If you ______ an umbrella, you ______ wet.

4 You're a hard worker, so you passed your exams.
You ______ your exams if you ______ a hard worker.

5 David missed the bus. That's why he isn't at home now.
David ______ at home now if he ______ the bus.

4 **Decide which two sentences are correct. Correct the mistakes in the three incorrect sentences.**

1 If I weren't such a fast runner, I wouldn't have missed the bus this morning.
2 If it weren't so wet, we could have gone to the park today.
3 If I didn't have my calculator today, I wouldn't have taken much longer with this homework.
4 You would be in trouble now if you haven't done your homework.
5 If you had taken a headache tablet as I suggested, you would be out cycling now.

5 **Write questions using mixed conditionals.**

0 Today's a weekday, but what (you / do / this morning / if / Saturday)
would you have done this morning if it were a Saturday?
1 The internet was launched in the 1980s, but (if / they / not invent / it / how / life / be / different)
2 You aren't a millionaire, but (where / you / go / on holiday / last summer / if / be / millionaire)
3 You haven't left school yet, but (if / you / already / leave / where / live)
4 Mobile phones became popular in the 1990s, but (how / you / communicate / with your friends / if / they / not become popular)

6 **Ask and answer the questions in Exercise 5.**

VOCABULARY Phrasal verbs: the media

1 **Match the sentence halves.**

EP

1 I managed to **get** the point **across**
2 He **followed up** his TV interview
3 The news item **brought up** an
4 I got out my tablet and **caught up on**
5 These points were **left out**
6 His family **backed** him **up**
7 The programme **looked into**
8 We need to **clear up**

a with a Twitter conversation for fans.
b to the audience.
c of the article about guerrilla marketing.
d the issue of fees for higher education.
e interesting point about equality.
f after he confessed he was lying.
g a few problems before we can move on.
h all the latest gossip on social media.

2 **Replace the underlined words and phrases in the email with a phrasal verb from Exercise 1 with a similar meaning.**

Dear Jonas,

While I'm [1] learning the latest information about how everyone's getting on, I just want to confirm your responsibilities as the newsletter editor. Your main role is checking the content of the blogs. I [2] mentioned the issue of sources when I spoke to some of the writers a while back, so do make sure you [3] emphasise to them the importance of using accurate sources. They mustn't [4] forget to include their references either. It's the webmaster's job to learn about and [5] solve problems, such as photos that don't upload, so don't worry about those. Let me know if you want me to [6] check the accuracy of any sources and references. I'm here to [7] support you, as you know. If you want, we can [8] take further action connected to this email with a meeting to talk about things in more detail.

See you soon,
Clare

3 **In pairs, make sentences with the phrasal verbs from Exercise 1.**

WRITING A review

1 **Read the first paragraph of a magazine review.**

1. Who do you think the review is aimed at?
2. Do you think the style is lively or serious? Which words and phrases tell you this?

THINK INK: NEWS AND VIEWS FOR TEENAGERS

Are you into writing and art, but tired of the same boring old magazines? Then you should check out 'Think Ink'. It's a new magazine especially for teenagers who are into writing, art and photography. It's full of interesting articles and original stories. The photos are amazing, too.

2 **Read two options, A and B, for the rest of the review and answer the questions.**

1. Which has a similar style to the first paragraph?
2. Which option do you think is more appropriate for a review? Why?

A

It seems to be the case that magazines for teenagers tend to concentrate on celebrities and fashion. Arguably, publishers fail to understand their market if they see celebrity culture as a teenager's chief concern and don't look into other issues which concern young people. However, 'Think Ink' is not in this category because its readers are treated like adults. What's more, the content is entirely created by its readers, which makes it unique and genuinely attractive to a teenage audience.

Nevertheless, it has to be said that the poetry section is rather disappointing. If the poems hadn't seemed so childish, they would be a little more appealing. On the other hand, the articles feature many original topics, and the fiction is generally excellent. While 'Think Ink' isn't perfect, it is a thoroughly good read and highly recommended.

B

As we know, most magazines for teenagers are stuffed full of articles about celebrities and fashion. Do publishers really think we only want to read trivial gossip? Teenage magazines get very boring after a while, but 'Think Ink' is refreshingly different. For a start, it treats its readers like adults, and brings up fascinating points which are backed up with detailed arguments. That makes a nice change, and I know you'll really love its style! And the best thing is that we, the readers, write everything that's in it, giving us the opportunity to get across ideas that a teenage audience will relate to.

I feel that the poetry section lets the magazine down a bit. Who wants to read poems aimed at children? But then again, the creative fiction really stands out, and the articles are excellent as well. 'Think Ink' is definitely worth a read, so look out for it!

3 **Read the *Prepare to write* box, and read review B again. Underline examples of:**

- **a** informal phrases
- **b** direct questions
- **c** phrasal verbs
- **d** a friendly tone

PREPARE TO WRITE Language for reviews

Reviews written for teenagers will generally

- have a friendly tone rather than a formal one.
- contain informal phrases, such as *really cool* and *stuff like that*.
- use direct questions, which address the reader personally.
- include phrasal verbs, such as *get across* and *stand out*.

PREPARE FOR THE EXAM

Writing Part 2 (A review)

4 **Read the task and plan your answer.**

You see a notice on an international students' forum asking for reviews of news websites.

Submit a review!

We are looking for reviews of news websites. Write us a review of a website you know well, telling us:

- why you use this website
- what information you have found on the website and why it is interesting
- who you would recommend the website to and why.

Write your **review**.

5 **Write your review.**

- Use the tips in the *Prepare to write* box.
- Give your review a title and organise it into paragraphs.
- Express your opinion and make a recommendation.
- Check your grammar and spelling.
- Write 140–190 words.

18 CREATIVE CAREERS

ABOUT YOU

▶ 14 Watch the video and answer the questions.

Have you ever worked during the school holidays? What did you do?

Have you ever done any work experience? What was it like?

How do you think that schools and parents can help young people prepare for their futures?

VOCABULARY The world of work

1 **Read the list of aspects a job might have. Then look at photos A–F and decide which aspects apply to these jobs.** EP

a having to work long hours
b using a hobby to make a living
c being able to take lots of time off
d doing something that is rewarding
e having to meet deadlines
f being well paid
g being badly paid
h having to work shifts

2 **Can you think of another job for each of the aspects in Exercise 1?**

80 **3** **Listen to Sofia, Martin and Tara. Which of the jobs in the pictures A–F would be most appropriate for each person?**

80 **4** **Listen again. Why is each job appropriate for each person? Use the aspects of work in your answers.**

Sofia: artist. She wouldn't need to meet deadlines or work shifts …

5 **Discuss the questions.**

1 Which person is most like you? Why?
2 Which aspects from Exercise 1 will be important to you in your future job?

READING

1 **Read the blog post quickly. Which career does Emily seem to be most attracted to?**

PREPARE FOR THE EXAM

Reading and Use of English Part 5

2 **Read the blog post again. For questions 1–6, choose the answer (A, B, C or D) which you think fits best according to the text.**

1 From the first paragraph, we understand that Emily
A believes she still has a chance of becoming famous.
B is worried about how much she'll earn in the future.
C is undecided about her future plans.
D thinks most teenagers want to become famous.

2 In line 23, 'making it' means
A becoming successful in a chosen field.
B being discovered at a very young age.
C deciding to follow up on a hidden talent.
D having the chance to earn some money.

3 What does Emily think about having a career in finance?
A The work might be too difficult for her.
B The hours would be too physically demanding for her.
C The job wouldn't be appropriate for her.
D The career is morally unacceptable to her.

4 What do Emily's parents agree is important to her career choice?
A that she gains further qualifications
B that she tries out a number of different jobs
C that she avoids the mistakes they both made
D that she finds something she is enthusiastic about

5 Emily feels that law and medicine
A are careers she can't take seriously.
B require too much studying.
C are professions she wouldn't be able to do.
D have a predictable career path.

6 What steps has Emily taken towards finding work?
A She's arranged some work experience.
B She's shown her blog to some local newspapers.
C She's researched the kinds of work she'd like to do.
D She's applied for a degree in journalism.

81

THE BIG DECISION

BY EMILY PARKER Posted 8th April

With just over a year of school to go, sooner or later I'll be making some decisions about my future. This has left me wondering whether I want to spend another few years studying or whether I'm actually ready to start making a living. The only thing that's clear to me right now is that my vague teenage dreams of making films, singing in a band, competing in the Olympics or generally earning a fortune while socialising with celebrities are becoming more and more unlikely. It's probably nothing unusual, but I've just come to the realisation that, although I'm good at lots of things, I'm not *brilliant* at anything.

I'm not upset by this. Research about teenagers' career ambitions reveals that those prioritising fame and fortune above other ambitions are likely to earn 20% less in adult life than teenagers who have realised that their futures may be less glamorous. And even if I did have a genuine talent, the statistics aren't encouraging. In baseball, for example, by far the largest sport in the US, only the top 250 amateur players out of every 300,000 will be selected for the professional leagues. For musicians, there's even less chance of **making it**. Unless you are discovered before your twenties, which is incredibly unlikely, you'll probably struggle to make a living from your talent.

At school recently, we did an online questionnaire about our academic strengths, interests and career priorities. The aim was to give us all some ideas for the future. OK, so economics and maths are my best subjects. But while having a career in finance might be well paid and earn me far more than most people get, is it really rewarding and would I be able to take plenty of time off?; two things I consider important in a job. And besides, don't people like bankers have to get up really early in the morning? I can do that, but really, *every* morning?

My parents, trying desperately not to influence my decisions, have so far offered limited guidance. My dad, who went into construction straight from school and doesn't regret a thing, talks about being passionate about whatever you do. My mum, a teacher, holds the same view. However, on balance, she feels that qualifications gave her more options when she was ready to decide. But, now and then, I get the feeling she'd rather have done something different.

Most of my friends are in the same position as me. One or two have decided on degrees in medicine or law. Until recently, I might have laughed at them – it takes a long time to qualify in those subjects. I don't mind hard work, but only for something I definitely want to do. And saving someone's life in an operating theatre or giving speeches in a court seems so grown up. Now I'm actually jealous of their plans. Forgetting about the hard work for the moment, or even whether I'd be capable of doing those jobs, their futures are more or less decided: a degree, training and then work. In ten years, they'll all have enjoyable careers.

One thing I do feel positive about is the response I've had to this blog. People seem to enjoy reading it, so I've been wondering whether journalism might be my 'thing' and whether I could make a living with my writing. I've already written to several local newspapers to arrange some work experience and, in my applications, I've been able to prove my interest in journalism by referencing my blog and asking them to take a look at it. I haven't had any replies yet, but I remain hopeful. I've also been looking into relevant courses at local colleges and at some universities, but the length of time required to do a full degree is putting me off. Naturally, I'll keep you updated, so come back soon and I might have some exciting news about my future!

TALKING POINTS

Have you started planning for your future yet?

Do you think it's important for young people to follow their parents' advice when planning their futures?

GRAMMAR Uses of verb + *-ing*

1 **Match the examples to the rules.**

1 People seem to enjoy **reading** my blog.
2 This has left me wondering whether I want to spend another few years **studying**.
3 **Giving** speeches in a court seems so grown up.
4 My dreams of **making** films are unlikely.
5 I've been **looking into** relevant courses.
6 My parents, **trying** desperately not to influence my decisions, have so far offered limited guidance.

We use verb + *-ing*
a as part of continuous verb forms.
b after prepositions.
c after certain verbs, e.g. *like, admit, keep.*
d as the subject, or part of the subject, of a verb.
e after certain phrases, e.g. *spend time.*
f in participle clauses, to give more information about a noun.

» GRAMMAR REFERENCE AND PRACTICE PAGE 165

2 **Complete the story with the *-ing* form of the verbs in the box.**

be	beat	~~invent~~	live	realise
study	think	turn	win	

Hannah Herbst discovered that she liked [0] *inventing* things when she was just 13, after [1] ________ a robot-making competition. At 15, Hannah found out from her penfriend in Africa that many people [2] ________ there didn't have electricity. She started [3] ________ about how she could help and came up with BEACON (Bringing Electricity Access to Countries through Ocean Energy), an invention which captures energy from waves.

Hannah, [4] ________ that many millions of people without electricity live close to the sea, created a simple device that would change their lives. It consists of a plastic tube with a propeller at one end and a hydroelectric generator at the other. The flow of the water creates power by [5] ________ the propeller, which is connected to the generator. [6] ________ light, portable and cheap makes the device particularly practical. [7] ________ hundreds of other young inventors, Hannah was named 'America's Top Young Scientist' for BEACON. Now in her late teens, Hannah is [8] ________ computer science at university. Her future looks bright!

3 **Correct the mistakes in the sentences. There may be more than one mistake.**

1 Your idea about find a job before start college is great.
2 We had loads of fun design a new toy for children.
3 Offer greater bonuses has contributed to raise the motivation of our young sales team.
4 Mason likes use his brain and enjoys do puzzles.
5 Teresa, believe she would help me do my work more quickly, actually slowed me down.

4 **Work with a partner and complete the sentences about you. Use the *-ing* form of a verb.**

1 I can't stand ...
2 I spend a lot of time ...
3 I don't think it's worth ...
4 I'm thinking of ... one day.

VOCABULARY Word pairs

1 **Read about word pairs. Then read the examples and match the word pairs to the meanings.**

EP

Word pairs are two words that are joined by a conjunction (usually *and* or *or*). They often have a similar meaning or opposite meanings.

1 **Sooner or later**, I'll be making some decisions.
2 We walked **up and down** the corridor, but couldn't find the careers office.
3 My dreams are becoming **more and more** unlikely.
4 **Now and then**, I get the feeling she'd rather have done something different.
5 The teacher told us **over and over again** how important it is to get qualifications.
6 **One or two** have decided on medicine or law.
7 Their futures are **more or less** decided.
8 Ideas go **round and round** in my head, but I still haven't decided on a career.

a almost or approximately
b sometimes, but not very often
c a few
d eventually
e increasingly; as time passes
f in one direction and then in the opposite direction
g moving in a circle without stopping
h happening or done many times

2 **Complete the sentences with the words in the box.**

down	later	less	more (x3)
now	one	over (x2)	round (x2)
sooner	then	two	up

1 We speak online ________ and ________, but in general, we're not in touch any more.
2 We walked ________ and ________ the park for over an hour, but couldn't find you.
3 You should think about it now. ________ or ________, you'll need to make a decision.
4 James has ________ or ________ decided. He's almost definitely going to university.
5 When she heard the news, she started jumping ________ and ________ with excitement.
6 It's becoming ________ and ________ expensive to do a degree.
7 I've got ________ or ________ ideas about my future. But I'm far from certain.
8 I rang the number ________ and ________ again, but got no answer.

3 » **Work in pairs. Turn to page 140.**

LISTENING

PREPARE FOR THE EXAM

Listening Part 4

1 **You will hear an interview with a boy called Aiden Cass, who started up his own T-shirt business. Read the questions and <u>underline</u> the words that might help you when you listen.**

1 What gave Aiden the idea for his business?
A One of his parents suggested it.
B His neighbours couldn't supply him with enough clothes.
C He realised selling used items could be very profitable.

2 The most **significant** problem that Aiden encountered was that
A he ran out of space to keep the T-shirts in.
B there weren't enough good T-shirts to sell.
C the T-shirts took too long to repair.

3 How does Aiden's business work now?
A His brother creates the T-shirts that it sells.
B He buys T-shirts from other countries.
C He sells T-shirts with original designs.

4 How does Aiden feel about paperwork?
A grateful to receive help with it
B surprised by his lack of skill with it
C pleased that there isn't very much to do

5 The hardest thing for Aiden about combining school and work is that
A he doesn't always do his best at school.
B he often finds his business more interesting.
C his school isn't very flexible.

6 In general, how do Aiden's friends feel about his business?
A They're eager to make useful suggestions.
B They're fed up because they can't spend time with him now.
C They're not as interested in it as he expected.

7 Summer jobs taught Aiden
A how working hard is the key to success.
B how to deal with people well.
C the importance of making a living.

2 82 **Listen to the interview. For questions 1–7, choose the best answer (A, B or C). Then listen again and check.**

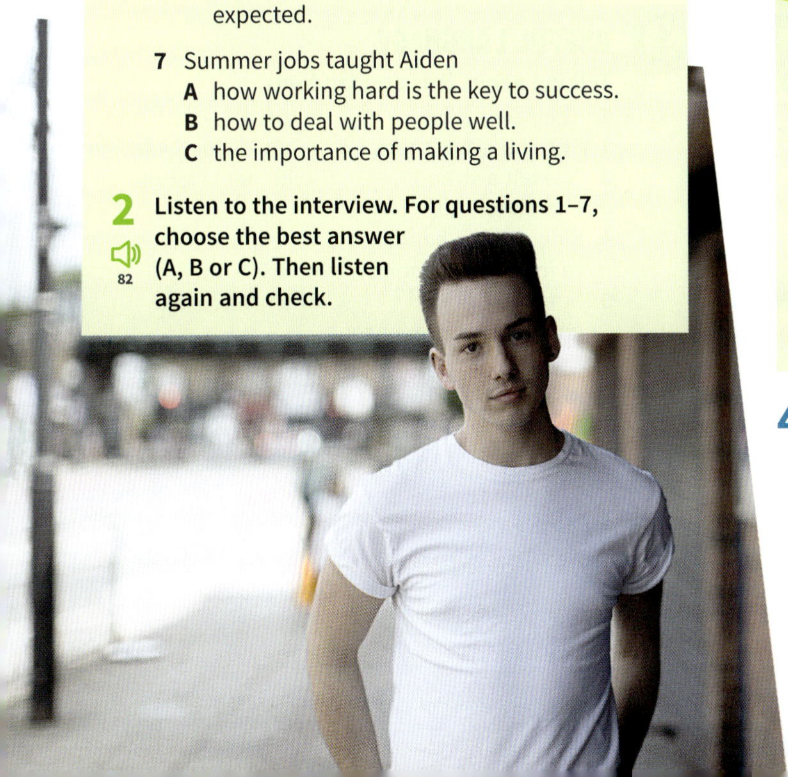

SPEAKING Agreeing and disagreeing

1 **Work in pairs. Look at the photos of summer jobs. Answer the questions.**

1 What are the good and bad things about each job?
2 Would you like to do this as a job? Why? / Why not?

83 **2** **Listen to Conor and Leila discussing five of the jobs in the photos. Answer the questions.**

1 Which jobs do they talk about?
2 Do they take turns to talk?
3 Do they ask each other's opinions?

83 **3** **Read the *Prepare to speak* box. Then listen again. Who uses each phrase? Write C (Conor) or L (Leila).**

PREPARE TO SPEAK | Agreeing and disagreeing

Agreeing
I'm with you on that.
That's a good point.
Absolutely!
Fair enough.

Disagreeing
I'm not sure about that.
I can't really see the point of …
I'm not convinced.
I agree up to a point, but …
I'd rather I didn't …

4 **Discuss the questions. Use phrases from the *Prepare to speak* box to agree or disagree with each other.**

1 What kind of things might you learn from the summer jobs in Exercise 1?
2 Which would you most or least like to do?
3 Do you think it's a good idea for teenagers to do summer jobs? Why? / Why not?

CULTURE

FAN CULTURE

1 Ask and answer the questions with a partner.

1 Are you a big fan of anything?
2 What do you think 'fan culture' means?

2 Read the article on page 107 quickly. Which of the following are mentioned?

1 the origins of the word *fandom*
2 examples of fandoms
3 things that participants in fandoms do
4 searching for the right fandom for you
5 how to start a fandom
6 advantages and disadvantages of fandoms

3 Read the article again and answer the questions.

1 Which group of fans are not normally considered to be members of a 'fandom'?
2 How does 'fan fiction' differ from normal fiction?
3 How can feeling a connection with a character, celebrity or show help people?
4 How do members of fandoms help each other?
5 What are the signs of an obsessive fan?

4 Match the highlighted words and phrases in the article to the meanings.

1 a series of films that have the same or similar titles and are about the same characters
2 sharing the same opinions, ideas or interests
3 very likely
4 feeling that you are in the right place or group
5 when too much of something pleasant becomes unpleasant

84 **5 Listen to an interview about spoilers. Number the topics in the order you hear them.**

A a brief history of spoilers in entertainment
B reasons why some people like to see spoilers
C what a spoiler is
D trying to keep the details of a film secret

84 **6 Listen to the interview again and decide whether the statements are true (*T*), false (*F*) or not mentioned (*NM*).**

1 The presenter doesn't know what her guest is going to talk about.
2 People tell spoilers about books, films, TV shows, etc. because it makes them feel powerful.
3 Spoilers have only existed since the arrival of social media.
4 Filmmakers always avoid putting spoilers in trailers.
5 The social media campaign against spoilers by fans of *Fantastic Beasts* was a success.
6 In the study mentioned by the lecturer, spoilers made the story less enjoyable to readers.

7 Complete the sentences with the words in the box.

admiration	characters	connection
lose	obsessive	participants

USEFUL LANGUAGE

Talking about fans and fandoms

1 They are active ________ in the *Whovian* fandom.
2 The subject of their ________ is Taylor Swift.
3 She felt a strong ________ with her favourite character.
4 *Shipping* is when fans want people or ________ to form relationships.
5 Sometimes fans ________ themselves in a character's experience.
6 ________ fans are often referred to as 'stans'.

FAN OR FANATIC?

Did you know the word 'fan' is short for 'fanatic'? This is because in the past, many people held negative views about fans, confusing their passion with obsessive behaviour. But things have changed, and psychologists now talk about fans as 'active participants in a culture or community'. This change in attitude has drawn our attention to 'fandoms', which is a subculture made up of people who are fans of the same thing, who share a common interest and who connect with other fans. The subject of their admiration could be a TV series, a band, a series of books, a movie franchise, a celebrity or any other form of culture or interest. Although supporters of a sports team or sportsperson can be said to be members of fandoms, the term isn't usually used for sports fans. Popular fandoms include *Potterheads* (yes, you guessed it – for Harry Potter fans), *Whovians* (Doctor Who fans) and *Swifties* (Taylor Swift fans).

Members of fandoms often take part in activities like attending Comic Cons, which are conventions for fans of comic genres, or creating and sharing new 'fan fiction'. This is when fans themselves write their own short stories using the characters from their favourite TV, book or film series, or even their favourite singers or actors. The term *shipping* is often used in fandoms and it comes from the word 'relation**ship**'. This is when fans would like to see real-life people or fictional characters form a romantic relationship. Fans create fan fiction or art of the imaginary relationship and often publish it on the internet.

Fandoms are not a new idea – in the late 19th Century, fans of Sherlock Holmes created what's considered to be the first fandom.

85

FANTASTIC FANDOMS

People become fans for many different reasons. But, undoubtedly, a big reason is to feel a strong connection with a favourite character, celebrity or show. Their story or struggle can feel like our own, and fans experience being a part of something much bigger than themselves. Some fans also find that they can let go of their own identity and 'lose' themselves in a character's experiences. They can step into Harry Potter's shoes and empathise with his fears and triumphs. This can be beneficial, as it allows them to momentarily forget about the worries and problems in their own lives. In addition, studies have found that many fans contribute to the real world in positive ways. They participate in social activism and form networks with other fans where they can help each other with advice and support.

Human beings have an almost universal need to form and maintain some kind of interpersonal relationship with others. Fandom participants can increase their sense of belonging by building large communities – spaces where fans can be enthusiastic about their passions – with like-minded people from all over the world. And many fans also get together in real life at conventions.

TAKING FANDOM TOO FAR?

Fandoms are not without their negative side, though, and too much of a good thing can also lead to unwanted consequences. Obsessive fans, often referred to as 'stans', can find it really hard to feel empathy for people in other groups, or towards anyone who doesn't share their interest. Feeling frustrated and disliking or even hating non-fans is a sure sign that someone is experiencing the negative side of fandom.

While having interests and being part of a community are good for our psychological well-being, fans shouldn't let their fandom become their whole world. It's important to have a range of different interests and hobbies.

PROJECT
Researching a fandom

Work in groups of three or four to research a fandom. Use these steps to help you.

1. Search for and then agree on a fandom you all want to know more about.
2. Research information about the fandom.
   - What does it call itself?
   - Does it have conventions or fan meetings?
   - What do the fans wear?
3. Find some images or videos of the fans.
4. Create a presentation.

Present your research to the class.

15 NOW WATCH THE CULTURE VIDEO

19 POINTS OF VIEW

ABOUT YOU

Do you have strong opinions and beliefs?
What issues in the news concern you the most at the moment?

VOCABULARY Opinions and beliefs

1 **Look at photos A–D. What issue do you think each photo represents?**

86 **2** **Listen and match the conversations to photos A–D. What issue is being discussed in each conversation?**

3 **Match the sentence halves.**

EP
1 You have to bear in mind
2 I've never been
3 They could,
4 You should keep an open mind
5 I'm totally against students
6 I'd go along with

a convinced by that argument.
b about allowing mobile phones in schools.
c that their careers are short.
d using their phones at school.
e that view.
f to my mind, easily get another job after playing.

7 What are your views on
8 It's hard to deny that it
9 As far as I'm concerned,
10 I suspect this is true,
11 There's no doubt
12 I firmly believe in

g that you're more independent when you're older.
h enjoying yourself while you've got the chance.
i people just need to eat less meat.
j vegetarianism?
k must be better for you.
l to be honest.

86 **4** **Listen again and check.**

5 **Work in pairs. Look at photos A–D again. What is your opinion on these issues? Discuss your opinions. Use phrases from Exercise 3.**

READING

1 **Read the article about the teenage brain quickly, ignoring the gaps. According to the article, which statement is true?**

A Teenagers need to spend less time thinking about their emotions.
B Teenage brains have some advantages and disadvantages over adult brains.
C The differences between adult and teenage brains are now becoming understood by scientists.
D Adults need to make more of an effort to understand the way teenagers think.

PREPARE FOR THE EXAM

Reading and Use of English Part 6

2 **Six sentences have been removed from the article. Choose from the sentences A–G the one which fits each gap (1–6). There is one extra sentence which you do not need to use.**

A This is the area we use for thinking carefully about something in order to make a decision.
B Dramatic conclusions like this might have made good headlines at the time, but we now know that evidence for any truth in them is weak.
C If teenagers spend more time with adults, there is more opportunity for them to learn how to make thoughtful decisions.
D It is able to absorb huge amounts of information, and the opportunity is there to make the most of this by putting energy into learning, experimenting and seeking out new experiences.
E All participants were asked to identify the feelings their expressions represented.
F During the discussions, the young people reacted more emotionally than the adults, and researchers concluded that emotions develop faster than the parts of the brain that help people to manage them.
G However, a number of studies using brain scanning equipment have since led to an understanding that it is the teenage brain itself that is not the same as an adult one.

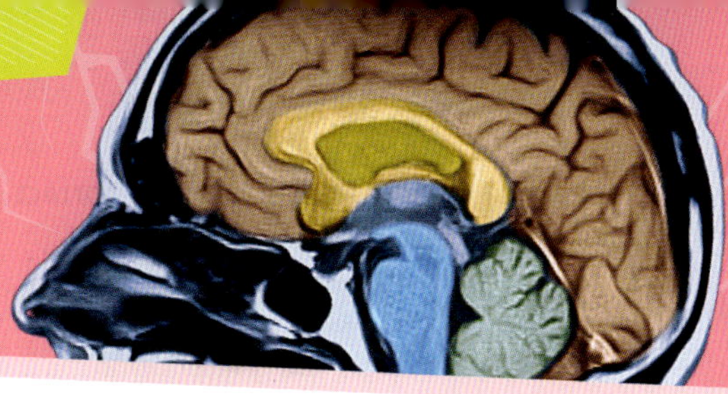

EXPLAINING YOUR BRAIN

Being a teenager is not unique to humans, although this stage in life lasts longer than the similar phase does for, say, primates or whales. But why do animals, and in particular humans, go through this stage? Scientists have offered different views on this: some believe long human lifespans have simply made room for this growth phase. Others think these years are needed to learn about the complex ways in which humans behave socially. The truth is that no one is even close to knowing about the brain, but scientists are getting nearer to understanding its complexities.

By the age of 12, the human brain is fully grown in size, and scientists once firmly believed that it was also fully developed. While they recognised that teenage behaviours and thoughts often differ from those of adults, including things like sleeping patterns and ideas about the world, scientists blamed these on hormones, the chemicals that control the way the human body grows and develops. [1] ________ In short, scientists now believe there is no doubt that teenagers' brains work quite differently to adults' brains.

In one study, teenagers and adults were shown photos of people's faces. [2] ________ The results surprised researchers. One of the pictures was of someone with an apparently obvious look of fear on their face. All the adults in the test were able to recognise this, but the teenagers believed the face was either surprised or angry. What accounted for this difference in interpretation?

Using scanning equipment, scientists observed which parts of the brain were active during the experiment. The adults used the part of their brain called the frontal cortex. [3] ________ In contrast, the teenagers' brain activity was in the amygdala, the region that handles instant reactions, which are often emotional. What's more, the older the teenagers in the group were, the more they used the frontal cortex for mental processing, just as adults do.

Another study asked groups of teenagers and their parents to talk about potentially controversial subjects, such as the amount of freedom teenagers should be given. The researchers found that young people with a larger amygdala are likely to have stronger opinions on such subjects than those who don't and, as a result, parents and teenagers are more likely to end up in conflict with each other. [4] ________ This explains why teenagers genuinely feel angry or upset by events that adults may think are insignificant.

Initially, some people used the research to support the argument that it could be biologically unhealthy for teenagers to play video games or watch a lot of TV. [5] ________ Fortunately, such ideas have since been abandoned. However, most scientists stress that while considerable progress has been made in our understanding of the teenage brain, our overall knowledge of the brain is still very limited. They encourage us to bear in mind that drawing too many conclusions from research is irresponsible.

As far as scientists are concerned, it is clear that the teenage stage is significant for the brain because of its flexibility. [6] ________ This may be by studying, by gaining new skills such as creating music or art, or by exploring the world. The important news is that the teenage years are a time of great change for the brain and a time when young people start to develop to their full potential as they move towards adulthood.

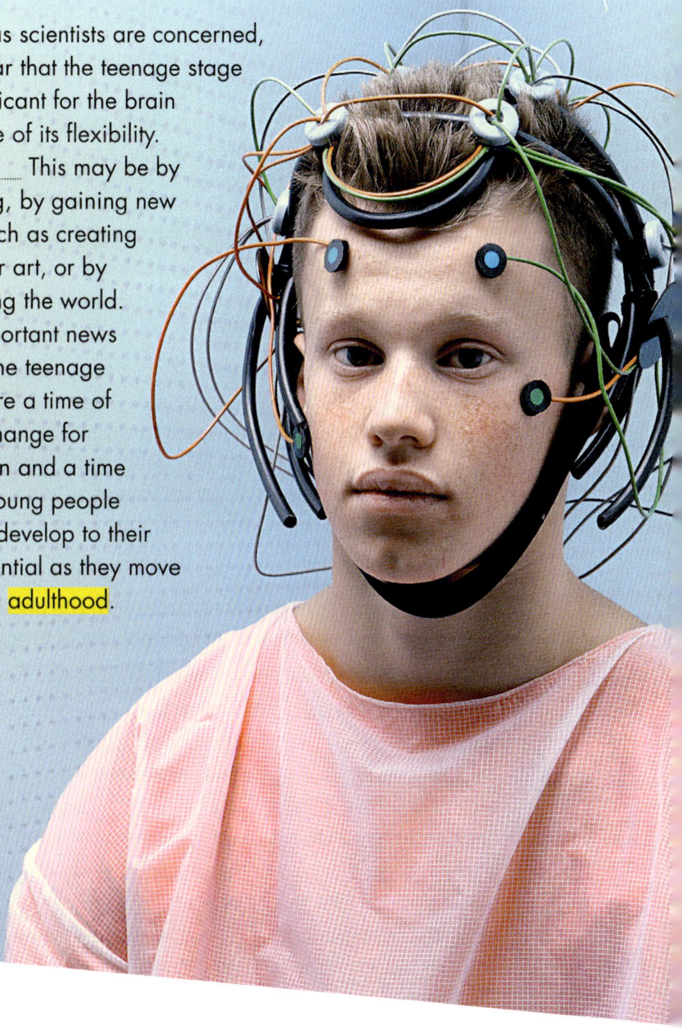

3 **Match the highlighted words and phrases in the article to the meanings.**

1. causing disagreement
2. the particular ways that something is often done
3. the time when someone is an adult
4. experience a difficult or unpleasant situation or event
5. emphasise something in order to show that it is important

TALKING POINTS

In what ways do teenagers and adults think differently?

What can scientists learn by studying people's brains?

GRAMMAR Subject–verb agreement

1 Read the examples and choose the correct options.

1 However, <u>a number of studies</u> ***has*** / ***have*** since led to an understanding that …
2 The truth is that <u>no one</u> ***is*** / ***are*** even close to knowing about the brain.
3 <u>One of the pictures</u> ***was*** / ***were*** of someone …
4 <u>Drawing too many conclusions</u> from research ***is*** / ***are*** irresponsible.
5 <u>The important news</u> ***is*** / ***are*** that the teenage years are a time of great change for the brain …

2 Match the examples in Exercise 1 to the rules.

We use a singular verb
a when the subject of the verb is an *-ing* form.
b with uncountable nouns, including those that end in *-s*, e.g. *physics*.
c after words such as *everyone*, *someone*, *anyone*, etc.
d after the expression *one of*.

We use a plural verb
e after the expressions *both of*, *a couple*, *a number of*.

With collective nouns, we can use a singular or plural verb, e.g. *My family live/lives in Spain.*
But the noun *police* always takes a plural noun, e.g. *The police are looking for two men.*

» GRAMMAR REFERENCE AND PRACTICE PAGE 166

3 Choose the correct verb form.

1 One of my friends always *go* / *goes* to school by car.
2 The information you gave me *was* / *were* useful.
3 If anyone *have* / *has* any questions, ask them now.
4 Living abroad for the last few years *has* / *have* made it impossible to keep up with everyone.
5 I've tried to keep an open mind, but I can't help thinking that maths *is* / *are* just pointless!

4 Complete the first part of the article with the present simple singular or plural form of the verbs in brackets.

You've changed my mind!

You've just been to the cinema and all of your friends [1] ________ (agree) that the film was brilliant. But one of you [2] ________ (feel) differently: you! Do you express your real views, or do you go along with the crowd? Plenty of us [3] ________ (do) the latter and it's hard to deny that everyone [4] ________ (tell) a little white lie from time to time to fit in. However, news [5] ________ (come) from an experiment in the United States that agreeing with people like this actually [6] ________ (have) a strong effect on your mind and can even change it permanently!

5 Read the second part of the article and correct six mistakes with subject–verb agreement.

If, to our mind, someone are attractive, a region of our brain called the orbitofrontal cortex becomes active. In an experiment, a number of people was shown photos of faces and gave scores based on how attractive they thought the faces were. Next, everyone were told they had given much lower scores than a nationwide survey of the same faces. The process of scoring the faces were repeated, and the scientists observed the activity in the orbitofrontal cortex. The scores on this occasion were higher than the first time and the activity in the orbitofrontal cortex was also higher. Therefore, one of the researchers' conclusions were that following the opinion of a larger group lead to people changing their own opinion.

6 Work in groups. Find something that …

1 all of you are convinced by.
2 a number of you firmly believe in.
3 one of you is totally against.
4 no one believes in.
5 some of you suspect is true.

VOCABULARY Plural nouns

1 The nouns in the example are always plural. Can you think of any other nouns that are always plural?

He spent his **savings** on lots of new **clothes**.

2 Read the sentences. Which nouns should be plural? Change the nouns, then match them to the meanings.

0 Please help yourselves to ~~refreshment~~, everyone. *refreshments*
1 This term in English, we've been looking at the lyric of some famous songs.
2 Look in the content at the beginning and find the unit about money.
3 Leaving my belonging all over the house is guaranteed to drive my parents mad.
4 We live on the outskirt of London, near the river.
5 I'd love to study in such beautiful surrounding.

a a list in a book that tells you what the book contains
b the place where someone or something is and the things that are in it
c the areas of a town or city furthest away from the centre
d food and drinks available at an event, meeting, etc.
e the words of a song
f the things that someone owns

3 **» Work in pairs. Student A, turn to page 139. Student B, turn to page 141.**

WRITING An essay (4)

1 **What time does your school start and finish each day? Should it start or finish earlier or later?**

2 **Read the task and answer the questions.**

> **'Students who are 15 and older should start and finish school an hour later.'**
> **Do you agree?**
>
> **Notes**
> Write about:
> 1 health
> 2 learning
> 3 *transport* (your own idea)

1 The student has added their own idea. What other ideas could you add?
2 What advantages and disadvantages can you think of to do with health, learning and transport?

3 **Read the essay. Which of your ideas are mentioned? What other ideas are mentioned?**

Changing the timing of the school day is a complex issue. However, such a policy might benefit teenagers, who are often so busy with after-school activities and homework that they are rarely in bed before 11 pm.

In my country, students need to get up by 7 am in order to arrive at school for 8 am. As a result, teenagers get fewer than eight hours' sleep, whereas the recommended minimum is 9.5 hours per night. This may well start to affect their health. In addition, while some young people manage to eat breakfast before they leave home, others arrive at school hungry and, consequently, do not always pay full attention in lessons. Some even pretend to be ill to gain more time in bed, therefore missing important work in class. Starting later would help in this respect.

On the other hand, other problems might occur. Teenagers who rely on their parents for transport could experience difficulties, as the parents might have already left for work. Furthermore, even though teachers might support the change, their working hours would be longer.

On balance, despite the drawbacks, it seems worth experimenting in selected schools. A decision could then be made based on the results.

4 **Read the *Prepare to write* box and find examples of the different kinds of linking words in the essay. Then choose the correct options below.**

PREPARE TO WRITE Organising essays

We use linking words to link clauses and make sentences longer. Linking words can express

- contrast: *although, even though, whereas, despite*
- purpose: *so, so that, in order that*
- reason: *because, as, since, for this reason*
- result: *consequently, therefore*

1 He left early *so / despite* he could catch the last bus.
2 *So that / Even though* she left early, she missed the bus.
3 I got home very late and *because / consequently* I felt exhausted the next day.
4 I was late for school, *as / although* I overslept.
5 I got a bad mark in the exam, *despite / since* all the work I did.
6 Some people work well in the mornings, *therefore / whereas* others work better later in the day.
7 I couldn't get a lift to school, *as / in order that* my parents had already left for work.
8 *In order to / Since* the exam has to be fair, everyone must do it at exactly the same time.

PREPARE FOR THE EXAM

Writing Part 1

5 **Read the task. Add more information and your own idea to the notes.**

> **'Having a lot of homework discourages students from wanting to learn.'**
> **Do you agree?**
>
> **Notes**
> Write about:
> 1 the time spent on doing homework
> 2 how useful homework is
> 3 .... (your own idea)

6 **Write your essay. Use all the notes and give reasons for your point of view.**

- Organise your essay into paragraphs (see page 13).
- Use language to compare and contrast (see page 57).
- Use linking words to link clauses and make your sentences longer (see page 89).
- Check your grammar and spelling.
- Write 140–190 words.

20 SPEAK UP

ABOUT YOU

What idioms do you know in your own language?

What idioms do you know in English?

VOCABULARY Idioms

1 **Look at the list of idioms. Which meanings do you think are the most likely? Why?**

EP

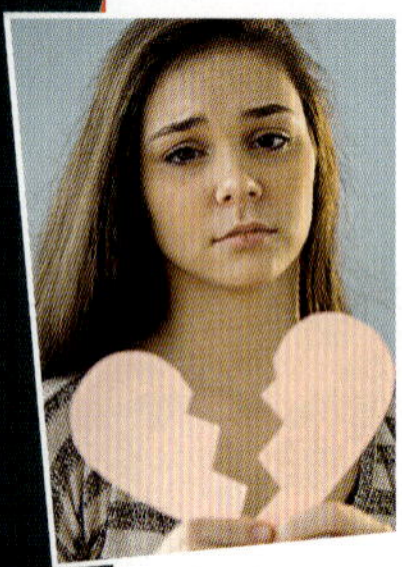

1 break the ice
- a make people feel more relaxed in a social situation
- b explain why people feel a certain way

2 break someone's heart
- a make someone feel nervous
- b make someone feel extremely sad

3 take your breath away
- a make you feel anxious and impatient
- b make you feel surprise and admiration

4 be a piece of cake
- a be sweet and tasty
- b be very easy

5 cross your mind
- a come into your thoughts for a short time
- b make you change your mind

6 have an eye for something
- a want something very much
- b be good at noticing certain things

7 be a pain
- a be very sore
- b be annoying

8 lose track of time
- a not be aware of what time it is
- b not be able to find time for something

88 **2** **Listen and choose the correct meanings in Exercise 1.**

3 **Discuss the questions.**

1 What is the best way to break the ice when you meet new people?
2 Have you ever seen something that took your breath away? What?
3 Is there anything that your friends find difficult that you think is a piece of cake?
4 When was the last time you were late because you'd lost track of time?

READING

1 **Read the title of the article on page 113. What might the article be about? Then read the article quickly and check your ideas.**

PREPARE FOR THE EXAM

Reading and Use of English Part 3

2 **For questions 1–8, read the first three paragraphs of the article. Use the word given in capitals to form a word that fits in the gap.**

3 **Read the article again and answer the questions.**

1 Why do teenagers have an influence on language change?
2 What examples does the text give of how English has changed lately?
3 What are the standard question tags for these questions? What question tag do some young people use instead?
   - a *You texted me,* .... ?
   - b *You like this game,* .... ?
4 How does the language of texting differ from standard English?
5 How does texting affect texters?
6 How does the saying, 'Everything rolls on, nothing stays still' relate to languages?

4 **Match the highlighted words in the article to the meanings.**

1 planned or controlled by a particular person or thing
2 the ability to read and write
3 hurting or damaging
4 informal language that is only used by people who belong to a particular group
5 although

5 **Discuss the questions.**

1 Do you use slang when you are speaking to your friends? Give some examples.
2 Are you sometimes criticised for using the 'wrong' language? In what situations?
3 Think of examples of words in English and in your own language that
   - a are borrowed from other languages.
   - b are often shortened.
   - c come from technological developments.

'TEEN SPEAK' We love it!

Do you use some words or **(0)** *expressions* (**EXPRESS**) with your friends and other ones with your family? Maybe you use very different language in **(1)** ________ (**COMPARE**) with older generations, or perhaps you receive **(2)** ________ (**CRITICISE**) from teachers for using the 'wrong' language at school.

Slang that is **(3)** ________ (**SPECIFY**) to teenagers is common in most languages, as are complaints about it from older people. However, in spite of the claims made by some adults that teenagers are 'ruining' their language, in fact changes to standard grammar and vocabulary are nothing new, and aren't, therefore, particularly **(4)** ________ (**REMARK**). Since the time of the Ancient Greeks, there have always been plenty of **(5)** ________ (**OBJECT**) to young people's language use.

Groups with similar interests adapt language to suit their purposes: think of the **(6)** ________ (**SPECIALISE**) language used in the legal and **(7)** ________ (**MEDICINE**) worlds. Known as 'jargon', these words mark out those who use them as belonging to a specific group. **(8)** ________ (**NATURE**), teenagers also want to make it clear which social group they belong to, and changing the language you use is a great way to do this.

One way in which teenagers change their language is to introduce new vocabulary or change the meaning of existing words. Some recent examples of 'teen speak' show how big these changes in meaning can be. For young people, *wicked* doesn't mean *very bad* as it does for older generations, but *wonderful; bad* can mean *good*, and *sick* has taken on the meaning of *very cool.* These uses don't always last for long. Indeed, words come in and out of use very quickly, and it can be hard to keep up.

Young people also make changes to grammar. One example of a teen-led change to English grammar is the use among some young people of *innit* (a shortened form of *isn't it*) as a substitute for all question tags, e.g. *You texted me, innit?* or *You like this game, innit?* It has been suggested that this 'simplification' is a by-product of texting and instant messaging. Although some people are concerned that this trend towards 'text speak' is harming the language, well-known linguist Professor David Crystal doesn't agree. According to Crystal and many other linguists, the fact that teenagers use text speak, acronyms (LOL) and emojis 🙂 doesn't mean the end of the language. Says Crystal, 'Texting is just a new type of English that has evolved as a result of internet technology. It hasn't had any impact on the rest of the language. The big myth is that texting is somehow harming the language. There is no evidence of that. All the recent research shows the best texters are actually the best spellers. The more they text, the better their literacy is, as it gives them the practice in reading and writing they wouldn't otherwise have.'

Although teenagers are often criticised for ignoring linguistic rules and destroying the language by those keen on imposing standard grammar rules, we should bear in mind that languages aren't fixed. All languages change over time, albeit at different rates and for a lot of different reasons. Vocabulary evolves as speakers need new words to describe new concepts or consumer goods, for example. Where would we be without all those new words such as *app* and *e-reader* that have come into the language as a result of modern technologies? Grammar also changes over time, which explains why many present-day native English-speakers find Shakespeare's 16th-century plays difficult to read. Our use of language changes naturally as we go through life, too; we continually pick up new words and phrases and integrate them into our speech.

Some adults may not always like the way teenagers speak to each other, but realising that language change is inevitable and that teenagers are integral to this process might help older generations feel better about it. People have always complained that standards are declining among the younger generation, but as the Greek philosopher Heraclitus observed more than 2,500 years ago, 'Everything rolls on, nothing stays still.'

TALKING POINTS

How have modern ways of communicating changed the way we use language?

GRAMMAR Determiners

1 Read the examples and choose the correct options. Check your answers in the rules.

1 Perhaps you receive ***the*** / ***–*** criticism from teachers for using ***the*** / ***a*** 'wrong' language at ***–*** / ***the*** school.
2 There have always been ***much*** / ***plenty of*** objections to young people's language use.
3 All languages change over time … for ***a bit of*** / ***a lot of*** different reasons.
4 This explains why ***much*** / ***many*** present-day speakers find Shakespeare's 16th-century plays difficult to read.
5 Changing the language you use is ***–*** / ***a*** great way to do this.

We use
a *a* or *an* before a singular countable noun, for referring to one of many things, or one that is not specific.
b *the* before any noun, for referring to something in particular or something already mentioned.
c – before any noun, for referring to things generally.
d *some*, *any*, *plenty of*, *a lot of*, *lots of* before uncountable and plural countable nouns.
e *much*, *(a) little*, *a bit of*, *a small/large amount of* before uncountable nouns.
f *many*, *(a) few*, *several*, *a small/large number of* before plural countable nouns.

» GRAMMAR REFERENCE AND PRACTICE PAGE 167

2 Read the sentences and explain the difference in meaning between them.

0 **a** She has **a little** money to spend.
b She has **little** money to spend.
a She has some money to spend. ('A little' means a small amount but it is enough.)
b She doesn't have very much to spend. ('Little' means a very small amount and it is not enough.)

1 **a** They gave me **little** help.
b They gave me **a little** help.

2 **a** **Few** people here can speak Chinese.
b **A few** people here can speak Chinese.

3 **a** We get **a little** rain in summer.
b We get **little** rain in summer.

4 **a** Latin is offered by **few** schools these days.
b Latin is offered by **a few** schools these days.

5 **a** I speak **little** French.
b I speak **a little** French.

3 Correct the mistake in each sentence.

1 We apologise for sending a wrong phone to you.
2 Hi, Ciaran! I have a good news for you!
3 Yesterday I went to shops and bought some new clothes.
4 There are few biscuits left if you'd like some with your coffee?
5 I don't think you'll have many fun on the language-exchange programme.

4 Complete the text with the correct determiners. There may be more than one correct answer.

FOREIGN-ACCENT SYNDROME

Olga Grigorieva, a Russian schoolgirl from Novgorod, passed out one day while she was in [1] ________ art class. When she came round, a nurse told her to drink [2] ________ of water and to get [3] ________ rest. When Olga thanked [4] ________ nurse and stood up, she noticed that [5] ________ of her classmates were giggling. Olga asked them what was wrong and then she noticed her own voice. She was speaking Russian with [6] ________ English accent!

Olga was suffering from 'foreign-accent syndrome', where people suddenly, sometimes after an operation or accident, start speaking with [7] ________ foreign accent. Like a large [8] ________ of other people with the syndrome, Olga was, naturally, upset. A person's speech forms part of their personality, after all.

Olga's case was even more unusual because she didn't speak [9] ________ English at all before her fall. It was her accent, not the language, that was different. Slowly her old Russian accent returned, but she has learned to say a [10] ________ things in English as well.

VOCABULARY Commonly confused words

1 Choose the correct options.

EP
1 Which is your favourite *way* / *means* of transport?
2 What is the best *means* / *way* to practise English?
3 I'll visit you if the *journey* / *way* isn't too long.
4 What is the best *way* / *journey* to the beach?
5 You'll have plenty of *possibilities* / *opportunities* to meet people at university.
6 There's *a possibility* / *an opportunity* my sister will be at the party.
7 Why won't you let me play my music? I'm only trying to have *funny* / *fun*.
8 I've never thought Logan was very *fun* / *funny*, but everyone else laughs at his jokes.

2 Complete the sentences with words from Exercise 1.

1 Did you have a good ________ or was the traffic bad?
2 I haven't had the ________ to read your blog yet.
3 He told us a very ________ joke!
4 I know the ________ to school from here.
5 There's a ________ I'll be late, I'm not sure yet.
6 I really enjoyed my holiday. It was great ________.

3 Complete the sentences with the verbs in the box.

damage	guess	harm	injure
know	observe		

1 How did you ________ your leg?
2 The rain won't ________ you or your equipment.
3 Please don't ________ the furniture.
4 Can you ________ how old I am?
5 The headteacher is going to ________ this class.
6 I have read the essay title, but I don't ________ what it means.

LISTENING

PREPARE FOR THE EXAM

Listening Part 1

1 90 **You will hear people talking in eight different situations. For questions 1–8, choose the best answer (A, B or C).**

1 You hear two friends talking about their college library. What does the boy think of it?
A Some sections don't have a variety of books.
B You should be able to borrow books for longer periods.
C Staff can be unhelpful in locating books.

2 You hear a linguist talking about endangered languages. What does she say about languages?
A Languages represent one of man's most important skills.
B Language loss could result in loss of historical knowledge.
C There will be fewer regional cultures if languages die out.

3 You hear two friends talking about a novel they have read. They agree that
A it was well-written.
B the writing was very descriptive.
C its main character was realistic.

4 You hear a teacher talking to her students about the school holidays. During the holidays, she wants them to
A make an effort to keep in touch with one another.
B catch up on any schoolwork they have missed.
C keep a brief record of experiences they have.

5 You hear two friends talking about speaking two languages. The boy says that people who speak two or more languages
A can interact better with people in other cultures.
B are able to do certain things better than other people.
C should be able to learn further languages without difficulty.

6 You hear a student adviser talking about young people starting university. The man advises new students to
A prepare themselves for a different approach to studying.
B find out as much as possible about the town or city they are going to.
C meet as many people as possible.

7 You hear two friends talking about a long-distance running race. What is the girl worried about?
A whether she will finish the race or not
B how big a problem her clothing will be
C who will see her take part in the race

8 You hear a boy telling a friend about a blog he writes. What does he regard as a priority?
A controlling the length of what he produces online
B increasing the number of followers that he has
C finding new topics to interest his readers

SPEAKING Comparing photographs (2)

1 **You are going to compare two photographs. Look at the photographs. What is the connection between them?**

1 Social conversation
2 Learning a foreign language
3 Communicating with others

A

B

91 **2** **Listen to Andrea talking about one of the photos. Which photo is he talking about?**

92 **3** **Read the *Prepare to speak* box and listen to Andrea talking about the other photo. Which phrases does he use?**

PREPARE TO SPEAK | **Speculating**

It looks as if/though they're … / It looks like …
He/She/They might/could be (learning …)
I think they're about to …
Perhaps/Maybe it's …
I get the impression that …
They seem/look …
They/It must be …
Clearly they're …

4 **Work in pairs. Speculate about the two photos. Use phrases from the *Prepare to speak* box.**

PREPARE FOR THE EXAM

Speaking Part 2

5 » **Turn to page 141 and complete the task.**

LIFE SKILLS STUDY SKILLS

PREPARING FOR EXAMS

1 **Ask and answer the questions with a partner.**

1 How do you feel when you have to take exams?
2 What routines or techniques do you use to prepare for exams?
3 How do you cope with exam-related stress?

2 **Read the article on the opposite page. Match the headings (A–E) to paragraphs 1, 2, 5, 8 and 9.**

A Get up and do something!
B Create a revision timetable
C Study when you're wide awake!
D Make flash cards
E Get some Zzzzzs

3 **What is the difference between an *early bird* and a *night owl*? Which one are you? Can you give some examples to explain why?**

4 **Read the article again and complete the sentences with two or three words in each gap.**

1 When you've calculated how long to spend on each subject, begin your revision as ______.
2 The recommended rest time for each 60 minutes you spend revising is ______.
3 If you study while listening to music, remember that ______ can make it difficult to concentrate.
4 You should try to eat a lot of ______ and snack regularly around exam time.
5 If you don't ______, you might forget what you studied the day before!

5 **Match the highlighted words and phrases in the article to the meanings.**

1 improvement or increase
2 try to learn a lot very quickly before an exam
3 short sleep, especially during the day
4 a plan that gives events or activities and the times that they will happen or be done
5 a combination of the correct types and amounts of food

LIFE SKILLS

Preparing for exams

Preparing for and taking exams can be both scary and stressful. Exams form a big part of university life too, and they are also a reality for many different professions. Learning how to prepare for them effectively is key to your future in many ways.

93 **6** **Listen to a study-skills tutor having a conversation with two students. Put the topics mentioned in the correct order.**

A Moving and stretching ___
B Focusing on progress ___
C Not panicking, planning instead ___
D Making a note of your worries before going into an exam ___
E Thinking positively ___

93 **7** **Listen again and complete the sentences with between two and six words.**

1 When she plans her revision schedule, Lucia feels …
2 If you're worried before an exam, the tutor suggests …
3 When you have exams, it's important to believe in yourself so that you don't focus …
4 Thinking about a memory that makes you happy will motivate you to …
5 Try not to be hard on yourself and celebrate …
6 Stretching and moving around will help you …

8 **Complete the sentences with the words in the box.**

achieving	cope	mindset
plan	well-being	

USEFUL LANGUAGE

Coping with exam stress

1 I want to find ways to help me ______ with exam stress.
2 Writing a study ______ will save time in the long run.
3 I'm trying to keep a positive ______ before my exams.
4 Thinking about a happy memory can give us a sense of ______.
5 Focus on making progress and not on ______ perfection.

TOP TIPS FOR EXAM SUCCESS!

There are lots of things you can do to prepare for exams. Try out these great tips and you'll see the difference when it comes to results time!

1 ______________________

Exams are often close together, so you'll probably be revising for various subjects at the same time. Work out how much time you can dedicate to each subject and make a chart of what you need to do when. Then start revising as early as possible, especially if you tend to cram at the last minute!

2 ______________________

Are you an early bird? Or perhaps you're a night owl? Planning your revision timetable around when your mind is most alert will make revising much easier! But no matter what time of day you study best, you ought to take a 15-minute break for every hour of study in order to give your brain some much needed rest.

3 STUDY TECHNIQUES MATTER

Some people use model exam answers to review what they've studied. You might find that studying with music really helps you concentrate, although be careful, because the lyrics can also be a big distraction! Get together with friends from class to talk through what you've learned and explain difficult things to each other. But if it quickly turns into social chat, group study might not be for you.

4 KEEP YOUR NOTES TIDY

Organising your notes into different sections will make your life a lot easier. Make sure that you ask a classmate or teacher for notes on any classes that you've missed. Good notes should include plenty of visuals like mind maps. And always use different coloured pens to highlight important points.

5 ______________________

Reduce your notes to summaries, and then write the most important facts from the summaries. Some students like to use a Q&A format, with a question on one side and an answer on the other. Take these everywhere you go – you never know when you'll get a few minutes to test yourself. Use them regularly and you'll be amazed how much you remember!

6 DRINK PLENTY OF WATER

Your brain needs to stay hydrated to work well. It's easy to forget to drink when you're studying a lot, and you can get headaches and feel tired as a result. Avoid drinks with caffeine or excessive amounts of sugar, and drink lots of water or herbal teas instead.

7 EAT PROPERLY AND SNACK HEALTHILY!

Just like sugary drinks, sweets and chocolate give you a quick energy boost. However, at exam time, it's preferable to eat foods which give you a slow release of energy. Make sure you have a balanced diet which includes plenty of 'brain foods' like cereals, pasta, oily fish, chicken, vegetables and salads. And snack regularly on things like nuts or fruit.

8 ______________________

Your brain needs lots of oxygen to work well, and exercise moves oxygen around your body. Going for a walk, a swim or playing a team sport should form a part of your daily schedule. And don't forget to exercise your eyes by blinking and looking away from your books or screen regularly. Tired eyes aren't good for reading!

9 ______________________

As well as hydration, good food and oxygen, your brain needs plenty of rest. Sleep is key, especially the night before an exam, and without it, it's easy to forget what you've studied! You should aim for a good eight hours of quality sleep. A power nap of 15–30 minutes can also give you some energy before you start a revision session.

10 AVOID STRESS

Do your best to avoid any situations that you know you find stressful. And remember that the day before an exam, you're not studying to learn new things, but to review what you've already studied.

PROJECT

A campaign about exam preparation

Work in groups of three or four to prepare a campaign to improve exam preparation. Use these steps to help you.

1 Brainstorm advice and techniques for preparing for exams and coping with exam-related stress.
2 Decide together on the three best ideas to include in your campaign.
3 Come up with a main message and slogan for your campaign.
4 Decide how you will promote the campaign to students in your school. Choose from different media such as posters, a web page, presentations, etc.
5 Include some personal stories about your own exam preparation experiences.

Present your work to the class.

REVIEW 5 UNITS 17–20

VOCABULARY

1 Complete the sentences with the words in the box.

comment	injured	keep
keeping	mind	suspect

1 How do you ________ up to date with what's happening in the world?
2 To my ________, it's important to be aware of news so you can ________ on current events intelligently.
3 I ________ you may have ________ your ankle when you jumped off that wall. Let's take a look at it and find out.
4 I like chilling out with a good book. A great adventure series is ________ me amused at the moment!

2 Complete the sentences with the jumbled verbs in the box.

ahctc	evela	igrnb	kbac	teg

1 I hate to ________ this up, but you owe me £10.
2 My holiday gave me time to ________ up on sleep.
3 Please help me make a list for the party. I might ________ out something important.
4 I tried to ________ my point across at the meeting, but I'm not convinced people understood.
5 When I tell Mum about the stain, will you ________ me up that it wasn't my fault?

3 Match the two parts of the phrases.

1	make	**a**	deadlines
2	meet	**b**	shifts
3	be	**c**	a living
4	take lots	**d**	something rewarding
5	work	**e**	of time off
6	do	**f**	well paid

4 Complete the sentences with the idioms. Make changes to the idioms as necessary.

be a pain   be a piece of cake   break my heart
lose track of time   take my breath away

1 I finished the test 15 minutes early. It ________.
2 Is it two o'clock yet? I've ________.
3 My phone's battery rarely lasts the whole day. Having to recharge it during the day ________.
4 It ________ when the last series of that programme ended. I used to love it so much.
5 The view from our hotel room ________. We could see right across the whole city.

GRAMMAR

1 Complete the mixed conditionals with the correct form of the verbs in brackets.

1 I wouldn't be here now if Abby ________ (not mention) the game.
2 If we had sorted out the problems earlier, we ________ (not be) in this mess today.
3 I ________ (take) the summer job if it were a bit better paid. But I had to turn it down.
4 Tom could apply for medicine if he ________ (study) biology, but he did maths, physics and chemistry.
5 If my brother ________ (not be) such a pain, I might have invited him to the festival. He's too young.

2 Complete the sentences with the correct form of the verbs in brackets. Use the *-ing* form, the infinitive with *to*, or the infinitive without *to*.

1 I hate ________ told what ________. (be, do)
2 ________ in mind how long it will take ________ there, I think we should leave now. (bear, get)
3 Despite Ollie ________ the best cook, we took turns ________ the meals on holiday. (be, make)
4 He denies ________ Joe, but admits he's been ________ about it. (tell, think)
5 ________ in a shop made me ________ how much I would hate that kind of job. (work, realise)

3 Choose the correct verb forms.

1 I like most of my classmates, but a couple *is* / *are* a pain.
2 The news about his accident *has* / *have* really upset me.
3 I think starting your own business *sound* / *sounds* like hard work.
4 One of my friends *work* / *works* in that café.
5 *Is* / *Are* anything in those film reviews positive?

4 Choose the correct options. Sometimes there is more than one possible answer.

I've got [1] *a* / *the* / *some* summer work in a local pizza restaurant. [2] *A* / *The* / – job itself is OK, and at least I'm earning [3] *some* / *a bit* / *a few* money. I spend [4] *a lot of* / *several* / *much* time taking orders over the phone, but I also make [5] *much* / *a large number* / *a bit* of pizzas, too. There are always [6] *a few* / *a bit of* / *a little* pizzas left at the end of [7] *an* / *the* / – evening, but I've gone off them now!

5 Correct the mistake in each sentence.

1 I would have been happier right now if you had done your homework.
2 I don't enjoy to shop all the time.
3 I really want to spend time to go sightseeing.
4 Life nowadays is so full of things to be done, that people forget that their health are important.
5 Whilst spending a few time in Barcelona, I have been looking for different kinds of activities which you could do in a single week.

PREPARE FOR THE EXAM

Reading and Use of English Part 1

1 For questions 1–8, read the text below and decide which answer (**A**, **B**, **C** or **D**) best fits each gap.

The world's best summer job?

When an international holiday company **(0)** *advertised* a job for someone to test their water slides, they didn't expect so many people to apply. Incredibly, over 2,000 people did, but lucky Seb Smith, a British student, **(1)** ________ from them all.

Potential candidates needed to be 'mad about water parks', '**(2)** ________ to travel' and 'happy to get wet at work.' Seb **(3)** ________ his application with a funny video of himself testing a slide in his local park.

He will now spend three months travelling the world and judging new water slides which have been **(4)** ________ at the company's 20 water parks. **(5)** ________ in mind that all Seb's accommodation and travel expenses are free, it's hard to **(6)** ________ that the job is pretty well paid, too: Seb will earn an amazing £20,000!

'I'm absolutely over the **(7)** ________,' said Seb, 'and I can't wait to get started.' A spokesman for the company said Seb's enthusiasm made him the ideal person for the **(8)** ________ of water-slide tester.

	A	B	C	D
0	**A** composed	**B** published	**(C)** advertised	**D** broadcast
1	**A** put out	**B** came out	**C** brought out	**D** stood out
2	**A** agreeing	**B** obliging	**C** willing	**D** encouraging
3	**A** backed up	**B** cleared up	**C** faced up	**D** picked up
4	**A** begun	**B** launched	**C** served	**D** started
5	**A** Taking	**B** Crossing	**C** Bearing	**D** Thinking
6	**A** deny	**B** refuse	**C** decline	**D** reject
7	**A** sun	**B** moon	**C** Earth	**D** world
8	**A** part	**B** function	**C** purpose	**D** role

Reading and Use of English Part 3

2 For questions 1–8, read the text below. Use the word given in capitals to form a word that fits in the gap.

WHAT'S THE POINT OF LEARNING A LANGUAGE?

Many native English speakers are of the firm **(0)** *belief* **(BELIEVE)** that they needn't bother learning another language. As far as they are **(1)** ________ **(CONCERN)**, the people they come into contact with through business or travel already speak English. It isn't that they are **(2)** ________ **(TOTAL)** against the idea of learning languages, but simply that they don't see the point. They often get **(3)** ________ **(PATIENCE)**, too, when it's suggested that they should make more of an effort.

What they're missing out on is a **(4)** ________ **(MEAN)** of understanding other cultures, and a whole range of skills which would almost certainly benefit them. Language learners not only gain a sense of **(5)** ________ **(ACHIEVE)** from being able to communicate with others across the globe, but also have **(6)** ________ **(IMPROVE)** memory, enhanced listening skills and better job opportunities.

Learning another language can be highly **(7)** ________ **(REWARD)**, and it isn't necessary to reach fluency, either. Managing a conversation in another language, however basic, often leads to a great deal of **(8)** ________ **(SATISFY)** and pride.

Reading and Use of English Part 4

3 For questions 1–6, complete the second sentence so that it has a similar meaning to the first sentence, using the word given. **Do not change the word given.** You must use between **two** and **five** words, including the word given.

0 You keep talking and that's why I still have homework to do. **WOULD**
If it wasn't for you talking, I *would have done* my homework by now.

1 The media raised the issue of fake news, otherwise no one would know about it. **BROUGHT**
You wouldn't know about fake news if the media ________ the issue.

2 Jake takes ages getting ready to go out! **LOT**
Jake spends ________ getting ready to go out!

3 Several families have lived in this house over the years. **NUMBER**
Over the years, ________ families have lived in this house.

4 We're both going to go to the event at the town hall tomorrow night. **WILL**
Both ________ going to the event at the town hall tomorrow night.

5 The family doesn't have much money to spend on holidays. **ONLY**
The family has ________ money to spend on holidays.

6 Eventually, you will have to make a decision about what job you'd like to do. **ARE**
Sooner ________ going to have to make a decision about what job you'd like to do.

PREPARE FOR THE EXAM
B2 FIRST FOR SCHOOLS

READING AND USE OF ENGLISH

Reading and Use of English Part 1 Multiple-choice cloze (Unit 2, Unit 6, Unit 15, Review 1, Review 2, Review 4, Review 5)

EXAM INFORMATION

Reading and Use of English Part 1

- You will read a short text with eight gaps, each representing a missing word or phrase.
- There are eight four-option multiple-choice items, one for each gap.
- You should choose the correct answer to fill each gap.
- There is one example, to show you what to do.

1 Read the article quickly for general meaning. What alternative title could you give the article?

2 Look at the example (0). All four options are verbs. Why is A the correct answer?

3 Now read the exam instructions and complete the task.

For questions **1–8**, read the text opposite and decide which answer (**A, B, C** or **D**) best fits each gap. There is an example at the beginning (**0**).

EXAM TIPS

Look at the words around the gap to see if the missing word is part of a phrase or collocation. When you have finished, read the text again and check your answers.

	A	B	C	D
0	**(A)** rise	**B** widen	**C** move	**D** progress
1	**A** aim	**B** hunt	**C** search	**D** track
2	**A** occupied	**B** urban	**C** engaged	**D** crowded
3	**A** inhabitants	**B** populations	**C** members	**D** public
4	**A** well-paid	**B** affordable	**C** modest	**D** low-priced
5	**A** take	**B** get	**C** make	**D** keep
6	**A** occasions	**B** chances	**C** capabilities	**D** opportunities
7	**A** diverse	**B** separate	**C** assorted	**D** variable
8	**A** profit	**B** gain	**C** promote	**D** benefit

CITY LIVING

Today, over half of the world's population live in cities, and this percentage is likely to **(0)** *rise* significantly in the future. More and more people are moving to cities in **(1)** ________ of employment and a better life. Their lives are becoming more **(2)** ________ and less rural, with 'mega cities', which have over 10 million **(3)** ________, emerging around the globe.

Some cities are more **(4)** ________ to live in than others, but residents with earning power can **(5)** ________ the most of city living, as cities provide many attractions, such as excellent shopping **(6)** ________, trendy restaurants and numerous other leisure facilities. What's more, anyone who lives in a city can take advantage of how culturally **(7)** ________ it is, how convenient it is, and how many interesting people there are to meet. There are certainly negative aspects of living in a city, such as overcrowding and pollution, but the general picture is that cities greatly **(8)** ________ those who live there.

Reading and Use of English Part 2 Open cloze
(Unit 5, Unit 11, Unit 16, Review 1, Review 2, Review 3, Review 4)

EXAM INFORMATION

Reading and Use of English Part 2

- You will read a short text with eight gaps.
- You should decide which word fits in each gap.
- You should write only one word for each gap.
- There is one example, to show you what to do.

1 **Read the text quickly for general meaning. Then look at the example. What kind of word is it (noun, preposition, determiner, article, etc.)?**

2 **Now look at the gaps in the text. Which gap (or gaps) require …**

- a conjunction
- a verb form
- part of a comparative structure
- part of a phrase
- a determiner
- part of an infinitive
- a preposition

3 **Now read the exam instructions and complete the task.**

For questions 1–8, read the text below and think of the word which best fits each gap. Use only one word in each gap. There is an example at the beginning (0).

EXAM TIPS

Check your spelling before writing your answers. The words must be spelled correctly. When you have finished, read the whole text again and make sure the word you've chosen makes sense.

CROCODILES

Not **(0)** *all* crocodiles in Australia are threatening to humans. Freshwater crocodiles, known **(1)** ________ 'freshies', do not attack people, and being shy by nature, they prefer **(2)** ________ stay away from them altogether. Their habitat includes rivers and natural pools in northern regions of the country, and fish are therefore the creatures' main source **(3)** ________ food. Freshies do, however, consume a variety of small animals and insects as well.

Saltwater crocodiles (or 'salties'), on the **(4)** ________ hand, are dangerous creatures. They are also **(5)** ________ of the largest living creatures on our planet. Unlike freshwater crocodiles, which usually grow to around two metres in length, male adult salties **(6)** ________ been known to reach an incredible seven metres, **(7)** ________ this is rare. Like freshies, salties also eat fish and birds, but they are more **(8)** ________ happy to hunt larger animals, too, including horses and cattle. The 'saltwater' name is actually misleading, because these giant reptiles are just as content living in rivers and swamps inland.

PREPARE FOR THE EXAM
B2 FIRST FOR SCHOOLS

Reading and Use of English Part 3 Word formation
(Unit 9, Unit 17, Unit 20, Review 2, Review 3, Review 5)

EXAM INFORMATION

Reading and Use of English Part 3

- You will read a short text with eight gaps.
- There are eight words which you should change to fit the gap.
- You should only use the word which is on the same line as the gap.
- You must use all the words.
- There is one example, to show you what to do.

1 **Look at the example and gaps 1–4 in the text and read the explanations below. Notice that the answers require a suffix, a prefix or both.**

Example: The gap is followed by a noun, which suggests that the missing word is an adjective.
Question 1: The plural verb and *their* shows that the answer must be people (*psychologists*).
Question 2: The gap is after the main verb and an adverb is needed (*exactly*).
Question 3: A noun is needed after *There is* (*agreement*).
Question 4: Here, you must understand the meaning of the whole sentence to know that an adjective with a negative prefix is needed (*unlikely*).

2 **Look at question 5. What part of speech is needed in the gap: an adverb or an adjective? Choose *cheerfully* or *cheerful*.**

3 **Now read the exam instructions and complete the task.**

For questions 1–8, read the text below. Use the word given in capitals at the end of some of the lines to form a word that fits in the gap in the same line. There is an example at the beginning (0).

EXAM TIPS

Decide which part of speech is needed for each gap. Remember that you may need to make a word negative, and can use a prefix or suffix to do so. When you have finished, check your answers make sense and are spelled correctly.

Identity and the *Individual*

The whole concept of **(0)** *personal* identity is fascinating. A lot of meaningful	**PERSON**
research has been carried out in this area, and **(1)** ________ continue to spend	**PSYCHOLOGY**
their working lives exploring its deep questions. Do our personalities stay	
(2) ________ the same over time? Given that our childhood experiences are so	**EXACT**
different to what we encounter as adults, there is **(3)** ________ among experts	**AGREE**
working in the field that this is **(4)** ________ to be the case.	**LIKE**
Do we even have just one 'self' or various 'selves' according to who we are	
with? A teenage boy may engage in **(5)** ________ conversation with his elderly	**CHEER**
grandmother about hobbies and homework, whereas his **(6)** ________ could	**BEHAVE**
be somewhat different when he is with other teens. The **(7)** ________ of us will	**MAJOR**
act differently according to who we are with at any given time. Our desire to	
gain **(8)** ________ of a group often influences what we do and say in different	**MEMBER**
situations, whether this is for better or worse.	

Reading and Use of English Part 4 Key word transformation (Unit 4, Unit 10, Unit 14, Review 1, Review 3, Review 4, Review 5)

EXAM INFORMATION

Reading and Use of English Part 4

- You will read six separate questions, each with a pair of sentences, one complete and one incomplete.
- You should complete the second sentence using between two and five words, including the key word given in bold.
- The second sentence should have the same meaning as the first sentence.
- You must not change the key word.
- There is one example, to show you what to do.

1 **Look at the example below. What changes have taken place in the second sentence?**

0 Medical research recommends reducing the amount of salt you consume. **DOWN**
According to medical research, you *should cut down on* the amount of salt you consume.

2 **Look at questions 1 and 2 in Exercise 3. Which one tests a dependent preposition?**

3 **Now read the exam instructions and complete the task.**

For questions 1–6, complete the second sentence so that it has a similar meaning to the first sentence, using the word given. Do not change the word given. You must use between two and five words, including the word given.

EXAM TIPS

Make sure the second sentence means the same as the first. Then check your spelling and grammar carefully.

1 A majority of students selected Jackie as the best singer in the school's talent competition. **VOTED**
More students .... any other singer in the school's talent competition.

2 I'll only phone next week if it is absolutely necessary. **REALLY**
Next week, I won't phone .... to.

3 I didn't like the new fashion at first, but I don't mind it now. **USED**
It has taken me a while .... the new fashion.

4 Doing homework needn't be a chore if you work with your friends. **HAVE**
It .... be a chore doing homework if you work with your friends.

5 There wasn't much food left over after the party. **SMALL**
Only .... food was left over after the party.

6 To my mind, travel is a waste of time. **FAR**
As ...., travel is a waste of time.

PREPARE FOR THE EXAM
B2 FIRST FOR SCHOOLS

Reading and Use of English Part 5 Multiple choice
(Unit 7, Unit 12, Unit 18)

EXAM INFORMATION

- You will read a fiction or non-fiction text.
- There are six four-option multiple-choice questions.
- The questions are in the same order as the information in the text.
- You should read the text carefully and choose only one option per question.

1 **Read the article on page 125 quickly. What is *Southfields*?**

A a documentary about old skateboarding movies
B a documentary about the award-winning skateboarder Stuart Laker
C a documentary about skaters in an area of London

2 **Read question 1 below. Then look at the highlighted part of the first paragraph, which confirms the answer. Why are A, B and D wrong?**

3 **Now read the exam instructions and complete the task.**

You are going to read an article about a film-maker called Stewart Laker and a skateboarding film he has made. For questions 1–6, choose the answer (A, B, C or D), which you think fits best according to the text.

1 What made the writer want to watch the film *Southfields*?
A the fact that it was made for younger audiences
B the reputation of the person who directed it
C the location where the film is set
D the publicity she had read about it

EXAM TIPS

Read the relevant paragraph and underline where you think the answer is. Check that the other three options are wrong.

2 Stewart Laker tells the writer that *Southfields*
A explores certain aspects of growing up.
B draws attention to an unfamiliar side of urban life.
C highlights the value of having a particular passion.
D shows how people benefit from overcoming physical challenges.

3 In the third paragraph, the writer expresses admiration for the way *Southfields* shows how
A extreme the lifestyle of skateboarders can be.
B different skateboarders are from each other.
C separate skateboarders are from the rest of society.
D skateboarders use language imaginatively.

4 The writer suggests the action scenes in *Southfields*
A may well have benefitted from more careful planning.
B must have required many repeated attempts to get them right.
C would have been better if more advanced film equipment had been used.
D could only have been made by someone with in-depth knowledge of skateboarding.

5 What does 'have a knack for' in line 52 mean?
A have a talent for
B have an interest in
C have problems with
D have time for

6 How does Laker feel about skateboarding being included in the Olympic Games?
A concerned about how it will affect people already involved in the sport
B unsure whether it will attract more people to the sport
C confident that it will result in better facilities for the sport
D hopeful that it will lead to improved safety in the sport

SOUTHFIELDS

Jennie Burgess meets Stewart Laker, the director of a new skateboarding movie.

People have always filmed skateboarding. As a skateboarder myself, I've watched hundreds of videos of young skateboarders displaying their skills and many skateboarding movies – dramas, usually based in some urban landscape in the USA, in which the main characters are teenage skateboarders. These movies often aren't very good, and when I first read about *Southfields* – directed by a well-known, award-winning maker of adverts for skateboarding equipment – I suspected more of the same. It wasn't until someone told me it was about young people in my home town, London, that I thought I'd give it a try. I'm glad I did.

When I meet Stewart Laker, he has his skateboard with him. He skates every day and says it makes him feel good. 'You concentrate on bumps in the street, how steep a ramp is, how to jump over a concrete block, and not getting hurt. This takes your mind off other things. You see that in *Southfields*. By losing themselves in what they're doing, the skaters are often dealing with other issues – the changes they're experiencing as they move towards adulthood, complicated feelings about family and friends, the desire for independence. Those things are what the film's really about – skateboarding's the context.'

Most of Laker's cast are skateboarders from an area of the city the film is named after, and parts of the storyline are based on their real-life experiences. There's a tendency to view skateboarders as all weird, wild, long-haired teenage boys who wear torn clothes, communicate with strange words, and can't fit in with the way most people live. While two of Laker's skaters are like that, we also meet 14-year-old Sam, a promising pianist; Maria, who's studying medicine; and 22-year-old Fatima, who's a qualified accountant. Their fascinating individual stories are followed in convincing detail; what brings them together is their love for the sport.

How interesting non-skateboarders will find the skateboarding action scenes in *Southfields,* I can't be certain. They were clearly filmed by someone with a great deal of personal experience of the sport – they capture what it's really like. Many scenes are filmed from the ground looking upwards. The shots are often shaky, as if taken with a small, hand-held camera rather than the large, modern, sophisticated devices that Laker assures me he actually filmed with. We see the skateboarders practising the same trick again and again – usually failing, very occasionally succeeding. That's skateboarding, though – thrills, dangers, frustrations and rare satisfactions.

As in all skateboarding films, music plays a key part. Skaters' musical tastes vary, so it's no surprise that the soundtrack includes Scandinavian heavy metal, Colombian *reggaeton*, African jazz, UK hip-hop and Korean pop. There are also tunes that Laker has included in an attempt to recall the soundtracks of skateboarding films made 20, even 50 years ago; but, rather than achieving this aim, these songs make the film seem a
line 52 little dated. Laker does **have a knack for** arranging the songs to support the story – we see Maria, who is confident and dynamic, skating to fast, electronic dance music, while shy, sensitive Sam gets a quieter, thoughtful piece. These choices skilfully reflect the skaters' individual personalities and further highlight how diverse the skating community is.

One young skateboarder in the film talks about representing her country at the Olympic Games. How does Laker feel about skateboarding becoming an Olympic sport? Does it mean that more skateparks will be built? 'How many more courts have been built since tennis became an Olympic sport?' he replies. With media coverage of the Olympics, the general public will know what skateboarding is like and realise how impressive the top skaters are. However, it's not clear if this will translate into people actually taking up the sport. Will more regulations be introduced to make the sport safer? 'Some probably will,' Laker says. 'It's an extreme sport – accidents obviously happen. But if it becomes very regulated, we'll lose something special about it, although there isn't much danger of that happening.'

PREPARE FOR THE EXAM
B2 FIRST FOR SCHOOLS

Reading and Use of English Part 6 Gapped text (Unit 3, Unit 10, Unit 19)

EXAM INFORMATION

Reading and Use of English Part 6

- You will read a text from which six sentences have been removed.
- There are seven sentences to choose from.
- You should read the text carefully and choose only one sentence to fill each gap.
- There is one sentence which you do not need to use.

1 **Read the text quickly. Choose the best alternative title for the text.**

A How companies benefit from advertising
B How adverts encourage you to buy
C How to create a successful advert

2 **Choose the option which fits in the first gap. Why is this the correct option?**

3 **Now read the exam instructions and complete the task.**

You are going to read an article about advertising. Six sentences have been removed from the article. Choose from the sentences A–G the one which fits each gap (1–6). There is one extra sentence which you do not need to use.

EXAM TIPS

Look for meaning and language in the sentences which link to the text around the gap. Then read each paragraph with your answer in place to check it makes sense.

A Another proven advertising technique involves featuring a celebrity who gives a personal recommendation for their chosen brand.

B Advertisements like this are, predictably, broadcast more frequently at certain times of year.

C A sunny image of smiling teenagers enjoying their favourite soft drink by the pool may well persuade you to follow their example.

D By releasing such an impressive set of facts about this special feature, the advertiser expects you to commit to the product without a second thought.

E So, the orange juice that provides 75% of your daily requirement of vitamins will be bought in preference to other soft drinks where no such claim is made.

F In other words, they can create a need that you didn't even know you had.

G This personalisation of products helped them reconnect with the public, and convince those who had not tried the product before to give it a go.

The art of advertising

ADVERTISEMENTS work in different ways according to how they have been developed. Of course, the objective is the same – to persuade you, the consumer, to purchase a product – but the techniques employed to do this vary a great deal.

Some adverts are designed to appeal directly to your emotions, both positive and negative. **1** ______ The suggestion is that if you do so, you will end up feeling as satisfied as they are.

Witnessing pain and suffering can play on your feelings just as effectively. Seeing someone in an advert with a heavy cold who gains instant relief from the product being advertised should register in your memory that this is the remedy to seek out the next time you are sneezing helplessly. **2** ______ In this particular case, the advert would be shown during the peak period of winter coughs and colds.

A different approach that is adopted for other kinds of advert relies on convincing the consumer to buy a product based on real scientific evidence or statistics. **3** ______ This appeal to reason appears to be highly effective where personal health and fitness is concerned.

4 ______ Involving such people in this way gives a product status, and makes potential customers want to associate themselves with those promoting the product. Whatever image the person endorsing the brand has will supposedly be passed onto the consumer when they purchase the brand themselves.

One recent kind of advertising campaign involves the consumers themselves. For example, one big name brand, Coca-Cola, produced products with common first names on the label. **5** ______ Another popular brand, the chocolate nut spread Nutella, made it possible for customers to request an individual label with their own name printed on it.

There are many other strategies employed by brands to make you, the consumer, want to go out and purchase their products right away. **6** ______ In addition to promising happiness and status, advertisers also take advantage of consumers' FOMO (fear of missing out). So, if all your friends have the latest smartphone, the chances are, you'll want it too. Companies will even resort to scare tactics (if you don't buy this product, a particular problem will get worse) to make you buy a product.

PREPARE FOR THE EXAM
B2 FIRST FOR SCHOOLS

Reading and Use of English Part 7 Multiple matching
(Unit 1, Unit 8, Unit 13)

EXAM INFORMATION

Reading and Use of English Part 7

- You will read either a single text which is divided into sections, or several short texts about the same subject.
- There are ten questions which you should match to each section.
- You can use each section more than once.

1 Look at questions 1 and 2. Which asks about an opinion? Does it ask about a positive or negative opinion?

2 In this part of the exam, information which appears to be relevant may be found in another section of the text, but it will not answer the question correctly. Look at question 2. Then read texts A and B. Underline the information which appears to match the question. Then decide whether A or B is the right answer.

3 Now read the exam instructions and complete the task.

You are going to read an article about four teenage tennis players and their fitness. For questions 1–10, choose from the teenagers (A–D). The teenagers may be chosen more than once.

EXAM TIPS

Read the questions first and underline important words. Then read the texts quickly to find the information you need.

Which teenager

disapproves of an aspect of her fellow players' behaviour?	1
arranges additional matches as part of her fitness plan?	2
acknowledges that she could make more effort to be healthy?	3
admits that a chosen form of physical exercise could be risky?	4
is following a plan which has been created especially for her?	5
praises the advice and support she has been given on diet?	6
makes a particular effort to prepare well before a match?	7
would like to start working on a certain technique with her coach?	8
is confident that she can overcome a weakness in her performance?	9
believes some people think that the sport requires little effort?	10

TEENAGE TENNIS PLAYERS AND THEIR FITNESS

A ALEXANDRA

Being part of the top college tennis team means I have to stay in great shape. So, however hard I'm studying, not a day goes by without some form of exercise, although I might only actually do tennis practice three times a week. Swimming and long-distance running suit me better than organising extra games, allowing me to build up my strength. These activities also provide useful thinking time for essays, so my brain gets a proper workout. Our fitness trainer keeps an eye on general food intake and comes up with really helpful suggestions about what to eat and when. Not everyone listens to him, though, which I think shows little respect for what he's contributing to the team effort. Then again, I tend to ignore advice on sleep patterns, while the others are pretty good at observing the early nights rule, so I maybe shouldn't criticise them!

B KATE

Our team practice sessions are scheduled after school finishes and focus on movement around the tennis court and general technique. I also set up further sessions on court with friends, so there's no shortage of tennis! Some players do other sports to keep fit, but that's not my thing. I do lift weights, but my body's still growing, so I need to be careful how I do it, even though it's evidently good preparation for long matches. Up to a point, taking in high-energy products on court helps with any lack of stamina, but I can't deny that as time goes on through the match, it's tough to keep going. I'm doing extra workouts right now to tackle this and I expect to see some benefit from that soon. Maybe I should seek advice on eating a balanced diet, too. We don't get much official support on that, which could actually make all the difference in big matches.

C TAMARA

I always make sure I get myself ready properly for any match, whether I'm playing against someone experienced or someone without as much experience as me. I reckon that's great practice for when I turn professional – if I ever do! This means getting a good night's sleep and then eating the right stuff – some protein, fruit or energy bars. I've done my own research into what I should do and when, and I'm sure that's helped me improve my game. At the moment, I'm increasing my fitness levels with my coach, who's developed a training programme to suit my own personal needs. I do a series of jumps and sprinting, which reflect the movements you do on court. The professionals make the sport look easy, and friends seem surprised when I tell them how demanding it is. Tennis matches can go on for hours, so you can lose by not being fit enough.

D MICHELA

Every time I have a spare hour or two, you'll see me heading down to the courts by my house, looking out for someone to have a game with. I'm self-taught, which means I've picked up a few bad habits which I'm now trying to undo. I've just found a trainer at the local club who's agreed to do some sessions with me, and I'm making progress. I still need to develop a stronger serve, so that's what I want to look at next with him. So far, we've spent time building up my stamina so I can keep going for longer. I haven't taken any of it too seriously until now, but I'm quite keen to become a better player, though I know I'll probably never play professionally. I never really considered that what I ate had an impact on my playing ability, and I know I ought to eat fewer burgers and more lean protein, like fish.

PREPARE FOR THE EXAM
B2 FIRST FOR SCHOOLS

WRITING

Writing Part 1 Writing an essay (Unit 1, Unit 9, Unit 15, Unit 19)

EXAM INFORMATION
Writing Part 1

- You will be given a question or statement and asked whether you agree with it.
- You are also given two ideas which you must include in your essay.
- Your essay must also contain a third idea of your own which does not overlap with the first two ideas. This 'own idea' is **not** the conclusion.

1 **Read the task. Which two ideas below (A–C) would be relevant as a third idea?**

A developing talent **B** time in the day
C social skills

In your English class you have been talking about sport. Now your English teacher has asked you to write an essay for homework. Write your essay using **all** the notes and giving reasons for your point of view.

> **'Sport should be a compulsory subject for teenage schoolchildren.'**
> **Do you agree?**
>
> **Notes**
> Write about:
> 1 keeping fit
> 2 teamwork
> 3 ________ (your own idea)

2 **Complete the advice with the words in the box.**

conclusion	grammar	introduction	
language	paragraphs	plan	spelling

1 Make a ________ before you begin writing.
2 Start your essay with an ________, where you explain what it will cover.
3 Organise your essay in ________.
4 Include a ________ at the end.
5 Don't use ________ which is too informal.
6 Check your essay for ________ and ________.

3 **Now read the exam instructions and complete the task.**

You **must** answer this question. Write your answer in **140–190** words in an appropriate style.

EXAM TIPS
Remember to include a relevant third idea. Time how long it takes you to write your essay – you should spend no longer than 40 minutes on it.

Writing Part 2 A choice of writing task (Unit 3, Unit 5, Unit 7, Unit 11, Unit 13, Unit 17)

EXAM INFORMATION
Writing Part 2

- You are given a choice of four questions. These may include an article, a letter or email, an essay, a review or a story.
- You should choose **one** question only.
- Question 5 is about a set text. You shouldn't choose this question if you haven't studied the set text in class.
- You should write 140–190 words.

1 **Read the task, then answer the questions to help you think of ideas for your story.**

1 What do you think has happened in the room to cause Sofie to leave?
2 Where do you think Sofie will go next?
3 Has someone been unable to keep a secret?
4 How might a phone be involved in the story?

You have seen this announcement in an English-language magazine.

> **Write a story!**
> We are looking for stories about strong emotions to publish in the next issue of our magazine. Your story must **begin** with this sentence:
> *Sofie was so angry that she stood up and ran out of the room, shutting the door loudly behind her.*
> Your story must include:
> - a secret
> - a phone

2 **Which of these tips could you use for writing a story? Tick all that apply.**

have a clear storyline ☐
use descriptive vocabulary ☐
use a range of grammatical structures ☐
add lots of detail ☐
use direct speech ☐
use humour ☐
use narrative tenses ☐
write an unexpected or dramatic ending ☐

3 **Now read the exam instructions and complete the task.**

Write your story. Write your answer in **140–190** words in an appropriate style.

EXAM TIPS
Decide how you will continue from the first sentence before you start writing. Remember to include the two things listed.

LISTENING

Listening Part 1 Multiple choice
(Unit 6, Unit 20)

EXAM INFORMATION

Listening Part 1

- You will listen to eight unrelated extracts of about 30 seconds each.
- You will hear one or two speakers each time.
- There is one three-option multiple-choice question to answer for each extract.

1 **Read question 1. What is it important to listen out for?**

95 **2** **Listen to the extract for question 1. Choose the best answer (A, B or C). Why are the other options incorrect?**

1 You hear two friends discussing a novel.
What do they agree is impressive about it?
A how believable the characters are
B how clearly the plot develops
C how well the places are described

2 You hear a boy talking on the phone about some homework.
He is worried because he
A doesn't have the right materials.
B can't complete everything in time.
C hasn't got enough ideas to include.

3 You hear two friends talking about social media.
What do they both say about it?
A It's a good way to connect with new people.
B It helps them to remember past events.
C It occupies time which would otherwise be boring.

4 You hear a girl telling her friend about moving house.
How does she feel about it?
A sad about having left her old home
B upset not to have more space
C disappointed with the location

5 You hear a teacher talking to his class about being a good citizen.
What does he want them to do after the lesson?
A talk about what it means
B carry out some online research
C put some ideas into action

6 You hear an announcement at a railway station.
The purpose of the announcement is to inform customers that
A there are likely to be some delays.
B there is a replacement service available.
C some work is being carried out on the tracks.

7 You hear a boy talking to his sister about climbing.
What is he doing?
A advising her to do something
B reminding her to do something
C offering to help her do something

8 You hear two friends talking about the girl's temporary job.
The girl thinks that her work should be
A better organised.
B more highly paid.
C done at a different time.

96 **3** **Now read the exam instructions and complete the task.**

You will hear people talking in eight different situations. For questions 1–8, choose the best answer (A, B or C).

EXAM TIPS

Choose the answer you think is correct at the first listening. Check your answer when the recording is repeated.

PREPARE FOR THE EXAM
B2 FIRST FOR SCHOOLS

Listening Part 2 Sentence completion (Unit 8, Unit 12, Unit 16)

EXAM INFORMATION

Listening Part 2

- You will listen to one person speaking for between three and four minutes.
- There are ten questions in the form of incomplete sentences.
- As you listen, you should complete each sentence with a word or short phrase.
- The questions are in the same order as the information you hear.

1 Look at the title. What do you think the recording will be about? What do you think Jamal does?

2 Read the sentences. What kind of information would complete each sentence?

97 **3** Now read the exam instructions and complete the task.

You will hear a girl called Cristina talking about a musician called Jamal Edwards. For questions 1–10, complete the sentences with a word or short phrase.

EXAM TIPS

Read the sentences before listening to predict what kind of information is missing. Check your answers when you listen to the recording the second time.

JAMAL EDWARDS and his music website SBTV

The first video Jamal uploaded to the internet showed **(1)** ________ in London.

Jamal was interested in music which combined garage and **(2)** ________.

Some of Jamal's early music videos were filmed in **(3)** ________, which people found very original.

Jamal started saving money for equipment when he was working in a **(4)** ________.

Jamal set up his website when his videos had been viewed more than **(5)** ________ times.

Cristina likes looking at the **(6)** ________ which are posted on the SBTV website.

Jamal acknowledges that he wasn't good at **(7)** ________ when his business started to become serious.

Jamal used to **(8)** ________ staff because he was shy.

Cristina likes the fact that Jamal encourages people to build their **(9)** ________ in order to become successful.

Jamal was not keen on becoming **(10)** ________ after what happened to his mother.

Listening Part 3 Multiple matching (Unit 2, Unit 4, Unit 14)

EXAM INFORMATION

Listening Part 3

- You will hear five individual speakers, talking about a common theme.
- You should choose the option which matches what each speaker says.
- There are eight options (A–H) to choose from.
- There are three options which are not used.

98 **1** Read options A–H below. Which subject (A–C) do you think they all relate to? Listen to the first speaker and check your ideas.

A studying science
B wildlife holidays
C volunteering

2 Read the exam instructions in Exercise 3. Underline the key words in the options which you need to listen out for.

99 **3** Now complete the task.

You will hear five short extracts in which university students are talking about doing voluntary work on conservation projects in different parts of the world. For questions 1–5, choose from the list (A–H) what each speaker says they enjoyed most about the experience. Use the letters only once. There are three extra letters which you do not need to use.

EXAM TIPS

Be careful – sometimes an option seems possible, but it isn't a match. Check your answers when you listen to the recording the second time.

A saving the life of individual animals
B getting to see a wide variety of environments
C having the chance to do challenging tasks
D getting close to a very rare animal
E being responsible for collecting important data
F using relevant previously learned information
G learning more about various local traditions
H being able to view the beautiful surroundings

Speaker 1	1
Speaker 2	2
Speaker 3	3
Speaker 4	4
Speaker 5	5

Listening Part 4 Multiple choice (Unit 10, Unit 18)

EXAM INFORMATION

- You will hear an interview or conversation lasting between three and four minutes.
- There are seven multiple-choice questions with three options (A, B and C).
- You should choose the option which answers each question.

100 **1** **Listen to an interviewer introduce a guest called Maria Smith on a radio programme. What has Maria done recently?**

2 **Look at the questions. Which ones ask about people's emotions and opinions?**

101 **3** **Now read the exam instructions and complete the task.**

You will hear an interview with a teenager called Maria Smith, who's talking about carrying out a survey into her generation's views on the future. For questions 1–7, choose the best answer (A, B or C).

1 Maria says that she became interested in the topic of her survey after
- **A** hearing her friends discussing their plans.
- **B** feeling worried about her progress at college.
- **C** being encouraged to think about her future.

2 Maria's biggest challenge while working on her survey was
- **A** preparing suitably worded content.
- **B** analysing all the results thoroughly.
- **C** persuading enough students to complete it.

3 What did Maria identify as being of concern to many students?
- **A** being accepted at the right university
- **B** getting a job that is suitable for them
- **C** having an adequate standard of living

4 On the subject of technology, Maria says that many students seem to be
- **A** convinced that it will continue to develop.
- **B** dissatisfied with the range of products available.
- **C** uneasy about needing it for everything they do.

5 When Maria read responses to a question about success, she felt
- **A** surprised by what people considered important.
- **B** disappointed that people gave little detail.
- **C** pleased that people were so ambitious.

6 What does Maria plan to do with the data she has collected?
- **A** publish it online
- **B** write a report explaining her findings
- **C** encourage other people to read about what she did

7 How does Maria feel after having carried out the survey?
- **A** more confused than she was previously
- **B** confident that she will make good decisions
- **C** regretful that she has wasted valuable time

EXAM TIPS

Underline the key words in the questions before you listen. Check your answers when you listen to the recording the second time.

PREPARE FOR THE EXAM
B2 FIRST FOR SCHOOLS

SPEAKING

Speaking Part 1 Interview
(Unit 2, Unit 14)

EXAM INFORMATION
Speaking Part 1

- The examiner will ask you some questions.
- The questions will be about you, your interests and your life.
- You should answer the questions, expressing your opinion about various topics.

1 **Look at the questions. Which three topics are they about?**

- How often do you use social media?
- What do you like finding out about on the internet?
- How do you usually travel to school or work?
- Do you use public transport to travel around?
- What do you enjoy doing with your family and friends in your free time?
- Is there a new hobby you would like to do in the future?

102 **2** **Listen to Sara answering some of the questions. Which ones is she asked?**

3 **Read the questions below. Ask and answer them with a partner.**

1

What kind of books do you like?

I like fantasy books best.

What do you like about them?

They're really imaginative and take you into a different world.

2 What was the last special occasion you celebrated? What did you do to celebrate?
3 Do you have any interesting hobbies? Tell me what you like about it/them.
4 Who do you enjoy spending time with? What kind of things do you do when you spend time with him/her?
5 Tell me about a TV programme you've seen recently. Would you recommend it to other people? Why? / Why not?

EXAM TIPS
Give longer answers, not just *Yes* or *No* answers. Don't worry if you get stuck. The examiner will ask you another question. You will not lose marks for this.

Speaking Part 2 Long turn
(Unit 8, Unit 20)

EXAM INFORMATION
Speaking Part 2

- The examiner will give you two photographs.
- You should compare the photographs for about one minute and answer the question given.
- You will also be asked to comment (for about 30 seconds) on your partner's photos.

1 **You are going to compare two photographs. Look at photographs 1 and 2 on page 135. They show teenagers doing different things in their free time. Think of ideas for the question above them.**

103 **2** **Listen to Álvaro comparing photographs 1 and 2. How many of your ideas does he include?**

3 **Work in pairs.**

Candidate A: Look at photographs 3 and 4 on page 135. They show teenagers doing different outdoor activities. Compare photographs 3 and 4 and say what you think the teenagers are enjoying about these activities.

Candidate B: Which of these activities would you prefer to do? Why?

4 **Work in pairs.**

Candidate B: Look at photographs 5 and 6 on page 135. They show teenagers studying in different ways. Compare photographs 5 and 6 and say what you think the advantages are of studying in these different ways.

Candidate A: Do you prefer studying alone or in a group? Why?

EXAM TIPS
Compare the two photographs, making sure you answer the question you are asked about them. Be careful to make comparisons rather than simply describing the photos separately. Don't interrupt the other candidate when they are talking about their photos. The examiner will make it clear when it is your turn to speak.

What do people like about doing these activities?

1

2

What do you think the teenagers are enjoying about these activities?

3

4

What are the advantages of studying in these different ways?

5

6

PREPARE FOR THE EXAM
B2 FIRST FOR SCHOOLS

Speaking Part 3 Collaborative task
(Unit 12, Unit 16)

EXAM INFORMATION

Speaking Part 3

- You will have a conversation with another candidate lasting about three minutes.
- The examiner will give you a question to discuss, with five ideas to help you discuss the question.
- You will talk together for about two minutes, then the examiner will stop you.
- The examiner will then ask you to talk together for another minute before making a decision based on the task.

104 **1 Read the task, then listen to Sara and Álvaro. Do they think all of the ideas might be interesting to young people?**

Some young people would like to find out more about the history of the area where they live. Here are some ways they could find out about the history of their area and a question for you to discuss.

Talk to each other about how interesting young people would find these ways of finding out about history.

105 **2 Listen to the examiner. What do the candidates have to do next?**

106 **3 Listen to Sara and Álvaro make their decision. Which way of finding out about history do they choose?**

107 **4 Work in pairs. Listen to the examiner, then complete the task in Exercise 1.**

EXAM TIPS

Make sure you take turns in the conversation, and give your partner chances to speak. Don't be afraid to ask the examiner to repeat the questions if you need to hear them again.

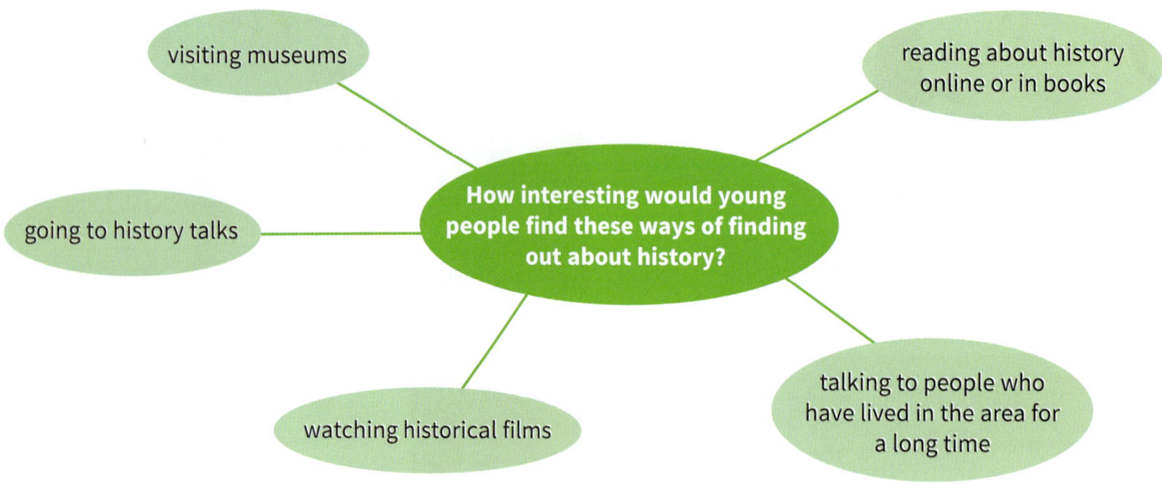

Speaking Part 4 (Unit 12, Unit 16) Discussion

EXAM INFORMATION

- You will continue the discussion on the topic you talked about in Speaking Part 3.
- The examiner will ask questions for you both to answer.

108 **1** **Read the questions, then listen to Sara and Álvaro. Which questions do they answer?**

- How can talking to the older generation help young people learn about the past?
- Do you think people should look to the future rather than the past? (Why?)
- Why are people so interested in their own family's history?
- Why do you think history museums should be interactive, with activities for visitors to do?
- How can history lessons be made interesting at school?
- Do you think certain periods of history are more important for young people to find out about than others? (Why? / Which ones?)

108 **2** **Listen again. What do they say about each question they are asked?**

3 **Ask and answer the questions in Exercise 1 with a partner.**

How can talking to the older generation help young people learn about the past?

Life was often harder in the past. I think older people can help young people feel hopeful about the future and teach them what they've learned in life.

EXAM TIPS

Remember to talk to your partner during the discussion. Give reasons for your answers.

EXTRA ACTIVITIES

UNIT 4 PAGE 26 VOCABULARY

2 **Complete the sentences with the correct form of the phrasal verbs in Exercise 1. Then discuss the questions.**

0 What kinds of things ___get___ you ___down___?
1 I felt really dizzy when I ______ after fainting.
2 Does it take you a long time to ______ arguments with good friends?
3 The smell of sour milk makes me want to ______. It's disgusting!
4 Have you ever ______ an illness because you've been outside in the cold for too long?
5 I eventually ______ after the argument, but I was really annoyed at the time.

3 **Ask and answer the questions with a partner.**

1 What kind of things get you down?
2 Have you ever come down with food poisoning?
3 Do you usually get over illness quickly?
4 Have you ever come round after fainting and wondered where you were?
5 Do you find it easy to calm down after an argument?
6 Have you ever thrown up on a long car journey?

UNIT 7 PAGE 44 VOCABULARY

3 **Complete the sentences about you. Then compare them with your partner.**

1 The year before last, I …
2 I haven't … for some time.
3 Before long, I'd like to learn how to …
4 I often … for hours on end.
5 I could learn to … in no time.

UNIT 8 PAGE 49 SPEAKING

PREPARE FOR THE EXAM

Speaking Part 2

5 **Work in pairs. The photographs show two cities at different times of year.**

Student B: Compare the two photographs. Say what the people might enjoy about living in the cities at these different times of year.
Student A: What time of year do you like best where you live? Why?

UNIT 9 PAGE 54 VOCABULARY

WHAT WAS **YOUR SCORE?**

All the statements are characteristics of optimistic people. Optimists have a belief that things will always turn out well. They believe they are in control of their future and when things go wrong, they tend to see others as the reason, rather than themselves. They look for new opportunities and see themselves as very able people in everything they do. They are goal-oriented and often determined to achieve their goals.

The more statements you agreed with, the more optimistic you are.

35–40: VERY OPTIMISTIC
You always look on the bright side of a situation. The positive attitude you bring to everything you do means your friends probably see you as someone whose presence cheers everyone up.

28–34: QUITE OPTIMISTIC
For the most part, you're someone who makes the most of things and looks forward to the future, but there is still a part of you that holds back. Perhaps a bit of realism is useful, though?

21–27: REALISTIC
For you, it's not about hoping for the best in situations or seeing the worst in people. It's about using reason to make decisions. You might not have the most exciting time, but your realism means you usually have a fairly accurate idea of what new experiences will be like.

14–20: QUITE PESSIMISTIC
You aren't a complete pessimist, but you tend to avoid new experiences, as generally speaking you think that something bad might happen.

8 (MINIMUM SCORE)–13: VERY PESSIMISTIC
If something can go wrong, your belief is that it will. And if you can blame yourself for the problem, you probably will too. Even if something good happens, you'll probably believe that it was only because of good fortune that things went well.

UNIT 9 PAGE 56 VOCABULARY

5 **Complete the questions using a form of the words in the box. Ask and answer the questions with a partner.**

driver enjoy personal recognise remark

1. What do you think are the advantages and disadvantages of ________ vehicles?
2. Who is the most ________ celebrity in your country?
3. What is the most ________ thing you have ever seen?
4. Are there any benefits to having a pessimistic ________?
5. What activities do you get the most ________ from?

UNIT 10 PAGE 60 VOCABULARY

4 **Ask and answer the questions with a partner.**

1. Do you know anyone who you would call 'an angel'?
2. When was the last time your parents or teacher grilled you about something?
3. Do you usually sail through things like exams or other challenges?
4. What lifts your mood when you're fed up?
5. Do you remember events clearly, or have you got a foggy memory?

UNIT 11 PAGE 66 VOCABULARY

3 **Ask and answer the questions with a partner.**

1. Are you a well-organised person?
2. Do you have many hi-tech gadgets?
3. Do you like to organise things well in advance, or do you prefer last-minute plans?
4. How important is it to get a well-paid job?
5. Do you eat a well-balanced diet?

UNIT 12 PAGE 70 VOCABULARY

4 **Read the speech bubbles aloud. Complete the sentences using *both*, *either of*, *either … or*, *neither of* or *neither … nor*.**

1
I'm really hungry!
I'm hungry too!
We're … !

2
I haven't got any money left.
I haven't got any either.
…

3
We don't have time to visit both museums. …

4
I'm so excited about our holiday! Poppy and Jake – are … ?

5
I'm not playing football today.
I'm not playing football today, either.
… Leroy … Heather is …

UNIT 19 PAGE 110 VOCABULARY

3 **Student A, read the sentences below. Student B will listen and say whether each sentence is correct or not. He/She will then correct the incorrect sentences.**

1. I've just heard some interesting new about Karl.
2. I love our school surrounding. They help me work hard.
3. I'm sure they'll serve some refreshments after the races.

Answers: **1** not correct – *news*
2 not correct – *surroundings* **3** correct

Now listen to Student B's sentences. Say whether each sentence is correct or incorrect. If the sentence is incorrect, say the sentence again, correcting the mistake.

EXTRA ACTIVITIES

UNIT 13 PAGE 76 VOCABULARY

WHAT WAS YOUR SCORE?

All the sentences are qualities of good leaders.

20–24: Wow! You're the kind of person that people look up to and you're on your way to becoming a great leader.

14–19: You're doing OK, but you probably have the potential to be even better. Look at the questions you scored the least on – is there anything you could do to improve your leadership skills?

8 (MINIMUM SCORE)–13: You're probably not a natural leader, but there's nothing wrong with that. All teams need good, positive team members!

UNIT 14 PAGE 82 VOCABULARY

4 **Take turns to read out the statements and report them using the correct form of the reporting verbs in the box.**

~~confess~~	enquire	forbid
insist	point out	recommend

0 'I stole the tablet from the technology lab,' she said.

She confessed that she had stolen the tablet from the technology lab.

1 'You are *not* allowed to go on your brother's motorbike. Not even for a short ride – absolutely not.'
My dad …
2 'You really must eat something,' my mum said.
My mum …
3 'You can't stop here – look, the sign says so,' Beth said to Charlie.
Beth …
4 'I suggest you park by the station,' the attendant said.
The attendant …
5 'Excuse me. Could you tell me where the nearest bus stop is?' asked the woman.
The woman …

UNIT 15 PAGE 88 VOCABULARY

3 **Work with a partner. Take turns to complete the sentences with your own ideas.**

1 I'm in favour of banning …
2 Many people think that … , but in actual fact …
3 When an exam is in progress, you shouldn't …
4 In the light of recent news about the acceleration of climate change, it's important that …
5 When working in groups, it's important to let everyone speak in turn, because …
6 In general I like … , but I'm not keen on …

UNIT 16 PAGE 92 VOCABULARY

3 **Ask and answer the questions with a partner.**

1 Do you eat a well-balanced diet?
2 At what age do you hope to become financially independent?
3 What do you do that is environmentally friendly?
4 Do you keep your social-media pages regularly updated?
5 Are any of your things made by globally recognised brands?

UNIT 18 PAGE 104 VOCABULARY

3 **Ask and answer the questions with a partner.**

1 What do you do to stop worries going round and round in your head?
2 Do you walk up and down while you're talking on the phone?
3 Have you got any dreams which are looking more and more unlikely?
4 Have you more or less decided on a career yet?
5 What activities do you only do now and then?

UNIT 19 PAGE 110 VOCABULARY

3 **Student B, listen to Student A's sentences. Say whether each sentence is correct or incorrect. If the sentence is incorrect, say the sentence again, correcting the mistake.**

Now read the sentences below. Student A will listen and say whether each sentence is correct or not. He/She will then correct the incorrect sentences.

4 The content is quite short, considering it's such a long book.
5 I love the lyrics of this song – they're so romantic.
6 My grandparents have just bought a flat on the outskirt of Paris.

Answers: **4** not correct – *contents* **5** correct **6** not correct – *outskirts*

UNIT 20 PAGE 115 SPEAKING

PREPARE FOR THE EXAM

Speaking Part 2

5 **Work in pairs. The photographs show people communicating with each other other using technology.**

Student A: Compare the two photographs. Say why the people might have decided to communicate with friends or family in these ways.
Student B: How do you prefer to communicate with friends? Why?

EP VOCABULARY LIST

adj = adjective	*adv* = adverb	
n = noun	*v* = verb	*pv* = phrasal verb
prep = preposition	*phr* = phrase	
id = idiom	*conj* = conjunction	
pron = pronoun	*det* = determiner	

UNIT 1

ARTS AND MEDIA

appearance /ə'pɪərəns/ *n* an occasion when someone appears in public
bestseller /ˌbest'selə/ *n* a very popular book that many people have bought
broadcast /'brɔːdkɑːst/ *v* to send out a programme on television or radio
cast /kɑːst/ *n* all the actors in a film, play or show
the charts /ðə 'tʃɑːts/ *phr* an official list of the most popular songs each week
classic /'klæsɪk/ *n* a piece of writing, a musical recording or a film which has been popular for a long time and is considered to be of a high quality
piece /piːs/ *n* an example of artistic, musical or written work
series /'sɪəriːz/ *n* a set of books published by the same company which deal with the same subject
shoot /ʃuːt/ *v* to use a camera to record a film or take a photograph
stream /striːm/ *v* to listen to or watch something on a device such as a computer, smartphone or smart TV directly from the internet
track /træk/ *n* one song or single piece of music

CREATIVE JOBS

comedian /kə'miːdiən/ *n* someone who entertains people by telling jokes
critic /'krɪtɪk/ *n* someone whose job is to give their opinion about something, especially films, books, music, etc.
editor /'edɪtə/ *n* a person who corrects or changes text, film, etc., or a person who is in charge of a newspaper or magazine
novelist /'nɒvəlɪst/ *n* a person who writes books about imaginary people and events
producer /prə'djuːsə/ *n* someone who controls how a film, play, programme or musical recording is made
programmer /'prəʊgræmə/ *n* someone who writes computer programs as a job
TV presenter /tiːˌviː prɪ'zentə/ *n* someone who introduces a television or radio show

UNIT 2

PERSONALITY: ADJECTIVE + PREPOSITION

addicted (to) /ə'dɪktɪd/ *adj* liking something very much
adventurous (with) /əd'ventʃərəs/ *adj* willing to try new and often difficult or dangerous things
aware (of) /ə'weə/ *adj* knowing that something exists, or having knowledge or experience of a particular thing
bothered (about) /'bɒðəd/ *adj* If you are bothered about something, it is important to you and you are worried about it.
cautious (about) /'kɔːʃəs/ *adj* taking care to avoid risks or danger
critical (of) /'krɪtɪkəl/ *adj* saying that someone or something is bad or wrong
decisive (about) /dɪ'saɪsɪv/ *adj* able to make decisions quickly and confidently, or showing this quality
hopeless (at) /'həʊpləs/ *adj* very bad at a particular activity
impressed (by) /ɪm'prest/ *adj* feeling admiration or respect for someone or something
jealous (of) /'dʒeləs/ *adj* unhappy and angry because you want something that someone else has
loyal (to) /'lɔɪəl/ *adj* always liking and supporting someone or something, sometimes when other people do not
mean (about) /miːn/ *adj* unkind or unpleasant

VERB + PREPOSITION

apologise (for) /ə'pɒlədʒaɪz/ *v* to tell someone that you are sorry about something you have done
compare with /kəm'peə wɪð/ *v* to say how one person or thing is different from another
cope (with) /kəʊp/ *v* to deal successfully with a difficult situation
depend on /dɪ'pend ɒn/ *pv* to need the help and support of someone or something in order to exist or continue as before
do without /ˌduː wɪ'ðaʊt/ *pv* to manage without having something
have heard of /həv 'hɜːd əv/ *v* If you have heard of someone or something, you know that that person or thing exists.
laugh at /'lɑːf ət/ *pv* to show that you think someone or something is stupid

UNIT 3

ABSTRACT NOUNS

agreement /ə'griːmənt/ *n* when people have the same opinion or have made the same decision
ambition /æm'bɪʃən/ *n* a strong wish to be successful, powerful, rich, etc.
belief /bɪ'liːf/ *n* an idea that you are certain is true
development /dɪ'veləpmənt/ *n* when someone or something grows or changes and becomes more advanced
drive /draɪv/ *n* energy and determination to achieve things
luck /lʌk/ *n* good and bad things caused by chance and not by your own actions
problem-solving /'prɒbləm ˌsɒlvɪŋ/ *n* the process of finding solutions to problems
success /sək'ses/ *n* If you achieve success, you are recognised and admired by many people for your skills and achievements or wealth.
thought /θɔːt/ *n* the act of thinking about or considering something, an idea or opinion, or a set of ideas about a particular subject

PHRASAL VERBS: LEARNING AND THINKING

back up /bæk 'ʌp/ *pv* to make a copy of information in a computer that is stored separately
face up to /feɪs 'ʌp tə/ *pv* to accept that a difficult situation exists
focus on /'fəʊkəs ɒn/ *pv* to give a lot of attention to one particular person, subject or thing
get in /get 'ɪn/ *pv* to succeed in getting a place on a course, especially at university or college
mix up /mɪks 'ʌp/ *pv* to mistake someone or something for someone or something else; to confuse two people or things
think through /θɪŋk 'θruː/ *pv* to carefully consider the possible results of doing something

UNIT 4

STRESS

faint /feɪnt/ *v* to suddenly become unconscious for a short time, usually falling down
feel dizzy /fiːl 'dɪzi/ *phr* to feel as if everything is turning round, so that you feel ill or as if you might fall

get in a panic /ˌget ɪn ə 'pænɪk/ *phr* to have a sudden strong feeling of fear that prevents reasonable thought and action

go over and over (sth) in your mind /gəʊ əʊvər ənd 'əʊvər ɪn jɔː 'maɪnd/ *phr* to think repeatedly about an event that has happened

have an upset stomach /hæv ən 'ʌpset 'stʌmək/ *phr* to have an illness in the stomach

have difficulty sleeping /hæv 'dɪfɪkəlti 'sliːpɪŋ/ *phr* to not be able to get to sleep easily or quickly and/or to wake up frequently during the night

lose your appetite /'luːz jər 'æpɪtaɪt/ *phr* to not feel like eating

lose your temper /'luːz jə 'tempə/ *phr* to suddenly become angry

PHRASAL VERBS: HEALTH

calm down /kɑːm 'daʊn/ *pv* to stop feeling upset, angry or excited

come down with (sth) /kʌm 'daʊn wɪð/ *pv* to become ill, usually with a disease that is not very serious

come round /kʌm 'raʊnd/ *pv* to become conscious again after an accident or operation

get (sb) down /get 'daʊn/ *pv* to make someone feel unhappy or depressed

get over (sth/sb) /get 'əʊvə/ *pv* to get better after an illness, or feel better after something or someone has made you unhappy

throw up /θrəʊ 'ʌp/ *pv* (informal) to vomit

UNIT 5

HISTORY

ancestor /'ænsestə/ *n* a relative who lived a long time ago

century /'sentʃəri/ *n* a period of 100 years

citizen /'sɪtɪzən/ *n* someone who lives in a particular town or city

decade /'dekeɪd/ *n* a period of ten years, especially a period such as 1860 to 1869, or 1990 to 1999

found /faʊnd/ *v* to bring something (e.g. a town, an organisation) into existence

get the vote /ˌget ðə 'vəʊt/ *phr* to be allowed to express your choice or opinion in an election

inhabitant /ɪn'hæbɪtənt/ *n* a person or animal that lives in a particular place

myth /mɪθ/ *n* an ancient story about gods and brave people, often one that explains an event in history or the natural world

tribe /traɪb/ *n* a group of people who live together, usually in areas far away from cities, and who share the same culture and language

EXPRESSING FREQUENCY

all the time /ɔːl ðə 'taɪm/ *phr* continuously

constantly /'kɒnstəntli/ *adv* all the time or often

from time to time /frəm 'taɪm tə 'taɪm/ *phr* sometimes but not often

most days/weeks/months /məʊst 'deɪz/'wiːks/'mʌnθs/ *phr* almost every day/week/month

occasionally /ə'keɪʒənəli/ *adv* sometimes but not often

(every) once in a while /('evri) 'wʌns ɪn ə 'waɪl/ *phr* sometimes but not often

rarely /'reəli/ *adv* not often

regularly /'regjʊləli/ *adv* often

seldom /'seldəm/ *adv* not often

UNIT 6

EXPRESSING EMOTIONS

anxious (about) /'aŋkʃəs/ *adj* worried and nervous

bad-tempered (about) /bæd'tempəd/ *adj* angry and annoyed

cheerful (about) /'tʃɪəfəl/ *adj* happy and positive

concerned (about) /kən'sɜːnd/ *adj* worried

content (with) /kən'tent/ *adj* pleased with your situation and not hoping for change or improvement

depressed (about) /dɪ'prest/ *adj* unhappy and without hope for the future

down (about) /daʊn/ *adj* unhappy and depressed

fed up (with) /fed 'ʌp/ *adj* annoyed or bored with something that you have experienced for too long

furious (with) /'fjʊəriəs/ *adj* extremely angry

irritated (by) /'ɪrɪteɪtɪd/ *adj* annoyed

optimistic (about) /ɒptɪ'mɪstɪk/ *adj* always believing that good things will happen

over the moon (about) /ˌəʊvə ðə 'muːn/ *id* very pleased

pessimistic (about) /pesɪ'mɪstɪk/ *adj* always believing that bad things are likely to happen

petrified (of) /'petrɪfaɪd/ *adj* extremely frightened

relieved (about) /rɪ'liːvd/ *adj* happy that something unpleasant has not happened or has ended

scared (of) /skeəd/ *adj* frightened or worried

ADVERBS: TYPE AND POSITION

definitely /'defɪnətli/ *adv* without any doubt

frequently /'friːkwəntli/ *adv* often

however /haʊ'evə/ *adv* despite whatever amount or degree

last week /lɑːst 'wiːk/ *adv* the week before the present one

outside /aʊt'saɪd/ *adv* not inside a building

quickly /'kwɪkli/ *adv* at a fast speed

UNIT 7

VERBS OF MOVEMENT AND SOUNDS

kneel down /niːl 'daʊn/ *pv* to go down into, or stay in, a position where one or both knees are on the ground

lean /liːn/ *v* to move the top part of the body in a particular direction

mumble /'mʌmbl/ *v* to speak too quietly and not clearly enough for someone to understand you

rush /rʌʃ/ *v* to hurry or move quickly somewhere, or to make someone or something hurry or move quickly somewhere

sigh /saɪ/ *v* to breathe out slowly and noisily, often because you are annoyed or unhappy

slap /slæp/ *v* to hit someone with the flat, inside part of your hand

swing open /swɪŋ 'əʊpən/ *phr* to open easily and without interruption

tap /tæp/ *v* to knock or touch something gently

tremble /'trembəl/ *v* to shake slightly, usually because you are cold, frightened or very emotional

wander /'wɒndə/ *v* to walk slowly in a relaxed way

whisper /'wɪspə/ *v* to speak extremely quietly so that other people cannot hear

whistle /'wɪsl/ *v* to make a sound by breathing air out through a small hole made with your lips, or through a whistle

TIME PHRASES

before (very/too) long /bɪˌfɔː 'lɒŋ/ *phr* soon

for hours/weeks on end /fər 'aʊəz/'wiːks ən 'end/ *phr* for hours/weeks without stopping

for some time /fə 'sʌm 'taɪm/ *phr* for a long period of time

in no time /ɪn 'nəʊ taɪm/ *phr* very soon

the week before last /ðə 'wiːk bɪˌfɔː 'lɑːst/ *phr* the week before the one that has just finished

VOCABULARY LIST

UNIT 8

COMMUNITY

affordable /ə'fɔːdəbəl/ *adj* (used about houses, etc.) able to be bought or rented by people who do not earn a lot of money
close /kləʊs/ *adj* A close community is one where people who live in the same area all know each other well.
diverse /daɪ'vɜːs/ *adj* varied or different
industrial /ɪn'dʌstriəl/ *adj* connected with industry, or having a lot of industry and factories, etc.
inner-city /'ɪnə 'sɪti/ *adj* in the central part of a city where people live and where there are often problems because people are poor and there are few jobs and bad houses
relaxed /rɪ'lækst/ *adj* A relaxed situation or place is comfortable and informal.
remote /rɪ'məʊt/ *adj* describes an area, house or village that is a long way from any towns or cities
residential /rezɪ'denʃəl/ *adj* A residential area has only houses and not offices or factories.
rural /'rʊərəl/ *adj* relating to the countryside and not to towns
trendy /'trendi/ *adj* modern and influenced by the most recent fashions or ideas
urban /'ɜːbən/ *adj* belonging or relating to a town or city
welcoming /'welkəmɪŋ/ *adj* friendly or making you feel welcome

AS IF / AS THOUGH

as if / as though /əz 'ɪf / əz 'ðəʊ/ *phr* in a way that seems to show something

UNIT 9

COLLOCATIONS

achieve your goals /ə'tʃiːv jə gəʊlz/ *phr* to succeed in doing something you have aimed to do, usually by working hard
go wrong /gəʊ 'rɒŋ/ *phr* to develop problems
have a go at (sth) /ˌhæv ə 'gəʊ ət/ *phr* to try to do something you have not done before
look bright /lʊk 'braɪt/ *phr* to appear to have the possibility of success or happiness
make a (big) difference /ˌmeɪk ə 'dɪfərəns/ *phr* to improve a situation (a lot)
make the best of (sth) /ˌmeɪk ðə 'best əv/ *phr* to make an unsatisfactory situation as pleasant as possible
make the most of (sth) /ˌmeɪk ðə 'məʊst əv/ *phr* to take full advantage of something because it may not last long
put an end to (sth) /ˌpʊt ən 'end tuː/ *phr* to make something stop happening or existing
see the best in (sb) /ˌsiː ðə 'best ɪn/ *phr* to look for the good qualities that someone has
see the worst in (sb) /ˌsiː ðə 'wɜːst ɪn/ *phr* to look for the bad qualities that someone has
strength /streŋθ/ *n* a good quality or ability that makes someone or something effective
take an opportunity /ˌteɪk ən ˌɒpə'tjuːnəti/ *phr* to use an occasion to do or say something
weakness /'wiːknəs/ *n* a particular part or quality of someone or something that is not good or effective

ADJECTIVE AND NOUN SUFFIXES

active /'æktɪv/ *adj* doing a lot of things, or moving around a lot
beneficial /ˌbenə'fɪʃəl/ *adj* helpful, useful or good
competition /ˌkɒmpə'tɪʃən/ *n* a situation in which someone is trying to win something or be more successful than someone else
dangerous /'deɪndʒərəs/ *adj* a dangerous situation or thing could harm you
driverless /'draɪvələs/ *adj* (of a vehicle) not having a person as a driver
emotional /ɪ'məʊʃənəl/ *adj* relating to emotions
enjoyment /ɪn'dʒɔɪmənt/ *n* the feeling of enjoying something
majority /mə'dʒɒrəti/ *n* more than half of a group of people or things
personality /ˌpɜːsən'æləti/ *n* the way you are as a person
professional /prə'feʃənəl/ *adj* relating to work that needs special training or education
recognisable /ˌrekəg'naɪzəbəl/ *adj* easy to recognise
relationship /rɪ'leɪʃənʃɪp/ *n* the way two people or groups feel and behave towards each other
remarkable /rɪ'mɑːkəbl/ *adj* very unusual or noticeable in a way that you admire
satisfaction /ˌsætɪs'fækʃən/ *n* the pleasant feeling you have when you get something that you wanted or do something that you wanted to do
settlement /'setəlmənt/ *n* a place where people come to live
useful /'juːsfəl/ *adj* helping you to do or achieve something
valuable /'væljʊbl/ *adj* Valuable information, advice, etc. is very helpful or important.

UNIT 10

PHRASES WITH *IN, OUT OF, AT, BY*

at fault /ət 'fɒlt/ *phr* responsible for something bad that has happened
at risk /ət 'rɪsk/ *phr* being in a situation where something bad is likely to happen
by accident /baɪ 'æksɪdənt/ *phr* without intending to
by chance /baɪ 'tʃɑːns/ *phr* when something happens because of luck, or without being planned
in advance /ɪn əd'vɑːns/ *phr* before a particular time, or before doing a particular thing
in all /ɪn 'ɔːl/ *phr* used to show the total amount of something
in detail /ɪn 'diːteɪl/ *phr* including or considering all the information about something or every part of something
in secret /ɪn 'siːkrət/ *phr* without telling other people
out of character /ˌaʊt əv 'kærɪktə/ *phr* unusual in terms of someone's personality
out of nowhere /ˌaʊt əv 'nəʊweə/ *phr* If someone or something appears out of nowhere, it appears suddenly or unexpectedly.

EXTENDED MEANINGS OF WORDS

angel /'eɪndʒəl/ *n* someone who is very good, helpful or kind
boiling /'bɔɪlɪŋ/ *adj* very hot
bright /braɪt/ *adj* having the possibility of success or happiness
flood /flʌd/ *v* to fill or enter a place in large numbers or amounts
foggy /'fɒgi/ *adj* vague and unclear
freeze /friːz/ *v* to suddenly stop moving, especially because you are frightened
frozen /'frəʊzən/ *adj* not moving, absolutely still
grill /grɪl/ *v* to ask someone a lot of questions for a long time
hit /hɪt/ *v* to affect something badly
lift (sb's) mood /ˌlɪft 'muːd/ *phr* to make someone happier
sail through (sth) /'seɪl θruː/ *pv* to succeed very easily in something, especially a test
stormy /'stɔːmi/ *adj* full of difficulties or fights
weigh up /weɪ 'ʌp/ *pv* to consider something carefully, especially in order to make a decision

UNIT 11

PHRASAL VERBS: RELATIONSHIPS

count on (sb) /ˈkaʊnt ɒn/ *pv* to be confident that you can depend on someone
fall out (with) (sb) /fɔːl ˈaʊt/ *pv* to argue with someone and stop being friendly with them
finish with (sb) /ˈfɪnɪʃ wɪð/ *pv* to end a romantic relationship with someone
go off (sb/sth) /gəʊ ˈɒf/ *pv* to stop liking or being interested in someone or something
hit it off (with) /hɪt ɪt ˈɒf/ *pv* If people hit it off, they like each other and become friendly immediately.
let (sb) down /let ˈdaʊn/ *pv* to disappoint someone by failing to do what you agreed to do or were expected to do
look down on (sb) /lʊk ˈdaʊn ɒn/ *pv* to think that you are better than someone
look up to (sb) /lʊk ˈʌp tuː/ *pv* to admire and respect someone
stick together /ˌstɪk təˈgeðə/ *pv* If people stick together, they support and help each other.
take after (sb) /teɪk ˈɑːftə/ *pv* to be similar to an older member of your family in appearance or character

COMPOUND ADJECTIVES

badly behaved /ˌbædli bɪˈheɪvd/ *adj* behaving in a way that is accepted as incorrect
grown-up /ˈgrəʊn ʌp/ *adj* If you say that someone is grown-up, you mean that they are an adult or that they behave in a responsible way.
high-tech /haɪ ˈtek/ *adj* using or involved with the most recent and advanced electronic machines, computers, etc.
last-minute /lɑːst ˈmɪnɪt/ *adj* done at the latest possible opportunity
long-distance /lɒŋ ˈdɪstəns/ *adj* travelling or communicating between two places that are a long way apart
middle-aged /mɪdl ˈeɪdʒd/ *adj* in the middle of your life before you are old
self-confident /self ˈkɒnfɪdənt/ *adj* feeling sure about yourself and your abilities
short-term /ˈʃɔːt tɜːm/ *adj* lasting a short time, or relating to a short period of time
well-balanced /wel ˈbælənst/ *adj* A well-balanced diet or meal includes all the different types of food that the body needs to be healthy.
well-built /wel ˈbɪlt/ *adj* having a large, strong body
well-organised /wel ˈɔːgənaɪzd/ *adj* planned and arranged in a good way, to a high or satisfactory standard
well-paid /wel ˈpeɪd/ *adj* earning or paying a lot of money

UNIT 12

VERBS OF COMMUNICATION

amuse /əˈmjuːz/ *v* to make someone laugh or smile
cheer (sb) up /ˈtʃɪər ˈʌp/ *pv* If someone cheers up, or something cheers them up, they start to feel happier.
congratulate /kənˈgrætjʊleɪt/ *v* to tell someone that you are happy because they have done something good or something good has happened to them
highlight /ˈhaɪlaɪt/ *v* to attract attention to or emphasise something important
promote /prəˈməʊt/ *v* to encourage the popularity, sale, development or existence of something
reassure /ˌriːəˈʃɔː/ *v* to comfort someone and stop them from worrying
speak out /spiːk ˈaʊt/ *pv* to say in public what you think about something such as a law, an official plan or an important issue
spread /spred/ *v* to make a lot of people have a certain feeling
stimulate /ˈstɪmjʊleɪt/ *v* to make someone excited or interested about something

BOTH, EITHER, NEITHER

both /bəʊθ/ *pron, det* (referring to) two people or things together
either /ˈaɪðə, ˈiːðə/ *pron, det* used when referring to a choice between two possiblities
either … or /ˈaɪðə, ˈiːðə … ɔː/ *conj* used to connect two choices
neither /ˈnaɪðə, ˈniːðə/ *pron, det* not either of two things or people
neither … nor /ˈnaɪðə, ˈniːðə … nɔː/ *conj* used when you want to say that two or more things are not true

UNIT 13

LEADERSHIP AND ACHIEVEMENT

bossy /ˈbɒsi/ *adj* A bossy person is always telling people what to do.
conscientious /ˌkɒnʃiˈenʃəs/ *adj* putting a lot of effort into your work
doubt /daʊt/ *v* to not feel certain or confident about something
drive /draɪv/ *n* energy and determination to achieve things
fairly /ˈfeəli/ *adv* If you do something fairly, you do it in a way which is right and reasonable and treats people equally.
motivated /ˈməʊtɪveɪtɪd/ *adj* enthusiastic and determined to succeed
put your mind to (sth) /ˌpʊt jə ˈmaɪnd tə/ *phr* to decide that you are going to do something and to put a lot of effort into doing it
self-esteem /ˌself ɪˈstiːm/ *n* belief and confidence in your own ability and value
stand out /stænd ˈaʊt/ *pv* to be better than or different to other people or things
sympathetic /sɪmpəˈθetɪk/ *adj* showing that you understand and care about someone's problems
target /ˈtɑːgɪt/ *n* something that you intend to achieve

PHRASAL VERBS WITH *UP*

come up /kʌm ˈʌp/ *pv* to move towards someone
keep up /kiːp ˈʌp/ *pv* to move at the same speed as someone or something that is moving forward
live up to /lɪv ˈʌp tuː/ *pv* to be as good as someone hopes
make (sth) up /meɪk ˈʌp/ *pv* to say or write something that is not true
set up /set ˈʌp/ *pv* to start a new company, organisation, system, way of working, etc.
speak up /spiːk ˈʌp/ *pv* to speak in a louder voice so that people can hear you
turn up /tɜːn ˈʌp/ *pv* to arrive or appear somewhere

UNIT 14

PHRASAL VERBS: TRANSPORT

break down /breɪk ˈdaʊn/ *pv* (of a vehicle or machine) to stop working for a period of time
drive off /draɪv ˈɒf/ *pv* to leave in a car or other vehicle
hold up /həʊld ˈʌp/ *pv* to make something or someone slow or late
keep up with (sb or sth) /kiːp ˈʌp wɪð/ *pv* to move at the same speed as someone or something that is moving forward so that you stay level with them
pull into /pʊl ˈɪntuː/ *pv* If a vehicle pulls in or pulls into somewhere, it moves in that direction and stops there.
pull out /pʊl ˈaʊt/ *pv* If a train pulls out, it starts to leave a station.

EP VOCABULARY LIST

pull over /pʊl 'əʊvə/ *pv* If a vehicle pulls over, it moves to the side of the road and stops.

pull up /pʊl 'ʌp/ *pv* If a vehicle pulls up, it stops, often for a short time.

run into /rʌn 'ɪntə/ *pv* to drive a vehicle into an object or a person in another vehicle by accident

run over /rʌn 'əʊvə/ *pv* If a vehicle or its driver runs over someone or something, the vehicle hits and drives over them or it.

slow down /sləʊ 'daʊn/ *pv* to become slower, or to make someone or something become slower

speed up /spi:d 'ʌp/ *pv* to go or happen faster, or to cause something to happen faster

REPORTING VERBS

agree /ə'gri:/ *v* to say you will do something that someone asks you to

confess /kən'fes/ *v* to admit that you have done something wrong or something that you feel guilty or bad about

enquire /ɪn'kwaɪə/ *v* to ask someone for information about something

forbid /fə'bɪd/ *v* to refuse to allow something, especially officially, or to prevent a particular plan of action by making it impossible

insist /ɪn'sɪst/ *v* to demand that something must be done or that you must have a particular thing; to say firmly that something is true

persuade /pə'sweɪd/ *v* to make someone do or believe something by giving them a good reason to do it

point out /pɔɪnt 'aʊt/ *pv* to tell someone about some information, often because they do not know it or have forgotten it

recommend /rekə'mend/ *v* to advise someone that something should be done

UNIT 15

GLOBAL ISSUES: NOUNS AND VERBS

ban /bæn/ *v* to forbid something, especially officially

ban /bæn/ *n* an official order that prevents something from happening

collect /kə'lekt/ *v* to ask people to give you money, or sometimes food or clothes, for something, for example a charity

collection /kə'lekʃən/ *n* when money, food or clothes are collected for something, for example a charity

cooperate /kəʊ'ɒpəreɪt/ *v* to work together with someone in order to achieve the same aim

cooperation /kəʊɒpər'eɪʃən/ *n* when you work together with someone or do what they ask you

criticise /'krɪtɪsaɪz/ *v* to say that someone or something is bad

criticism /'krɪtɪsɪzəm/ *n* when you say that something or someone is bad

elect /ɪ'lekt/ *v* to choose someone for a particular job or position by voting

election /ɪ'lekʃən/ *n* a time when people vote in order to choose someone for a political or official job

support /sə'pɔ:t/ *v* to agree with an idea, group or person

supporter /sə'pɔ:tə/ *n* someone who supports a particular idea, group or person

PHRASES WITH *IN*

in actual fact /ɪn ˌæktʃuəl 'fækt/ *phr* really

in favour of /ɪn 'feɪvər əv/ *phr* supporting or approving of something

in general /ɪn 'dʒenrəl/ *phr* considering the whole of someone or something, and not just a particular part of them

in the light of /ɪn ðə 'laɪt əv/ *phr* because of

in progress /ɪn 'prəʊgres/ *phr* happening or being done now

in turn /ɪn 'tɜ:n/ *phr* one after another

UNIT 16

ADVERTISING: NOUNS AND VERBS

ad break /'æd breɪk/ *n* a short interruption of a television or radio programme to broadcast advertisements

appeal to /ə'pi:l tə/ *v* to interest or attract someone

be aimed at /bi: 'eɪmd ət/ *v* If information is aimed at a particular group of people, it is made known in a way that influences them or makes them interested in something.

consumer /kən'sju:mə/ *n* a person who buys goods or services for their own use

launch /lɔ:ntʃ/ *v* If a company launches a product or service, it makes it available for the first time.

product placement /'prɒdʌkt ˌpleɪsmənt/ *n* a way of advertising a product by supplying it for use in films or television programmes

sample /'sɑ:mpl/ *n* a small amount of something that shows you what it is like

sponsor /'spɒnsə/ *v* to give money to someone to support an activity, event or organisation, sometimes as a way to advertise your company or product

ADVERB + ADJECTIVE COLLOCATIONS

ecologically safe /i:kə'lɒdʒɪkli seɪf/ not dangerous or damaging to ecology or the environment

environmentally friendly /ɪnvaɪərəˌmentəli 'frendli/ not harmful to the environment

financially independent /faɪ'nænʃəli ˌɪndɪ'pendənt/ having enough money to live, without needing other people to give you money or to pay for things for you

globally recognised/'gləʊbəli 'rekəgnaɪzd/ well known all over the world

incredibly economical /ɪn'kredɪbli i:kə'nɒmɪkəl/ using very little fuel, money, etc.

regularly updated /'regjələli ʌp'deɪtɪd/ If something is regularly updated, new information or facts are frequently added to it.

scientifically proven /ˌsaɪən'tɪfɪkli 'pru:vən/ shown to be true by science

well-balanced /ˌwel 'bælənst/ A well-balanced diet or meal includes all the different types of food that the body needs to be healthy.

UNIT 17

THE MEDIA

celebrate achievements /'selɪbreɪt ə'tʃi:vmənts/ *phr* to express admiration for something very good and difficult that someone has succeeded in doing

comment on current events /'kɒment ɒn 'kʌrənt ɪ'vents/ *phr* to give your opinions about events that are being reported in the news

cover a story /'kʌvər ə 'stɔ:ri/ *phr* to report the news about a particular event

gossip (about) /'gɒsɪp/ *v* to talk about other people's private lives

keep (sb) amused /ˌki:p ə'mju:zd/ *phr* to help someone feel interested and happy

keep (sb) up to date /ˌki:p ʌp tə 'deɪt/ *phr* to give someone the latest information

make fun of /meɪk 'fʌn əv/ *phr* to make a joke about someone or something in a way that is not kind

make headlines /meɪk 'hedlaɪnz/ *phr* to be a featured story in the newspapers or in TV/radio news

PHRASAL VERBS: THE MEDIA

back (sb) up /bæk 'ʌp/ *pv* to support or help someone
bring (sth) up /brɪŋ 'ʌp/ *pv* to start to talk about a particular subject
catch up on /kætʃ 'ʌp ɒn/ *pv* to learn the newest facts about something
clear (sth) up /klɪər 'ʌp/ *pv* to give or find an explanation for something, or to deal with a problem or argument
follow up /ˌfɒləʊ 'ʌp/ *pv* to find out more about something, or take further action connected with it
get (sth) across /get ə'krɒs/ *pv* to manage to make someone understand or believe something
leave out /liːv 'aʊt/ *pv* to not include someone or something
look into /lʊk 'ɪntuː/ *pv* to examine the facts about a situation

UNIT 18

THE WORLD OF WORK

badly paid /ˌbædli 'peɪd/ *adj* not earning or paying a lot of money
deadline /'dedlaɪn/ *n* a time/day by when something must be done
make a living /ˌmeɪk ə 'lɪvɪŋ/ *phr* to earn enough money to buy the things you need
rewarding /rɪ'wɔːdɪŋ/ *adj* making you feel satisfied that you have done something important or useful
shift /ʃɪft/ *n* When people work shifts, they work for set periods of time during the day or night.
take time off /teɪk taɪm 'ɒf/ *phr* to stop work in order to do something else
well paid /wel 'peɪd/ *adj* earning a lot of money
work long hours /ˌwɜːk lɒŋ 'aʊəz/ *phr* to spend a lot of time each day at work

WORD PAIRS

more and more /'mɔːr ən 'mɔː/ *phr* increasingly, as time passes
more or less /'mɔːr ɔː 'les/ *phr* almost or approximately
now and then /'naʊ ən 'ðen/ *phr* If something happens now and then, it happens sometimes but not very often.
one or two /'wʌn ɔː 'tuː/ *phr* a few
over and over (again) /'əʊvər ən 'əʊvə/ *phr* happening or done many times
round and round /'raʊnd ən 'raʊnd/ *phr* moving in a circle
sooner or later /'suːnər ɔː 'leɪtə/ *phr* used to say that you do not know exactly when something will happen, but you are certain that it will happen
up and down /'ʌp ən 'daʊn/ *adv* in one direction and then in the opposite direction, especially repeatedly

UNIT 19

OPINIONS AND BELIEFS

as far as I'm concerned /əz 'fɑːr əz 'aɪm kən'sɜːnd/ *phr* in my opinion
be convinced by (sth) /biː kən'vɪnsd baɪ/ *phr* to be certain that something is true
be totally against /biː 'təʊtəli ə'genst/ *phr* to strongly disagree with a plan or activity
bear in mind /'beər ɪn 'maɪnd/ *phr* to remember a piece of information when you are making a decision or thinking about something
believe in /bɪ'liːv ɪn/ *pv* to be confident that something is effective and right
firmly /'fɜːmli/ *adv* strongly
go along with (sth/sb) /ˌgəʊ ə'lɒŋ wɪð/ *pv* to support an idea, or to agree with someone's opinion
It's hard to deny (that) /iːts 'hɑːd te dɪn'aɪ/ *phr* used to say that something is clearly true
keep an open mind /ˌkiːp ən 'əʊpən 'maɪnd/ *phr* to not have a fixed opinion about something
suspect /sə'spekt/ *v* to think that something is probably true, or is likely to happen
there's no doubt /ðeəz 'nəʊ 'daʊt/ *phr* used to emphasise that what you are saying is true or likely to happen
to my mind /tə 'maɪ 'maɪnd/ *phr* used to emphasise that you are giving your own opinion
view /vjuː/ *n* opinion

PLURAL NOUNS

belongings /bɪ'lɑŋɪŋz/ *n* the things that a person owns, especially those which can be carried
clothes /kləʊðz/ *n* things such as dresses and trousers that you wear to cover, protect or decorate your body
contents /'kɑntents/ *n* a list in a book that tells you what different parts of the book contain
lyrics /'lɪrɪks/ *n* the words of a song
outskirts /'aʊtskɜːts/ *n* the areas that form the edge of a town or city
refreshments /rɪ'freʃmənts/ *n* food and drinks that are available at a meeting, at an event, on a journey, etc.
savings /'seɪvɪŋz/ *n* the money you keep, especially in a bank or other financial organisation, and which you do not use for day-to-day living
surroundings /sə'rɑʊndɪŋz/ *n* the place where someone lives and the conditions they live in

UNIT 20

IDIOMS

be a pain /biː ə 'peɪn/ *id* to be annoying
be a piece of cake /biː ə 'piːs əv 'keɪk/ *id* to be very easy
break (sb's) heart /'breɪk 'hɑːt/ *id* If an event or situation breaks your heart, it makes you feel very sad.
break the ice /'breɪk ðiː 'aɪs/ *id* to make people feel more relaxed in a social situation
cross (sb's) mind /'krɒs 'maɪnd/ *id* If something crosses your mind, you think about it for a short time.
have an eye for (sth) /ˌhæv ən 'aɪ fɔː/ *id* to be good at noticing a particular type of thing
lose track of time /luːz 'træk əv 'taɪm/ *id* to not be aware of what time it is
take (sb's) breath away /teɪk 'breθ ə'weɪ/ *id* to make someone feel surprise and admiration

COMMONLY CONFUSED WORDS

damage /'dæmɪdʒ/ *v* to harm, break or spoil something
fun /fʌn/ *n* pleasure, enjoyment or entertainment
funny /'fʌni/ *adj* humorous, causing laughter
guess /ges/ *v* to give an answer to a particular question when you do not have all the facts and so cannot be certain if you are correct
harm /hɑːm/ *v* to hurt someone or damage something
injure /'ɪndʒə/ *v* to hurt a person, animal or part of your body
journey /'dʒɜːni/ *n* the act of travelling from one place to another, especially in a vehicle
know /nəʊ/ *v* to have information in your mind, be certain
means /miːnz/ *n* a method or way of doing something
observe /əb'zɜːv/ *v* to watch someone or something carefully
opportunity /ɒpə'tjuːnəti/ *n* a situation in which it is possible for you to do something, or a possibility of doing something
possibility /pɒsə'bɪləti/ *n* a chance that something may happen or be true
way /weɪ/ *n* an action that can produce the result you want; a method; a route, direction or path

GRAMMAR REFERENCE AND PRACTICE

UNIT 1 SIMPLE, CONTINUOUS OR PERFECT

Present perfect

- We use the **present perfect** (***has/have*** + past participle) for events which happened some time before or up to the present if we do not mention when they happened. We often use it with ***still … not, not … yet, just, already, before, ever, never, the first*** (***second***, etc.) ***time, since*** and ***for***.
  *They **still haven't** repaired my bike.*
  *I**'ve just had** lunch.*
  *They **have never eaten** spicy food.*
  *We **haven't seen** him **since** last week.*
  *They **haven't repaired** my bike **yet**.*
  *The plane **has already left**.*
  ***Have** you **ever ridden** a motorbike?*
  *This is **the first time I've tried** this dish.*

Past perfect

- We use the **past perfect** (***had*** + past participle) for events which happened some time before or up to a point in the past. Like the present perfect, we often use it with ***still … not, not … yet, just, already, before, ever, never, the first*** (***second***, etc.) ***time, since*** and ***for***.
  *I phoned the shop, but they **still hadn't** repaired my bike.*
  *I**'d just had** lunch, so I didn't go for a swim.*
  *They**'d never eaten** such spicy food, but they really enjoyed it.*
  *We **hadn't seen** him **since** the previous week and were very relieved when he turned up.*

Past simple

- We use the **past simple** (regular form: verb + ***-ed***) for completed events in the past which answer the question *when?*.
  *I **visited** China twice **last year**.*
  *I **stayed** there **for three weeks**.*
  *I **swam every day last summer**.*

Practice

1 **Complete the answers with the correct form of the verbs in brackets: present perfect, past perfect or past simple.**

1. Where did you get the idea for that painting?
   I ________ (want) to do a landscape that ________ (look) like a place no one ________ (see) before.
2. How old were you when you started learning the guitar?
   I think I ________ (be) 11 because I ________ (already/start) secondary school.
3. What do you think of my car?
   I ________ (never see) anything like it! Where ________ (find/you) it?

Present continuous

- We use the **present continuous** (***am/is/are*** (***not***) + verb + ***-ing***) for events which are happening now; for temporary or changing situations; with ***always*** to express annoyance or for repeated events.
  *He**'s making** coffee.*
  *The price of coffee **is going** up.*
  *My brother **is always borrowing** my phone.*

Past continuous

- We use the **past continuous** (***was/were*** (***not***) + verb + ***-ing***) for past events which are happening at the same time; for events happening around the time of another past event (in the past simple); with ***always*** to express annoyance; for temporary or changing situations; and for plans which didn't succeed or were changed later.
  *He **was making** coffee and I **was opening** the biscuits.*
  *I **was opening** the tin when I cut my finger.*
  *My sister **was always borrowing** my phone.*
  *We **were staying** at the Grand Hotel before we found this house.*
  *They **were hoping** to win the election, but no one voted for them.*

Practice

2 **Underline the verbs in the sentence beginnings (1–6) and the endings (a–f), then match the halves.**

1. We want to move house because ☐
2. I'm taking sandwiches to school this week because ☐
3. My brother was sailing round Ibiza while ☐
4. When my parents got home, ☐
5. I want to get a new phone because ☐
6. I was planning to take a holiday after my exams, but ☐

a this one is always crashing.
b his school friends were doing exams.
c I didn't have enough money.
d the traffic is getting so bad round here.
e we were all eating pizza in the kitchen.
f the kitchen is closed for repairs.

3 **Match each sentence in Exercise 2 to the different uses (A–F).**

A for past events which were happening at the same time
B for an event happening around the time of another past event
C continuous tense with *always* to express annoyance
D for plans which didn't succeed
E for a temporary situation
F for a changing situation

UNIT 2 PRESENT PERFECT SIMPLE AND CONTINUOUS

We use the **present perfect simple** and **present perfect continuous** for events which happened some time before or up to the present (we do not mention when).
We use the **present perfect simple** to talk about

- a completed action, especially one which has a present result.
  *She**'s designed** this computer game. What do you think of it?*
  (The game is ready to play.)
- how often something has happened before now.
  *I**'ve visited** that shop three times.*

» SEE PAGE 148 FOR FORM OF PRESENT PERFECT

We use the **present perfect continuous** (***has/have*** (***not***) ***been*** + past participle) to talk about

- an action that may or may not be complete, where the focus is on the action more than the result.
  *He**'s been designing** a computer game.*
  (We don't know if it's ready to play, perhaps he's still working on it.)
- how long something has been happening, up to and possibly including the present moment.
  *She**'s been trying to find a bag like yours** for weeks.*
  (We don't know if she's found one yet.)

NOTE We do not use the present continuous to say how long something has been happening.
~~*She's trying to find a bag like yours for weeks.*~~
Some common verbs describe actions which normally last for a period of time, so their meanings are not usually different in the present perfect simple or continuous. They include: ***live, stay, study, wait, work***.
*I**'ve worked** in the fashion industry for 30 years.*
*I**'ve been working** in the fashion industry for 30 years.*

Practice

1 Complete the sentences with the present perfect continuous of the verbs in brackets.

0 The students *have been doing* (do) research on British fashion in the 1960s.
1 .... (you/wait) long?
2 You .... (not listen) to what I .... (tell) you.
3 My brother .... (mend) his bike in the kitchen. It's a terrible mess!
4 I .... (walk) round the shops all morning looking for a present for my mum.
5 The bathroom floor is very wet. .... (the children/play) in there?
6 We don't know where Erin is. She .... (not live) at this address for some time.

2 Which pairs of sentences mean the same and which are different? Where they are different, explain why.

1 I haven't worked here since last May.
I haven't been working here since last May.
....
2 I've cleaned the car.
I've been cleaning the car.
....
3 Have you been living in Africa for a long time?
Have you lived in Africa for a long time?
....
4 I've cooked lunch.
I've been cooking lunch.
....
5 I haven't driven that car.
I haven't been driving that car.
....

3 Choose the correct options. In some places, both forms are correct; which are they?

I'm working on my final art project at the moment and [1] *I've nearly finished / I've nearly been finishing*. For the past six weeks, [2] *I've designed / I've been designing* men's clothes for a variety of occasions, such as a wedding, a job interview and a trip to see a football match. [3] *I've looked / I've been looking* at websites of famous designers to see how they present their work. [4] *I've also visited / I've also been visiting* the Costume Museum in Bath twice, to get ideas from historical costumes. [5] *I haven't spent / I haven't been spending* too much money on the fabric samples. I love all kinds of interesting patterns and textures, and [6] *I've collected / I've been collecting* fabrics since I was quite young, so I had plenty to choose from.

4 Write sentences about yourself or a friend, using the words given and putting the verbs into the present perfect continuous.

1 live / my present address for …
....
2 study / English since …
....
3 support / … football team for …
....
4 wear / these clothes since …
....

GRAMMAR REFERENCE AND PRACTICE

UNIT 3 THE GRAMMAR OF PHRASAL VERBS

A phrasal verb is a verb + particle(s). A particle is an adverb or a preposition.

Phrasal verb patterns

verb + adverb with no object

- These phrasal verbs never have an object.
  *Most of the musicians were fairly good, but the drummer really **stood out**.*

verb + adverb + object / verb + object + adverb

- These phrasal verbs always have an object.
- The object can go after the adverb or between the verb and the adverb.
  *I had lots of good ideas, but the boss **turned** all my suggestions **down**.*
  *I had lots of good ideas, but the boss **turned down** all my suggestions.*
- When the object is a pronoun, it must go between the verb and the adverb.
  *I had lots of good ideas, but the boss **turned them down**.*
  NOT *… ~~but the boss turned down them.~~*

verb + preposition + object

- These verbs always have an object.
- The object must go after the preposition, even if it is a pronoun.
  ***Look after this document** carefully, it's very important.*
  NOT *~~Look this document after carefully, …~~*
  ***Look after it** carefully, it's very important.* **NOT** *~~Look it after carefully, …~~*

verb + adverb + preposition + object

- These verbs always have an object.
- The object must go after the preposition, even if it is a pronoun.
  *I missed a lot of classes, so it's hard to **catch up with** the other students.*
  *I missed a lot of classes, so it's hard to **catch up with** them.*
- If you look up a phrasal verb in a good dictionary, it will tell you which pattern it follows and give you examples of different meanings.

Phrasal verb meanings

- The meaning of some phrasal verbs is easy to understand.
  *The boy **picked up** the box.*
  *The students **handed in** their work to the teacher.*
- The meaning of many phrasal verbs is less easy to guess, but the context may help.
  *You can't **count on** Nigel in an emergency.*
  *In the end, it **turned out** that we didn't need his help.*
- Some phrasal verbs have more than one meaning.
  *I don't know what the boys are doing, they'**ve gone off** somewhere.*
  *She set her alarm to **go off** at 5.30, as she didn't want to oversleep.*
  *There was bad storm and all the lights **went off**.*
  *Put the milk in the fridge, or it'**ll go off**.*
  *She used to enjoy yoga, but she's **gone off** it recently.*

Practice

1 Rewrite the sentences, replacing the words in bold with a pronoun in the correct position.

0 He doesn't want to go to the dentist, but he can't put off **the appointment** again.
He doesn't want to go to the dentist, but he can't put it off again.

1 I borrowed £15 from Mum and I promised I'd pay back **the money** at the weekend.
______

2 Is this an idea you've heard from someone else, or did you make up **the story** yourself?
______

3 We've decided to go to Holland for a few days and we're really looking forward to **our holiday**.
______

2 Replace the verbs in bold with the correct form of the phrasal verbs in the box.

break down	come across	get down
get into	go by	pass on	~~stand by~~
take up	think about	

Dear Joe,

I'm writing to say thank you for [0]**supporting** *standing by* me these past few weeks. When my friendship with Peter [1]**ended** ______ , I never expected him to accuse me of those things. I may [2]**seem** ______ as if I'm calm now, but really I'm not. As you can imagine, the whole business has really [3]**made me feel sad** ______ me ______ . Other friends tell me to [4]**start** ______ some new hobby, but I can't [5]**become interested in** ______ anything yet. Perhaps when a few months [6]**have passed** ______ , I may [7]**consider** ______ it. Please [8]**give** ______ my best wishes to your brother.

See you soon I hope,

Mike

3 Complete these sentences with your own ideas.

0 No one has the right to look down on *people who have less money than them.*

1 Police officers sometimes have to put up with ______

2 Have you ever given someone a present to make up for ______

3 Emotional maturity means being able to face up to ______

4 Working in the hotel business, I have to get on with ______

5 The children of successful parents may have trouble living up to ______

UNIT 4

MODALS (1): NECESSITY, OBLIGATION, PROHIBITION AND ADVICE

Necessity, obligation, prohibition

Necessity = The speaker believes it is necessary to do this: ***need to*** / ***need*** + verb.
*You **need to** take a fitness test to join the team.*
***Do** I **need to** / **Need** I take a fitness test before I join the team?*
*I **don't need to** / I **needn't** take a fitness test before I join the team.*
NOTE ***need*** is not used alone in positive statements, you can't say ~~I need pass a fitness test~~.
Obligation = The speaker believes it is obligatory to do this, there is no choice: ***must*** / ***have to*** / ***'ve got to*** + verb.

- We can often use any of these forms:
  *You **must** / **have to** / **'ve got to** pass a fitness test to join the team.*
- We usually prefer ***must*** or ***'ve got to*** when the idea comes from the speaker, to give an order or express a feeling.
  *You **must** show me your new boots!*
  ***I've got to** buy some new shorts, these are too small.*
- We usually prefer ***have to*** when the obligation is not the speaker's idea, for example to explain a rule.
  *She **has to** wear a red sweatshirt for training.*
  *We **have to** play until the whistle is blown.*

NOTE For the past of ***must***, we use ***had to***.
Lack of obligation = The speaker believes it is not necessary to do this, although it is possible. There is a choice: ***don't have to*** / ***haven't got to*** / ***don't need to*** / ***needn't*** + verb.
*You **don't have to** / **haven't got to** / **don't need to** / **needn't** pass a fitness test to join the team.*
Prohibition = The speaker believes you are not allowed to do this: ***mustn't***.
*You **mustn't** play football in the classroom.*

Practice

1 Choose the correct modal verbs in the email.

> When I leave school, I want to study sports science, so I'm working in a fitness club twice a week. I [1]*must / had to / needed* have an interview before I began work, but I [2]*didn't have to / mustn't / haven't got to* have any experience. I [3]*have / needn't / got* to be at the club by 6 pm and I finish at nine, so it's not bad. I [4]*must / have to / had to* stand behind the desk and check the members' cards when they come in. They [5]*don't have / mustn't / needn't* to bring anything with them except sports clothes and trainers because we supply towels. Sometimes I [6]*need / must / needn't* to remind them about the club rules. They [7]*haven't got to / mustn't / don't have to* wear outdoor shoes in the gym, for example, because they damage the floor.

Advice

Giving advice = The speaker believes it is the right thing to do.

- ***Should(n't)*** / ***ought(n't / not) to*** + verb can usually be used in the same way.
  *You **should** / **ought to** discuss your training programme with your sports teacher.*
  *You **shouldn't** / **ought not to** miss football practice if you're in the team.*

Asking for advice = The speaker wants to know someone's opinion about what to do.

- ***Should I*** / ***Ought I to*** + verb?
  ***Should I** / **Ought I to** see the doctor before I play in a match?*
  *How much money **should** we / **ought** we **to** take with us?*

Practice

2 Complete the questions asking for advice, first using ***should***, then using ***ought to***.

1 buying new shoes for a party
Which pair .... buy?
Which pair .... buy?
2 choosing a present for a cousin you don't know well
What .... get for my cousin?
What .... get for my cousin?
3 eating a healthy diet
What kinds of food .... eat and what kinds .... avoid?
What kinds of food .... eat and what kinds .... avoid?

3 Write three pieces of advice for a friend who wants to be a professional sportsman or woman.

1 You should ....
2 You ought not to ....
3 You shouldn't ....

4 Write new sentences with the same meaning. Use a modal verb. Can you write more than one new sentence for some of them?

1 You can bring your own towel but it's not necessary.
You can bring your own towel but
....
2 I advise you to talk to your teacher.
You ....
3 You are not allowed to bring food into the shop.
You ....
4 This school insists that students wear uniform.
Students at this school
....
5 Do you advise me to phone my brother?
............?
6 I insist that you allow me to help you.
You ....

GRAMMAR REFERENCE AND PRACTICE

UNIT 5 PRESENT AND PAST HABITS

Present habits

- We often use the **present simple** with an adverb of frequency to talk about present habits.
  *He **drinks** coffee in the morning **once in a while**.*
  *He **doesn't always/usually/often/normally drink** coffee in the morning.*
  ***Does he drink** coffee in the morning **all the time**?*
- We use ***always***, ***constantly*** and ***continually*** with the **present continuous** to express a complaint or a criticism.
  *She**'s always using** my phone and she never offers to pay for her calls.*
  *He**'s constantly leaving** dirty dishes on the table.*
- We can use the **present continuous** to describe something that's happening a lot, but it's only temporary and it isn't necessarily in progress at the moment of speaking.
  ***I'm not going out** a lot because I'm studying for an exam.*
  ***Is** Sara **having fun** on her judo course? Yes, she**'s loving** it.*

Past habits

- We use the **past simple** (sometimes with an adverb of frequency) to talk about past habits.
  *She **hardly ever visited** her sister when she was in Milan.*
  ***Did she visit** her sister **once in a while** when she was in Milan?*
  *She **didn't always/usually/often/normally visit** her sister when she was in Milan.*
  *Jon **played** bass guitar when he was in a band.*
  ***Did** you **read** comics as a child?*
- We can also use ***would*** to describe a past habit.
  *He **would always tidy** his desk before leaving the room.*
  *They **wouldn't normally put** their bags on the table.*
- We use ***used to*** to describe a habit or state in the past.
  *He **always used to tidy** his desk before leaving the room.*
  *They **didn't normally use to put** their bags on the table.*
  *She **used to live** in Brighton.* **NOT** ~~*She would live in Brighton.*~~
- We use ***always***, ***constantly*** and ***continually*** with the **past continuous** to express a complaint or a criticism.
  *They **were continually asking** for more money.*

Practice

1 Write sentences criticising the people, using a continuous tense and the adverbs in brackets.

0 A driver who crashed his car. (constantly)
He was constantly crashing his car.

1 A company that advertises special offers. (always)
They ______

2 A student who handed her assignments in late. (always)
She ______

3 A man who shouts at his children. (continually)
He ______

4 A cat that brings mice into the house. (constantly)
It ______

5 A political party that promised jobs for everyone. (always)
They ______

2 Rewrite the sentences with the adverbs in brackets in the correct position.

0 The children go to bed before their parents. (seldom)
The children seldom go to bed before their parents.

1 My dad would have a snack in the afternoon. (regularly)
______

2 I didn't use to sleep more than six hours when I was young. (often)
______

3 Do you get enough sleep during the week? (usually)
______

4 A doctor wouldn't prescribe sleeping tablets for someone as young as you. (normally)
______

5 The factory workers were short of sleep and injured themselves as a result. (frequently / sometimes)
______

6 The students were yawning during lectures because they went to sleep before midnight. (continually / never)
______

7 I sleep very soundly, but I have nightmares and wake up shouting. (normally / from time to time)
______

8 Did you use to sleep in your parents' bed when you were little? (all the time)
______

3 Complete the sentences. Use the correct form of the verbs in bold.

1 I don't normally **walk** to school, but I ______ every day at the moment because my mum's car's broken down.

2 We hardly ever **go** to the beach these days, but we ______ all the time when I was younger.

3 We ______ a lot of fish at the moment, but we never used to **eat** it before.

4 ______ you ______ football after school when you were a kid? No, I've never **played** football.

UNIT 6 *BE/GET USED TO*

- ***be used to*** = be familiar with, be accustomed to (a permanent situation)
- ***get/become used to*** = become familiar with, become accustomed to (a changing situation)
  Get is used more often in speaking, ***become*** is used in more formal situations.
- Any tense of ***be/get/become*** can be used.
  *I'**m used to** … They **weren't used to** …*
  *You'**ll get used to** … She **hasn't got used to** …*
  *We **had become used to** …*, etc.
- ***be/get/become used to*** are followed by a noun or the *-ing* form of a verb.

*I'**m used to** spicy **food.***	→	*I'**m used to eating** spicy food.*
*They **weren't used to** such hard **work**.*	→	*They **weren't used to working** so hard.*
*You'**ll get used to*** city ***life*** soon.	→	*You'**ll get used to living*** in the city soon.
*She **hasn't got used to** this **laptop** yet.*	→	*She **hasn't got used to using** this laptop yet.*
*We **had become used to interruptions.***	→	*We **had become used to being interrupted.***

NOTE Do not confuse ***be/get/become used to*** + noun / *-ing* with ***used to do***, which is for past habits.

Practice

1 **Complete the paragraph with the verbs in the box.**

am used to | can't get used to | had been used to | have got used to | wasn't used to | were used to | weren't used to

I grew up in Birmingham, in a modern block of flats not far from the city centre. Two years ago, my parents decided to move to an old farmhouse deep in the countryside. My brothers and I [1] ______ country life now, but it was quite a shock at first. We [2] ______ being so far from shops, cafés and cinemas, and we [3] ______ spending our free time with our friends whenever we wanted. Now though, we know we must plan our social lives. When we first arrived, I [4] ______ the silence of the countryside at night. All my life, I [5] ______ hearing traffic, so it made me nervous. However, now I [6] ______ living somewhere so quiet, I [7] ______ the noise when I go to town!

2 **Complete the sentences about the experiences of Max, a medical student. Use *be/get/become used to* + a noun or *-ing*.**

0 Before he came to medical school, Max had never lived away from his parents.
He *wasn't used to living* away from his parents.

1 He still forgets to buy food for himself because his mother always did the shopping.
He ______ for himself.

2 He had never stayed up all night, but he often does night duty now.
He ______ all night.

3 He usually remembers to tidy his room, but not always.
He ______ his room.

4 He found it difficult to talk to patients at first, but now he enjoys it.
When he began his training, he ______ to patients.

GRAMMAR REFERENCE AND PRACTICE

UNIT 7 NARRATIVE TENSES

Past perfect simple v past perfect continuous

The **past perfect simple** and **continuous** are both used in describing events which were happening before the time of another past event.

We use the **past perfect simple**:

- to make clear a sequence of events in the past.
  *He didn't call me because he'**d lost** his phone.*
  (= 1 He lost his phone. 2 He didn't call me.)
- to contrast with past events introduced by ***by the time***, ***before***, ***as soon as*** or ***when***.
  *The band **had finished** their first song **by the time** we reached our seats.* (= 1 The band finished their first song. 2 We reached our seats.)
- with ***already***, ***just***, ***ever*** and ***never***.
  *When we arrived, everyone **had already started** dancing.* (= 1 Everyone started dancing. 2 We arrived.)
- to say how many times, or how often, something had happened before a point of time in the past.
  *I'**d visited** LA **four times** before my tenth birthday.*
  (= 1 I visited LA four times. 2 I had my tenth birthday.)

We use the **past perfect continuous** for describing events which were happening before the time of another past event. We use it

- to focus on the fact that the earlier event may or may not be complete.
  *We could tell that everyone **had been having** a good time.*
- when we talk about how long the event had been happening.
  *The tourists **had been walking** for two hours and wanted a chance to sit down.*

Practice

1 **Complete the sentences with past perfect simple or continuous of the verbs in brackets. Which verbs can be in either tense?**

0 Lizzie *had been staying* with her sister when her exam results came out, so they celebrated together. (stay)
1 Katie phoned her friends as soon as she ________ the tickets. (book)
2 The fields were covered in water because it ________ heavily for several days. (rain)
3 We ________ for the concert for weeks and were very disapponted when it was cancelled. (prepare)
4 I couldn't go to Jane's party because I ________ to babysit for my aunt. (already agree)
5 When I checked my phone, I discovered Simon ________ three times. (text)
6 We weren't surprised when we saw Nicky's new bike, because we knew she ________ to get one for ages. (want)

Past perfect v past simple

- We use the **past simple** and **past perfect** together to show that one event happened before another.
  *When I **walked** into the room, everyone **had stopped** talking.*
  (= 1 They stopped talking. 2 I walked into the room.)
  *Everyone **had been enjoying** the show when the rain **started**.*
  (= 1 They were enjoying themselves. 2 The rain started.)
- We use two past-simple verbs to show that two events happened at the same time.
  *When I **walked** into the room, everyone **stopped** talking.*
  (= They stopped talking at the moment I walked into the room – possibly because I walked into the room.)
  *Everyone **danced** when the band **played**.*
- We can use ***and*** to link the two past-simple verbs to suggest that one event caused another.
  *I **walked** into the room **and** everyone **stopped** talking.*
  (= They stopped talking at the moment I walked into the room – probably because I walked into the room.)
  *The rain **started and** everyone **went** indoors.*

Practice

2 **Complete the story with the past simple, past perfect simple or past perfect continuous of the verbs in the boxes.**

be (x2)	board	delay	give
go out	hear	move	wait

We had a dreadful journey home last night. There [1] ________ a thunderstorm earlier in the day, which [2] ________ lots of incoming flights, including our plane. We [3] ________ for three hours by the time we [4] ________ the plane. All the passengers [5] ________ in their seats, the flight attendants [6] ________ already ________ the safety talk and the plane [7] ________ onto the runway, when we [8] ________ a bang and all the lights [9] ________ .

arrive	be able to	cause	cheer	complete
eat	enjoy	get out	land	return	turn out

Of course, everyone was terrified. The plane [10] ________ to the departure building and we all [11] ________ . Luckily, it [12] ________ that a small electrical fault [13] ________ the problem. Once the safety checks [14] ________ , we [15] ________ take off.
It was seven hours since we [16] ________ at the airport and we [17] ________ anything all that time, so we [18] ________ the inflight meal more than we had expected to! And when we [19] ________ safely at the end of the flight, everyone [20] ________ !

Present tenses with future meaning

- We use the **present simple** for future events in a timetable and for people if they have a fixed schedule.
  The airport bus ***leaves*** *at ten minutes past every hour.*
  When ***does*** *the concert* ***start?***
- We use the **present continuous** for plans which have already been made.
  My brother and I ***are playing*** *football this afternoon.*
  (= We have already arranged this.)
  What ***are*** *the students* ***doing*** *tomorrow?*
  (= What have they arranged?)

going to and *will*

Going to and ***will*** can often be used in the same place with little or no difference in meaning.

We use ***going to***

- for plans which have already been made. (This use is similar to the present continuous.)
  My brother and I ***are going to play*** *football this afternoon.*
  (= We have already arranged this.)
  What ***are*** *the students* ***going to do*** *tomorrow?*
  (= What has been arranged?)
- for predictions when we believe we have present evidence for our prediction.
  *Alice is well ahead of the other skiers; she****'s going to win*** *the race!*
  *You don't speak French, so you****'re going to have*** *problems if you go to a French university.*

We use ***will***

- for actions which we decide as we speak.
  I'll have *a tuna sandwich, please.*
  I'll pay *for the tickets by credit card.*
- for actions which are likely but not certain, often introduced by ***I*** (***don't***) ***think***, ***I*** (***don't***) ***expect***, ***I hope*** or with ***probably***, etc.
  I think I'll walk *to school tomorrow.*
  I don't expect it'll rain*.*
  I'll probably meet *Andy after school.*
- for predictions which we believe, but cannot prove.
  *You****'ll enjoy*** *living in Italy.*
  No one ***will notice*** *if you leave the party early.*
  The government ***will raise*** *taxes again next year.*
- for future events which we cannot change.
  The weather ***will be*** *much hotter in three months' time.*

be about to

We use ***be about to***

- for actions which will happen immediately.
  Hurry up, the firework display ***is about to*** *start!*
  *Can I phone you back? We****'re about to*** *have lunch.*
- with ***not***, to suggest that someone does not intend to do something.
  *I've already planned my holiday and I****'m not about to*** *change it to suit you.*

Present simple and present perfect after time expressions

When we talk about future events with time expressions ***when***, ***until***, ***before***, ***after*** and ***as soon as***.

We use

- the **present simple** for events which happen **at the same time** as another future event.
  I'll call you when I ***get*** *home.* (**NOT** ~~*when I will get home*~~)
  As soon as the guests ***arrive****, we're going to light the candles.* (**NOT** ~~*As soon as the guests will arrive*~~)
- the **present perfect** for events which have already happened.
  I'll call you when I've spoken to my friends.
  (= 1 I will speak to my friends. 2 I'll call you.)
  Don't use the machine until you've read the instructions.
  (**NOT** ~~*until you will read*~~)

Practice

1 **Choose the correct options in the conversations.**

A

Maria: [1] *I'm meeting / I meet* some friends in a few minutes. Would you like to come? I expect [2] *we'll try / we're trying* the new café in town.

Anya: Thanks, but I can't. [3] *I'm about to start / I'm starting* my packing. My holiday [4] *begins / will begin* tomorrow, and [5] *I won't be / I'm not* ready when the taxi [6] *comes / is coming* in the morning.

Maria: What time [7] *will the taxi pick / is the taxi picking* you up?

Anya: Half past four. My flight [8] *leaves / is leaving* at seven and the check-in queues [9] *will be / are being* very long because tomorrow [10] *is / is going to be* a public holiday.

Maria: Yes, and the airline [11] *aren't holding / won't hold* the flight until [12] *you arrive / you'll arrive*!

Anya: OK, so [13] *I'll see / I'm seeing* you next term, then. Bye!

B

Tom: We can't look round the theatre now because a rehearsal [1] *is about to start / will start*.

Kai: Can we come back later when the actors [2] *are going to go / have gone*?

Tom: I think so. [3] *I'll go / I go* and find out.

Kai: OK, [4] *I'll get / I'm getting* us a drink. What would you like?

Tom: [5] *I'm having / I'll have* something cold. The weather is so hot today.

Kai: Yes, but I think [6] *we're going to have / we're having* a storm later. Look at those clouds over the mountains.

Tom: I hope the rain [7] *won't start / hasn't started* until [8] *we're / we'll be* back at our hotel.

Kai: No, [9] *we'll be / we're going to be* fine, don't worry.

GRAMMAR REFERENCE AND PRACTICE

UNIT 9 FUTURE (2): CONTINUOUS AND PERFECT

Future continuous

We use the **future continuous** (***will*** + ***be*** + present participle) for:

- an event going on at a point in time or over a period of time in the future.
  *This time next month, we'**ll be lying** on a beach.*
  *When I'm 30, I hope I **won't be working** here.*
- an event which is already planned for some time in the future.
  *We'**ll be travelling to Wales** on Saturday.*
  *I **won't be starting** my new job until January.*
  This use is very similar to the present continuous for planned events, but compare these sentences:
  *He'**s giving** a speech at 11 o'clock.* (= He begins at 11.)
  *He'**ll be giving** a speech at 11 o'clock.* (= He begins some time before 11 and finishes some time after 11.)
- a future event which is part of a regular pattern of events.
  *The coach **will be talking** to the team before the match.*
  (= He always talks to them before a match, and he will talk to them before the next match as usual.)

Practice

1 Complete the sentences with the future continuous of the verbs in brackets.

1. The information office ______________ (close) early on Friday and it ______________ (not open) at all over the weekend.
2. A team training session ______________ (take) place on Monday morning.
3. 'How's the goalkeeper? ______________ (he/play) next Saturday?' 'No, he ______________ (not play) in any matches until he's recovered from his injuries.'

Future perfect and future perfect continuous

- We use the **future perfect** (***will*** + ***have*** + past participle) to talk about an event which will be complete by a time in the future. We often introduce the time with ***before***, ***by*** (***the time***) or use an adverb such as ***soon***.
  By the time** we get to the cinema, the film **will have started.
  *I hope the shop **won't have sold** all the new phones **before** we get there.*
  ***Will** the flat **have been decorated when** you move in?*
- We use the **future perfect continuous** (***will*** + ***have*** + ***been*** + present participle) to talk about the length of time a future event will continue until a time in the future.
- We usually mention the time, often with ***before***, ***by*** (***the time***) or use an adverb such as ***soon***. We also usually mention the duration of the event.
  *Very soon, I'**ll have been studying** medicine for five years.*
  *How many years **will you have been studying** Chinese by the time you go to Hong Kong?*

Practice

2 Complete the text with the future perfect of the verbs in brackets. Which ones can also be future perfect continuous?

My brother Freddie is 18 and he's going to Spain for a holiday with his friends after their exams.
He's got 200 euros, but he [1] ______________ (spend) that before the end of the week. When he gets home, he'll have a suntan, because he [2] ______________ (sunbathe) for hours every day. He may be thinner, because he [3] ______________ (not/eat) properly for a week and he [4] ______________ (dance) all night every night. He [5] ______________ (not miss) us, but Mum hopes he [6] ______________ (text) us at least once to say he's OK.

3 Complete the sentences describing each situation. Use the future perfect or the future perfect continuous. Where can you use either tense?

1. My uncle and aunt got married in 1985.
   By 2025, they ______________
2. We moved to this house nearly ten years ago.
   At the end of this year, we ______________
3. Harry went to sleep at three o'clock.
   He'll get up at seven, so he ______________ ______________ for only four hours.
4. I'm making a cake, so the kitchen is a bit messy. I'll tidy up before lunch.
   By lunchtime, I ______________
5. The team left in a coach early on Saturday morning to go to an away match. They arrive there on Saturday evening.
   When they get off the coach, they ______________ ______________ all day.

4 Put a tick (✔) if the sentence is correct or a cross (✘) if it is incorrect.

1. The train will be leaving in 20 minutes. ☐
2. The train will have left in 20 minutes. ☐
3. The train will have been leaving in 20 minutes. ☐
4. He's writing so slowly he won't be finishing his homework before the class begins. ☐
5. He's writing so slowly he won't have finished his homework before the class begins. ☐
6. He's writing so slowly he won't have been finishing his homework before the class begins. ☐
7. Will you be having a break before you start your next assignment? ☐
8. Will you have had a break before you start your next assignment? ☐
9. Will you have been having a break before you start your next assignment? ☐
10. I hope someone will be inventing a cure for flu by the end of the century. ☐
11. I hope someone will have invented a cure for flu by the end of the century. ☐
12. I hope someone will have been inventing a cure for flu by the end of the century. ☐

UNIT 10 MODALS (2): MODALS IN THE PAST

would have done

- We use ***would have*** + past participle to speak about an event or feeling which we imagine in the past but which did not happen.
  *I was so fed up that I couldn't go to the concert. I **would have loved** to see that band.*
  *We missed the match, but our team played really badly, so we **wouldn't have enjoyed** it anyway.*
  *I'm sorry you didn't get an invitation to the wedding. **Would** you **have gone**?*

should have done

- We use ***should have*** + past participle to speak about an event in the past that we regret or want to complain about.
  *I didn't know you were allergic to cheese. You **should have told** me.*
  *You **shouldn't have given** your address to that man.*
  *I knew that bike wasn't very good when my friend bought it. **Should** I **have warned** him?*

needn't have done

- We use ***needn't have*** + past participle to talk about an action in the past which happened but which was not necessary.
  *My brother had a spare ticket, so I **needn't have bought** one.* (= I bought a ticket because I didn't know about the spare one, so I wasted my money.)

didn't need to do

- We use ***didn't need*** + ***to*** infinitive to talk about an action in the past which was not necessary and therefore didn't happen.
  *My brother gave me a spare ticket, so I **didn't need to buy** one.* (= I didn't buy a ticket, I used the one my brother gave me.)

Practice

1 **Complete the sentences with *would(n't) have*, *should(n't) have*, *needn't have* or *didn't need to* and the correct form of the verb in brackets.**

1. Alex ______ (shout) at the shop assistant; she was trying to help him, and he was quite rude.
2. I'm glad I didn't buy that sweatshirt, it ______ (look) right with these jeans.
3. It was Simon's birthday last Friday. I really ______ (send) him a card.
4. I don't think Ellie liked that bag I sent her for her birthday. What ______ (I/give) her?
5. I spent hours typing up my notes, but I ______ (bother) because the teacher never asked to see them.
6. ______ (you/give) the taxi driver a tip? He looked a bit disappointed.
7. Jade was nervous about meeting her new supervisor, but she ______ (not worry), because he was absolutely charming.
8. We didn't realise Lisa was ill, or we ______ (send) her some flowers.
9. I had an interview for art college, but I ______ (take) an exam; they just looked at my drawings.
10. I know you think these curtains are the wrong colour for this room, but what ______ (you/choose) instead?

2 **Complete the sentences with your own ideas.**

Your friends went to a concert last weekend. You had arranged to go to the beach, so you didn't go with them. They saw your favourite singer there and they bought you a T-shirt. Actually, you already have a T-shirt like that.
What did they say when they saw you?
'It was a great concert. You would [1] ______. We know you had already arranged to go to the beach, but you should [2] ______. You can go to the beach any weekend, you needn't [3] ______.'
What did you think when you saw the T-shirt?
'They needn't [4] ______ – but I won't say so!'

GRAMMAR REFERENCE AND PRACTICE

UNIT 11 RELATIVE CLAUSES

Defining relative clauses

- give essential information about things or people.
  *The photo **that** is on the table is the oldest one we have.*
  We need the words ***that is on the table*** to understand which photo the speaker is referring to.
- can begin with a relative pronoun: ***who*** (for people), ***which*** (for things), ***that*** (for things and people).
  *There's the woman **who** is interested in local history.*
  *She showed me a website **which** she uses.*
  *I can email you the link **that** I told you about.*
  *There's the woman **that** I mentioned.*
- can have ***who***, ***which*** or ***that*** as their ***subject***.
  *The woman **who/that** is in the photo is my great grandmother.*
  or as their **object**.
  *There's the woman **who** I mentioned.*
  *She showed me a website **which/that** she uses.*
- often omit the relative pronoun when it is the object of the relative clause.
  There's the woman I mentioned.
  She showed me a website she uses.
- are never separated from the rest of the sentence by commas
  (**NOT** ~~*There's the woman, who I mentioned.*~~
  ~~*She showed me a website, that she uses.*~~)

Non-defining relative clauses

- give extra information about things or people.
  *This is a photo of my parents, **who** met in 1999.*
  If we take out ***who met in 1999***, we still know that the photo shows the speaker's parents.
- must begin with the relative pronoun ***who*** (for people) or ***which*** (for things).
  *My dad, **who** owns a software company, travels all over the world.*
  *The company, **which** is quite well known, employs about a hundred people.*
- can have ***who*** or ***which*** (but never ***that***) as their subject.
  *My dad, **who** is in this photo, helped my mum set up the business.* (**NOT** ~~*that is in this photo*~~)
  *The head office, **which** is in the north of England, is extremely modern.* (**NOT** ~~*that is in the north of England*~~)
- can have ***who*** or ***which*** (but not ***that***) as their **object**.
  *Some regular customers, **who** my dad knows well, come to our house.*
  *Our house, **which** we like very much, is near the sea.*
- never omit the relative pronoun. (**NOT** ~~*Our house, we like very much, is near the sea.*~~)
- must be separated from the rest of the sentence by commas.
  *Some regular customers**,** who my dad knows well**,** come to our house.* (**NOT** ~~*Some regular customers who my dad knows well come to our house.*~~)

Both defining and non-defining relative clauses

- can begin with ***whose*** (instead of *his/her/their*), ***when*** (for times) and ***where*** (for places).
  *My brother, **whose wife is an architect**, has a beautiful house.*
  *Here it is in this photo from the year **when they bought it**.*
  *My parents' house, **where I still live**, is much bigger than my brother's.*
- usually have any prepositions at the end of the clause.
  *This is the desk **which** my grandad worked **at**.*
  *I have a group of friends I go cycling **with**.*
  *Peter, **who** my dad went to university **with**, has his own business now.*

NOTE The object pronoun (***her***, ***him***, ***it***, etc.) is never used in a relative clause.
I know most of the people that my dad employs.
(**NOT** ~~*the people that my dad employs them*~~)
The next photo shows my Aunt Margaret, who my uncle married in 2005. (**NOT** ~~*who my uncle married her in 2005*~~)

Practice

1 Write relative clauses. Put the relative pronoun in brackets if you can leave it out.

1 my sister / is / at university / can / drive
....

2 I / followed / the instructions / you / gave / me
....

3 my phone / is / brand-new / has / a broken screen
....

4 I / loved the DJ / played / at your party
....

5 I / 'm having / dinner / with my best friend / who / I / introduced / you to last month
....

6 she / can / tell you / to go shopping for a bargain
....

2 Correct the mistake in each sentence.

1 Have you ever visited the island, that your grandparents came from?
....

2 John's bicycle, that was stolen last week, has turned up in the next street.
....

3 Is that the coat you wanted to buy it?
....

4 This is the website who I told you about.
....

5 The city, where I went to university, is a very lively place.
....

6 The singer who I like her most is from Argentina.
....

7 The friend I stayed with her in Geneva is a painter.
....

UNIT 12 THE PASSIVE (1): REVIEW

- The passive is formed with the correct form of ***be*** + a past participle.
  Breakfast ***isn't served*** *until 7.30.*
  We ***were offered*** *a choice of rooms.*
  The dining room ***hasn't been cleaned*** *yet.*
  The doors ***were being repaired****.*
  We heard the building ***had been damaged****.*
  Are *you* ***being given*** *enough help?*
- The person or thing that does the action is called **the agent**. We use ***by*** to introduce the agent.
  We ***were offered*** *a choice of rooms* ***by*** *the hotel manager.*
  We heard the building ***had been damaged by*** *the storm.*
- We use the passive
  - if we do not know the agent.
    *My phone****'s been stolen****!*
  - if the agent is unimportant.
    The new chairs ***will be delivered*** *tomorrow.*
  - if the agent is obvious.
    The thief ***was sent*** *to prison.*
  - if we don't want to mention the agent, for example if we want to avoid blame.
    The ice cream ***has*** *all* ***been eaten****.*
  - to emphasise the subject of the passive verb instead of the agent.
    The film star ***was being interviewed*** *by a journalist.*

Practice

1 **Read the email, then complete the blog opposite with verbs in the correct passive tenses.**

To: Megadeal Corporation Management team
Subject: Top secret – Successful takeover of Smallway & Co
Reply Forward

Yesterday, we bought our competitor Smallway & Co. The firm had resisted our offers for three months, but we made a new offer last week, and this time we included a special payment for the Managing Director. He has not told his colleagues about this payment, but he has persuaded them to accept the offer.

We will give a month's notice to all the staff at Smallway & Co and will put our accountant in charge. We are selling the buildings and we will use the money to pay for the new Megadeal Corporation headquarters.

A. Crookson, CEO, Megadeal

SECRET DEAL BY MEGADEAL CORPORATION REVEALED

by business journalist Zoe Garrett

Smallway & Co **(1)** .... by Megadeal Corporation yesterday. Their offers **(2)** .... for three months, but a new offer **(3)** .... last week, and this time a special payment for the Managing Director **(4)** .... His colleagues **(5)** .... about this payment, but they **(6)** .... by him to accept Megadeal's offer.
All the staff at Smallway & Co **(7)** .... a month's notice, and Megadeal's accountant **(8)** .... in charge. The buildings **(9)** .... and the money **(10)** .... to pay for the new Megadeal Corporation headquarters.

CAUSATIVE *HAVE/GET*

- We use ***have/get something done*** when someone else does something for us.
- It is not usually necessary to mention the agent.
- The use of ***get*** instead of ***have*** sounds more informal.
  *I****'m going to have/get*** *the sitting room* ***painted****.*
  (= Someone **is going to paint** the sitting room for me.)
  They want to ***have/get*** *their car* ***fixed****.* (= They want a mechanic *to* **fix** their car.)
  I ***had/got*** *my hair* ***coloured****.* (= The hairdresser **coloured** my hair.)
  I ***had/got*** *my hair* ***coloured by my cousin.*** (Emphasises that my cousin did it for me.)
- We use ***get someone to do something*** when we ask or persuade someone to do something for us.
  Jenny ***got*** *her dad* ***to give*** *her a lift because it was raining.*
  *I****'ll get*** *my assistant* ***to show*** *you the way to the office.*

Practice

2 **Complete the sentences with *have/get* + past participle or *get* + *to* + verb. Use the words in brackets.**

1. My new phone didn't work, so I .... (the shop / replace) it with a new one.
2. My coat has a dirty mark on it, so I .... (it / clean).
3. My brother kicked a football through the neighbours' window and they .... (my parents / pay) for a new one.
4. I had to work very late, but I .... (my boss / call) a taxi to take me home.
5. My sister was away on Mum's birthday, but she .... (a bunch of flowers / deliver) to the house.

GRAMMAR REFERENCE AND PRACTICE

UNIT 13 THE PASSIVE (2): OTHER STRUCTURES

Passive infinitive

We form the passive infinitive with (**not**) (**to**) **be** + past participle.
*I don't like **to be thought** of as mean by my friends.*
*This envelope is **not to be opened** until your birthday.*
*Petra asked **to be taken** to the airport.*

verb + passive infinitive

- Some verbs are followed by the passive infinitive, e.g. ***aim***, ***appear***, ***ask***, ***begin***, ***continue***, ***expect***, ***hope***, ***refuse***, ***seem***, ***tend***, ***try***, ***want***, ***wish***, ***would like***.
  *He **aims to be elected** next year.*
  *We**'ve asked to be given** a larger room.*
  *They **hoped to be offered** a refund.*
  *You **seem to be amused** by that email.*

verb + object + passive infinitive

- Some verbs are followed by an object + the passive infinitive, e.g. ***expect***, ***intend***, ***like***, ***prefer***, ***want***, ***would like.***
  *We **expected him to be stopped** at the gate by the guards.*
  *Do you **want the lettuce to be washed** now?*
  *I**'d like this jacket to be cleaned**, please.*

modal + passive infinitive without *to*

- These are ***could***, ***may***, ***might***, ***should***, ***would*** + ***be*** + past participle.
  *Another doctor **could be asked** for her opinion.*
  *We **might be told** the truth by somebody one day.*

***the first, second, only, last,* etc. + noun + passive infinitive**

- The words ***the first***, ***the second***, ***the third***, etc. and ***the last*** can be followed by a passive infinitive.
  *He was **the first to be chosen** for the team.*
  *This box was **the last to be delivered**.*
- The words ***the first***, ***the second***, ***the third***, etc. and ***the only*** and ***the last*** can be followed by a noun or ***one*** + passive infinitive.
  *This is **the third club to be opened** in our town this year.*
  *My suitcase was **the only one not to be inspected** by the customs officer.*

-ing passive

We form the *-ing* passive with ***being*** + past participle.
*I don't remember **being asked** my name.*
*We enjoyed **being entertained** by the dancers.*

verb + *-ing* passive

- Some verbs are followed by the *-ing* passive, e.g. ***avoid***, ***bear***, ***deny***, ***forget***, ***imagine***, ***risk***, ***remember***.
  *The children **avoided being found** by hiding under a bed.*
  *Sandy **won't forget being sent** home by the head teacher.*
  *Can you **imagine being refused** entry to a restaurant?*

verb + preposition + *-ing* passive

- Some verbs are followed by a preposition + the *-ing* passive, e.g. ***ask about***, ***enquire about***, ***insist on***, ***laugh about***, ***look forward to***.
  *Let's **ask about being given** a better room.*
  *He **insisted on being referred to** by his surname.*
  *Fergus doesn't care what people say. He just **laughs about being told off**.*

Practice

1 **Complete the sentences with the correct passive form (infinitive or *-ing* form) of the verb in brackets.**

1 They don't appear ________ by your jokes. (amuse)
2 You can laugh about ________, but it's not a joke. (tell off)
3 I think we should ________ a choice of essay topics. (give)
4 They prefer the drinks ________ very cold. (serve)
5 She was the third woman ________ a degree by Cambridge University. (award)
6 I'm looking forward to ________ to a meal in a nice restaurant by my parents after the exams. (treat)
7 My name was the last ________. (call)
8 We might ________ to lead the parade. (choose)
9 I can't bear ________ by strangers. (hug)
10 I would like ________ next time you want to use my phone. (ask)
11 Did he deny ________ in the fight? (involve)
12 The way you drive, we risk ________ by the traffic police! (stop)
13 These rooms tend ________ for seminars. (use)
14 They intended the invitations ________ immediately. (deliver)
15 They enquired about ________ to use the school hall for a party. (allow)

UNIT 14 REPORTED SPEECH

Tenses in reported speech

We usually change the tense of reported verbs when the reporting verb (e.g. *say, ask*) is in a past tense.

*'**I've been swimming** for an hour.'* → *He **said** he **had been swimming** for an hour.*

*'What **will you do?**'* → *She **asked** what **I would do.***

We usually do **not** change the tense of reported verbs

- when the reporting verb (e.g. *say, ask*) is in a present tense.
  - *'I **like** this music.'* → *He **says** he **likes** this music.*
  - *'**Did you enjoy** the film?'* → *She**'s asking** whether you **enjoyed** the film.*
  - *'We **won't be** away long.'* → *They **say** they **won't be** away long.*
- when the reporting verb is in a past tense, but the events reported are not past.
  - *'**I'm coming** with you this evening.'* → *She said **she is coming** with us this evening.*
  - *'What time **will you be** home?'* → *He wanted to know what time **we'll be** home.*
- when the reporting verb is in a past tense, but the events reported are true for any time.
  - *'The traffic **is** always bad on Fridays.'* → *She reminded me that the traffic **is** always bad on Fridays.*
  - *'You **can change** money at your hotel.'* → *He said that we **can** change money at our hotel.*

In the examples above, it is not wrong to change the reported verbs to a past tense, but it sounds more formal and it may make the meaning less clear.

*She said **she was coming** with us this evening.*

*He said that we **could** change money at our hotel.*

Practice

1 Put the sentences into reported speech. Do not change the tenses unless you have to.

0 'I'll come skiing with you next weekend.'
Alison has agreed *to come skiing with us* next weekend.

1 'We saw Ahmed at the football match.'
They mentioned that .... at the football match.

2 'I hate shopping at weekends.'
My dad claims .... at weekends.

3 'They went to Morocco in the winter.'
He says .... in the winter.

4 'Let me see the report!'
She demanded .... the report.

5 'Where is the ticket office?'
We asked ....

2 Write the reported speech as direct speech.

0 They said we can have a refund.
'You can have a refund.'

1 He said he was enjoying the movie.
....

2 Tom asked where he could charge his phone.
....

3 Nina wanted to know what the score was.
....

4 I said I'd been to the library a few times.
....

5 The teacher asked me what I needed.
....

6 She's asking if you saw the film.
....

3 Complete the email with the correct form of the reporting verbs in the box.

agree deny enquire persuade praise suggest

To: Drama club supporters
Subject: Holiday theatre club project
Reply Forward

I've talked to several people about helping us to set up a drama club for local teenagers during the summer holidays, and these are the results so far.

The town council has finally [1] .... to let us use the old cinema building, which is a big relief. Interestingly, the official I first spoke to now [2] .... saying the building wasn't fit to use. So it was worth speaking to all the councillors personally. I met Mr Baktiar, the head of our school, last month, and he [3] .... us for persevering with the project and [4] .... advertising the drama club on the local news website and local radio, so that lots of people hear about it. The local radio station mentioned the club on the breakfast show this week, and several people have [5] .... about the course since then. Freda Jones, our drama teacher, is going to run some workshops for us, and she has [6] .... her husband, who is a DJ, to lend us his sound system for our performances!

So, I think that's good progress so far. Has anyone else raised any money yet?

GRAMMAR REFERENCE AND PRACTICE

UNIT 15 MODALS (3): DEDUCTION

Deduction in the present and future

- To express deductions about the present and future, we use ***may***, ***may not***, ***might***, ***might not***, ***could***, ***could not***, ***can't***, ***must*** + verb.
- When we think something is **possible**, but we are not sure, we use ***may***, ***might*** or ***could***.
  Where's Nadia?
  *She **may be** in the garden.*
  *She **could be** in the garden.*
  *She **might be** in the garden.*
- When we think something is **possibly not true**, we use ***may not*** or ***might not***.
  I want to see her.
  *She **may not want** to see you.*
  *She **might not want** to see you.*
- When we feel **certain** that something is true, we use ***must***.
  *Alan passed his driving test. He **must be** very happy.*
- The opposite of ***must be*** is ***can't***/***couldn't be*** (**NOT** ~~mustn't be~~).
  *Ben failed his driving test. He **can't be** happy about that. / He **couldn't be** happy about that.*

Deduction in the past

- To express deductions about the past, we use ***may have***, ***may not have***, ***might have***, ***might not have***, ***could have***, ***couldn't have***, ***can't have***, ***must have*** + past participle.
- When we think something was **possible** in the past, but we are not sure, we use ***may*** (***not***) ***have***, ***might*** (***not***) ***have*** or ***could have***.
  Where was Nadia when I called?
  *She **may have been** in the garden.*
  *She **could have been** in the garden.*
  *She **might have been** in the garden.*
- When we think something was **possibly not true**, we use ***may*** (***not***) ***have*** or ***might*** (***not***) ***have***.
  I wanted to see her.
  *She **may not have wanted** to see you.*
  *She **might not have wanted** to see you.*
- When we feel **certain** that something was true, we use ***must have***.
  *Cathy borrowed some money from me. She **must have forgotten** about it.*
- The opposite of ***must have been*** is ***can't***/***couldn't have been*** (**NOT** ~~mustn't have been~~).
  She borrowed it last weekend.
  *She **can't have borrowed** money from you last weekend; she was away.*
  *She **couldn't have borrowed** money from you last weekend; she was away.*

Practice

1 **Complete the conversations using *must* / *can* / *could* / *may* / *might* / *can't* / *couldn't* / *may not* / *might not* + verb.**

Marta: There's a parcel for you.
Yves: It [1] ______________ for me. No one knows I'm here.
Marta: Someone [2] ______________, because it's got your name and this address.

Grandpa: Why isn't my phone working?
Jim: The battery [3] ______________ flat. You know you often forget to charge it.
Grandpa: But it [4] ______________ flat. I charged it last night.
Jim: Well, so you [5] ______________ a signal here.
Grandpa: There [6] ______________ a signal. We're in the middle of a city! It's impossible to be out of range here.
Jim: But these buildings are very tall. They [7] ______________ the signal. Let's walk to the end of the street. It [8] ______________ OK there.

2 **Match the pairs of sentences.**

1 There's the doorbell. ☐
2 Don't wait for me this evening. ☐
3 Chloe left before the end of the show. ☐
4 Otto is very late tonight. ☐
5 Where are the car keys? ☐
6 Josh didn't answer my text. ☐

a She can't have enjoyed the music.
b You could have left them in your bag.
c I may be working late.
d He might not have got it.
e It must be my taxi.
f He must have met some friends.

3 **Choose the correct options in the conversations.**

Eva: There's no milk in the fridge. Did you finish it?
Fran: I can't remember. It [1]*could have been / might be* me, or it [2]*must be / might have been* Jen – she was up early this morning.
Eva: No, it [3]*can't have been / must not have been* her. She doesn't drink milk.

Gilda: Look at this photo. Who is it?
Kay: I'm not sure, [4]it *could be / might have been* my grandparents when they were young.
Gilda: But the woman's wearing a long skirt. Your granny [5]*mustn't be / can't be* as old as that!
Kay: Oh, of course, it [6]*might be / must be* my great-grandparents. Yes, they [7]*could be / must have been* on their honeymoon. See the signpost? It's in Austria. I know they went there.

UNIT 16 CONDITIONALS (1): REVIEW

Zero conditional

- We use the **zero conditional** to state general truths.
- ***If*** and ***when*** have the same meaning.
  If/When + present tense (comma) present tense
  OR present tense ***if/when*** + present tense
  If/When *you* ***drive*** *fast, you* ***use*** *more petrol.*
  You ***use*** *more petrol* ***if/when*** *you* ***drive*** *fast.*

Practice

1 Complete the sentences with suitable verbs.

1 If you ______________ in a hot climate, you don't need many pullovers.
2 Students ______________ bored if they only study grammar.
3 When trains are cancelled, everyone ______________ home late.

First conditional

- We use the **first conditional** to describe a real possibility.
  If + present tense (comma) future tense
  OR future tense ***if*** + present tense
  If *you* ***drive*** *too fast, I'****ll be*** *sick.*
  *I'****ll be*** *sick* ***if*** *you* ***drive*** *too fast.*
- We can also use the imperative + ***and/or*** + future tense to make offers, promises and threats.
  Drive *too fast* ***and*** *I'****ll be*** *sick.*
  Drive *more slowly* ***or*** *I'****ll be*** *sick.*
- *If* does **not** mean the same as *when* in first conditional sentences. Compare these examples.
  If *my sister* ***leaves****, I'****ll be*** *lonely.* (= The speaker thinks her sister may leave.)
  When *my sister* ***leaves****, I'****ll be*** *lonely.* (= The speaker knows her sister is going to leave.)

Practice

2 Match the sentence halves.

1 Hurry up	a if we're late.
2 The driver won't wait	b or we'll miss the bus!
3 If it starts raining,	c and I'll call a taxi.
4 Lend me your phone	d you'll need a coat.

Second conditional

- We use the **second conditional** for an imaginary possibility in the present or future, which we believe to be impossible or very improbable.
  If + past tense (comma) ***would/'d*** + verb
  OR ***would/'d*** + verb ***if*** + past tense
  If *you* ***left*** *now, I'****d feel*** *sad.* (I believe you're unlikely to leave now.)
  *I'****d buy*** *a new car* ***if*** *you* ***gave*** *me some money.* (But I don't expect you will give me any money.)
- We often use ***If I were you*** to give advice or warnings.
  If I were *you, I* ***wouldn't buy*** *that car.*
- We sometimes use ***I were*** instead of ***I was*** in second conditional sentences.

Practice

3 Complete the second sentence so that it has a similar meaning to the first.

1 I advise you to take a smaller suitcase.
If I ______________
2 It's a good idea to check the weight limit.
I'd ______________
3 It's dangerous to walk along this road at night.
I wouldn't ______________
4 You should take a torch with you.
If I ______________

Third conditional

- We use the **third conditional** for an imaginary possibility in the past, which we know to be impossible.
  If + past perfect (comma) ***would/'d have*** + past participle
  OR ***would/'d have*** + past participle ***if*** + past perfect
  If *the sun* ***had shone****, we'****d have eaten*** *outdoors.* (= It did not shine, so we ate indoors.)
  *I'****d have texted*** *you* ***if*** *I'****d seen*** *your bag.* (= I didn't see your bag, so I didn't text you.)

Practice

4 Complete the second sentence so that it has a similar meaning to the first.

1 Angie didn't go to the party, so she didn't see the band.
Angie would ______________
2 Lewis entered the tournament and he won it.
Lewis wouldn't ______________
3 Matty felt fine at the end of the race because he had trained carefully.
If Matty hadn't ______________

5 Choose the correct verb forms.

Last week, I spent a whole day waiting at home for a new TV to be delivered. If I'd realised that, I [1]*would have asked / wouldn't have asked* the shop to deliver it. I'd have asked my brother to collect it for me. The problem is that I live in a small village, and there are few road signs, so people never [2]*find / found* the house if I [3]*don't give / didn't give* them directions. And of course, it [4]*would be / will be* easier if the houses [5]*had / have* numbers like they do in cities.
However, the shop had detailed directions from me, so it was their fault. If they [6]*'d remembered / remembered* to tell the driver, he [7]*wouldn't have got / didn't get* lost. When he eventually arrived, he said, 'They always forget to give me directions, they just give a postcode. If the shop manager [8]*didn't forget / hadn't forgotten* so often, we [9]*would save / saved* a lot of time.'

GRAMMAR REFERENCE AND PRACTICE

UNIT 17 CONDITIONALS (2): MIXED

Mixed conditional (present affected by past)

We use this mixed conditional to describe an imaginary possibility in the present or future which is affected by the past.

- ***If*** + past perfect (comma) ***would/might/could*** + verb
  *If you **had remembered** to book a table, we **would be** in the restaurant now.*
  (= You didn't remember to book a table, so we aren't in the restaurant.)
  *If we **had seen** the beginning of the film, **we might understand** what is happening.*
  (= We didn't see the beginning of the film, so we don't understand what's happening.)
- ***would/might/could*** + verb ***if*** + past perfect
  *I **could visit** my grandparents tomorrow if I **hadn't started** tennis club.*
  (= I started tennis club, so I can't visit my grandparents tomorrow.)
  *Where **might** you **live** now if you **hadn't come** to London?*
  (= You came to London, but where else might you have chosen?)

Practice

1 **Complete the sentences with the verbs in brackets. Use *would/might/could* + verb and the past perfect.**

1 If my brother ______ (not eat) all the pizza, I ______ (not be) so hungry.
2 We ______ (go) to the beach if it ______ (not start) to rain.
3 If a friend ______ (tell) me a story like that, I ______ (not repeat) it to everyone I know.
4 How ______ (we play) those games if we ______ (not install) broadband?
5 The students ______ (get) more out of this trip to Paris, if they ______ (study) French for longer.
6 If I ______ (finish) all my assignments, I ______ (relax) this evening.

Mixed conditional (past affected by present)

We use this mixed conditional to describe an imaginary possibility in the past which is affected by the present or by permanent conditions.

- ***If*** + past simple (comma) ***would/might/could*** + ***have*** + past participle
  *If you **were** a better player, they **would have picked** you for the team.*
  (= You aren't a very good player, so they didn't pick you for the team.)
  ***If** I **didn't know** my rights, I **might have lost** a lot of money.*
  (I know my rights, so I didn't lose a lot of money.)
- ***would/might/could*** + ***have*** + past participle ***if*** + past simple
  *They **wouldn't have spent** so much time watching TV **if** they **were** really busy.*
  (= They spent a lot of time watching TV, so I don't believe they are really busy.)
  *How **could** I **have made** this cake **if** I **was** no good at cooking?*
  (= I am good at cooking, so I could make this cake.)

Practice

2 **Complete the sentences with the verbs in brackets, using *would/might/could* + *have* + past participle and the past simple.**

1 We ______ (go) to the cinema, if we ______ (have) some money.
2 If the school ______ (be) up to date, we ______ (use) the internet to research this project.
3 If you ______ (not exaggerate) so often, I ______ (believe) the story you told me last night.
4 Where ______ (your friends / stay) if you ______ (not have) a spare room?
5 The teacher ______ (give) us more help if she ______ (have) more time between lessons.

3 **Complete the sentences, using the verbs in brackets to make a mixed-conditional structure.**

1 I wouldn't be top of the class if I ______ (not work) every weekend.
2 These politicians ______ (not be) in power now if voters had known their plans for the economy.
3 ______ (Rosa / have) more friends if her family hadn't moved house so often?
4 If my parents gave me money every week, I ______ (save) up for a new phone by now.
5 We ______ (have) a coffee with our breakfast if the electricity hadn't gone off an hour ago.
6 How many people would have heard of Jane Austen if there ______ (not be) so many films of her books?
7 If we ______ (bring) less luggage, we wouldn't be so tired.
8 The boys ______ (be) at the match now if the bus hadn't broken down.
9 Might the music we listen to now be different if The Beatles ______ (never exist)?
10 If the roads were safe, the children ______ (walk) to school every day, but they all had to go by bus.
11 What ______ (cities / be) like now if cars hadn't replaced horses?

UNIT 18 USES OF VERB + -ING

Verbs + -ing after verbs

- When one verb follows another, the second verb is often the *-ing* form.
  *He **denied stealing** the money.*
  *They **admitted being** impressed.*
  *Would you **consider staying** for one more day?*
- These verbs can all be followed by the *-ing* form.

admit	*deny*	*love*
advise (underlined)	*dislike*	*mention*
allow (underlined)	*enjoy*	*(not) mind*
appreciate	*fancy*	*miss*
avoid	*feel like*	*permit* (underlined)
begin	*finish*	*postpone*
can't bear	*forbid* (underlined)	*practise*
can't face	*give up*	*prefer*
can't help	*hate*	*put off*
can't stand	*imagine*	*recommend* (underlined)
carry on	*involve*	*resist*
consider	*keep*	*risk*
continue	*keep on*	*start*
delay	*like*	*suggest*

NOTE The underlined verbs are followed by the *to* form if they have a direct object.
I advise leaving early tomorrow. OR *I advise **you to leave** early tomorrow.*
(**NOT** ~~*I advise you leaving early tomorrow.*~~)

- The *-ing* form is used as part of continuous verb forms.
  *They've been **looking** for a solution.*

Practice

1 **Complete the sentences with your own ideas, using the *-ing* form of a verb and any other words you need.**

1 If you have important exams, you should avoid … .
2 I'm tired and hungry. Do you fancy … ?
3 They have a beautiful house. It's hard to imagine … .
4 If you're short of time, I don't mind … .
5 The weather's terrible. I don't think we should risk … .

Verb + -ing after prepositions and phrases

- We use the *-ing* form after prepositions, e.g. ***by, for, without***.
  *You start the machine **by pressing** this lever.*
  *These cloths are **for cleaning** the tables only.*
  *Don't leave **without saying** goodbye.*
- We use the *-ing* form after some time prepositions, e.g. ***after***, ***before***, ***since***, ***when***, ***while***.
  ***After leaving** school, she worked as a lifeguard.*
  ***Since passing** my driving test, I've been able to drive to work.*
- We use the *-ing* form after some expressions, e.g. ***be/get fed up with***, ***have enough of***, ***have*** (***no***) ***difficulty/trouble***, ***pass the time***, ***spend*** (***time***), (***not***) ***be worth***, ***a waste of time/money***.
  *He**'s fed up with being told** what to do.*
  *With your qualifications, you**'ll have no trouble finding** a job.*

Practice

2 **A junior chef is talking to some new employees in the kitchen of a famous restaurant. Complete what he says using the words and phrases in the box.**

after	by x2	get fed up with
have no difficulty	it's not worth	
pass the time	since	spend time
when	without	

'OK, so as this is your first day in the restaurant kitchen, I'll just run through the way we do things here.
High standards are very important, so the first thing you do [1] ………… arriving is put on a clean apron.
For the first week, you do nothing [2] ………… being given an order. This is the food processor. It's operated [3] ………… turning this handle. Be careful of your fingers [4] ………… using it, the blades are very sharp. Chef expects everyone to concentrate on their own work, not to [5] ………… chatting. We [6] ………… finding people who want to work here, so [7] ………… annoying the chef. You'll get two breaks during the day. You can [8] ………… watching the chef, as long as you don't get in his way. If you don't [9] ………… working here by the end of the week, we'll give you some more interesting jobs to do. [10] ………… starting here two years ago, I've learned a lot just [11] ………… observing what the chef does.'

Participle clauses

- When two clauses have the same subject, one of them often starts with the *-ing* form.
- This sometimes replaces a relative clause and can give more information about a noun.
  *The teacher, **realising** that we didn't understand, repeated her explanation more slowly.*
  (= The teacher, who realised that …)
- It often links an action and its explanation.
  *He phoned his brother, **hoping** for some helpful advice.*
  (= He phoned his brother because he hoped for …)
  ***Not looking** where I was going, I nearly stepped into the road.*
  (= Because I wasn't looking where I was going, …)

Practice

3 **Rewrite the sentences, using the *-ing* form.**

1 I sat at the back of the hall, so I couldn't see the show very well.
………………………………………
2 Because I'm not interested in rugby, I didn't go to the match with my cousins.
………………………………………
3 My dad, who wanted to know why I wasn't home, phoned the school office.
………………………………………

GRAMMAR REFERENCE AND PRACTICE

UNIT 19 SUBJECT–VERB AGREEMENT

Singular nouns which end in -s

A number of English nouns end in -*s*, but take a singular verb. They include:

- some common words: **crossroads**, **means** (= method), **news**.
  *The **crossroads is** about a kilometre further on.*
- some sports: **athletics**, **gymnastics**.
  ***Gymnastics is** a very demanding sport.*
- some academic subjects: **economics**, **maths/mathematics**, **physics**, **politics**.
  ***Maths is** my main subject, but **physics is** also part of the course.*
- some countries which have plural names but take a singular verb because we think of them as individual countries: **the Philippines**, **the United Arab Emirates**, **the United States**.
  ***It's** not where I was born, but **the Philippines is** my home now.*

Everyone, anyone, someone, etc.

***Anyone/anybody**, **everyone/everybody**, **someone/somebody**, **no one/nobody**:*

- take a singular verb
  *Can you answer the door if **anybody comes** to the house?*
  ***Someone is** eating all the biscuits.*
  ***Nobody likes** being made to look stupid.*
- are usually referred to by plural pronouns.
  *Can you answer the door if anybody comes to the house? Tell **them** I'm not here.*
  *Someone is eating all my biscuits. **They** should buy their own.*

Clause as subject

When a clause is the subject of a sentence, it takes a singular verb.
***Keeping** all my notes up to date **takes** at least an hour every day.*
***Playing** football matches with my mates **is** my way of keeping fit.*

Both of, all of, plenty of, etc.

- Most expressions with ***of*** are followed by plural nouns and pronouns and take a plural verb. These include ***both of***, ***all of***, ***plenty of***, ***most of***, ***a number of***, ***a couple of***, ***the majority of***.
  ***All of my friends play** computer games.*
- The expression ***one of*** is followed by plural nouns and pronouns but takes a singular verb.
  ***One of my friends likes** cooking.*
- Some expressions can be followed by a singular or plural noun and take a singular or plural verb. These include ***a lot of***, ***the majority of.***
  ***A lot of people like** this game.*
  ***A lot of music is** enjoyed by people of different ages.*

Collective nouns

- Nouns which can take a singular OR plural verb include ***band***, ***class***, ***club***, ***family***, ***government***, ***group***, ***staff*** and ***team***.
  *My **family is** moving house next weekend.*
  *My **team is** playing very well this season.*
- When we think of them as a number of individuals, we usually use a plural verb.
  *My **family** often **argue** about politics.*
  *My **team are** playing very well this season.*

Practice

1 Nine of these sentences have mistakes in them. Find the five correct sentences, then correct the mistakes in the others.

1 Nowadays, our usual means of communication is texting.

2 The city is very quiet because everybody are on holiday this week.

3 Revising for exams were preventing my brother from doing any sport.

4 The United States is a great place to live if you have plenty of money.

5 No one has come to see me for ages. I must have done something to upset him.

6 Spending time with friends has always been very important to me.

7 A number of my friends is taking part in a riding competition on Saturday.

8 My phone's dead. Have anyone brought their charger with them?

9 The majority of people in this town works at the electronics factory.

10 The class was texting their friends as they came out of the exam.

11 The swimming club has put up its membership fees.

12 Learning about other people are an important part of growing up.

13 Both of my parents works long hours, but we have plenty of fun together at weekends.

14 My parents were born in the United Kingdom, but they've lived in Spain for most of their lives.

UNIT 20 DETERMINERS

The definite article

The is used before any noun when:

- we mention the only one(s).
  Most young people care about ***the environment****.*
- we refer to the particular one(s).
  My sister likes shopping in ***the local market****.*
- we refer to a thing or things previously mentioned.
  The market *has all kinds of clothes.* ***The clothes*** *are quite cheap.*
- both the speaker and listener know which thing(s) we are referring to.
  She's gone to ***the park****.* (= the park we know)

The indefinite article

A/an is used before a singular countable noun when:

- we mention one of many things.
  Most towns in this region have ***a market*** *once a week.*
- we introduce a new item of information.
  I want to buy ***a rucksack*** *before I go away.*

The zero article

We do not use an article before an uncountable noun or a plural countable noun when:

- we refer to all or every kind of that thing in general.
  Exercise *is important whatever your age.*
  Markets *are good places to look for* ***bargains****.*
- the quantity is uncertain or unimportant.
  Do you want ***bread*** *with your soup?*

Plenty of, a lot of, etc. + noun

The quantifiers ***some***, ***any***, ***plenty of***, ***a lot of***, ***lots of*** go before

- a plural countable noun.
  Some people *never eat in restaurants.*
- a singular uncountable noun.
  There's ***plenty of room*** *for everyone in our car.*

(*not*) *much,* (*a*) *little,* etc. + noun

- The quantifiers **(*not*) *much***, **(*a*) *little***, ***a bit of***, ***a small/large amount of*** go before uncountable nouns.
  I've got ***a bit of work*** *to do before I go out.*
  There's ***not much music*** *here in the evenings.*
- ***Much*** is not often used in positive statements; it is rather formal.
  Much work *has gone into this project.*
- ***Little*** is negative; ***a little*** is positive.
  I have ***little money*** *to spend on clothes, so I look out for bargains.*
  I have ***a little money****, I can lend you some.*

Many, (*a*) *few, several,* etc.

The quantifiers **(*not*) *many***, **(*a*) *few***, ***several***, ***a small/large number of*** go before plural countable nouns.

We have ***several restaurants*** *in the city centre.*
*There are****n't many places*** *for teenagers to go round here.*
Many is not often used in positive statements; it is rather formal.
Many students *find physics difficult, but I enjoy it.*
Few is negative; ***a few*** is positive.
I have ***few friends*** *in this area, so I get a bit lonely sometimes.*
I've made ***a few friends****, so I don't miss my family now.*

Practice

1 **Choose the correct options in the email.**

Hi, Sara

How are you? We had [1]*a / the* great trip to Turkey. Thanks for recommending [2]*a / the* little hotel by [3]*the / –* harbour. We really liked it. [4]*The / A* staff were so helpful and friendly, and [5]*the / –* breakfasts were excellent. We found [6]*several / few* good places for [7]*– / the* dinner nearby. [8]*Some / The* tourists only eat in [9]*the / –* hotels when they go abroad, but not us. Even the smallest cafés had [10] *plenty of / several* choice on the menu, and [11]*the / –* Turkish food is absolutely delicious, as you know.

One day, we went on [12]*a / –* boat trip. [13]*A / The* boat was quite small, but we had [14]*lots of / a few* fun. We were able to jump into [15]*the / a* sea from [16]*the / a* boat and swim to [17]*the / a* sandy beach. There were [18]*few / a few* other tourists there, and we soon realised why: there was [19]*a very little / very little* shade and [20]*the / –* sun was extremely hot!

Later, we went to [21]*a / the* village where we'd heard there were a [22]*several / number of* carpets at [23]*– / the* good prices. In the end, we didn't buy anything, as we hadn't got [24]*plenty of / much* money left. I'd already bought [25]*few / a few* souvenirs anyway.

Write soon and tell me how [26]*the / a* new job is going.

Love, Marta

Acknowledgements

The authors would like to thank everyone who worked on the first edition of *Prepare*, and also Melissa Wilson and Alyson Maskell for their hard work on the second edition. Helen Chilton thanks Dave for all his support and encouragement. James Styring dedicates this book to Jude Robert Alver Styring. Nicholas Tims thanks Clare, Ismay and Elodie for their endless support.

The authors and publishers are grateful to the following for reviewing the material during the writing process:

Italy: Roberta Tornaghi; Mexico: Diana Gabriela González Benítez; Spain: Helena Sánchez Olivares and Reyes Bellmunt Pons

The authors and publishers acknowledge the following sources of copyright material and are grateful for the permissions granted. While every effort has been made, it has not always been possible to identify the sources of all the material used, or to trace all copyright holders. If any omissions are brought to our notice, we will be happy to include the appropriate acknowledgements on reprinting and in the next update to the digital edition, as applicable.

Key: C = Culture, EA = Extra Activities, LS = Life Skills, PE = Prepare for the Exam, R = Review, U = Unit.

Text

U1: Tenith Adityaa for the text about Tenith Adityaa. Copyright © Tenith Adityaa. Reproduced with permission; **C1:** Freddie Harrel for the text about Freddie Harrel. Copyright © Freddie Harrel. Reproduced with kind permission of Tom Harrel; **U7:** Adapted text from *Sherlock Level 4 Intermediate Cambridge Experience Readers* by Richard MacAndrew. Copyright © Cambridge University Press 2013. Reproduced with permission; **U13:** Adapted text from *Three-dot-dash. Global teen leaders.* Threedotdash.org. Copyright © We are family Foundation 2014. All rights reserved; **U15:** Adapted text from 'Case Study – Charity Mhende MYP for Solihull 2008-2010', www.ukyouthparliament.org.uk. Reproduced with permission of British Youth Council; **U18:** Hannah Herbst for the text about Hannah Herbst. Copyright © Hannah Herbst. Reproduced with permission of Julie Herbst; **U20:** Adapted text from http://www.nsf.gov/news/special_reports/linguistics/change.jsp. Courtesy: National Science Foundation; Newsquest Media Group Limited for the quote by Professor David Crystal from 'texting a great big mwah' by Oliver Evans, *Oxford Mail* 6.3.2012. Copyright © Newsquest Media Group Limited; PE: Jamal Edwards for the text about Jamal Edwards. Copyright © Jamal Edwards. Reproduced with kind permission.

Photography

The following photographs are sourced from Getty Images.

U1: Hinterhaus Productions/DigitalVision; martin-dm/E+; Mike Marsland/WireImage; Barry King/Getty Images Entertainment; vm/E+; Guido Mieth/Moment/Getty Images Plus; **U2:** Kirill Rudenko/Moment; Casarsa/iStock/Getty Images Plus; Hero Images; Andrii Shurpenkov/500px Prime; lechatnoir/E+; RyanJLane/E+; SolStock/E+; SensorSpot/E+; Isabella Antonelli/EyeEm; **C1:** Darren Gerrish/WireImage; Darren Gerrish/Getty Images Entertainment; Peter White/Getty Images Entertainment; John Phillips/Getty Images Entertainment; **U3:** Ben Cranke/Oxford Scientific/Getty Images Plus; Joe Raedle/Getty Images News; martin-dm/E+; gchutka/E+; Justin Tallis/AFP; **U4:** Francesco Carta fotografo/Moment; altrendo images/Getty Images Plus; Science Photo Library; eyenigelen/E+; Isabella Antonelli/EyeEm; Juanmonino/E+; Andersen Ross/Photodisc; Ariel Skelley/DigitalVision; oleg66/E+; Eric Audras/ONOKY; **LS1:** AndreyPopov/iStock/Getty Images Plus; Elke Meitzel/Moment; eclipse_images/E+; **R1:** Ben Gabbe/Getty Images Entertainment; **U5:** Wisconsin Historical Society/Archive Photos; Science & Society Picture Library; Print Collector/Hulton Archive; Hulton Deutsch/Corbis Historical; Adene Sanchez/E+; d3sign/Moment; Alberto Guglielmi/The Image Bank/Getty Images Plus; **U6:** Fuse/Corbis; filadendron/E+; Satoshi-K/E+; ondacaracola photography/Moment; timnewman/E+; adamkaz/E+; Hero Images; **C2:** Danita Delimont/Gallo Images/Getty Images Plus; ICHAUVEL/Moment; **U7:** Purple Collar Pet Photography/Moment; **U8:** Roy JAMES Shakespeare/Photodisc; Neale Clark/robertharding/Getty Images Plus; Rafael Eduardo Chavez/EyeEm; asiseeit/E+; **LS2:** skynesher/E+; Lucy Lambriex/DigitalVision; **U9:** Flashpop/DigitalVision; stock_colors/iStock/Getty Images Plus; drbimages/E+; Corey Ford/Stocktrek Images; Giulia Marchi/Bloomberg; Keystone-France/Hulton Archive/Getty Images Plus;Hero Images; **U10:** MASSIVE/Stone/Getty Images Plus; GCShutter/E+; Romy Arroyo Fernandez/NurPhoto; **C3:** pixonaut/E+; chaofann/iStock/Getty Images Plus; wragg/E+; **U11:** Doug Menuez/Forrester Images/Photodisc; H. Armstrong Roberts/Retrofile RF; OwenPrice/E+; pkazmierczak/iStock/Getty Images Plus; Westend61; **U12:** The Image Bank/Getty Images Plus; Mattia Marchi/Moment; ROBERT MICHAEL/AFP; PeopleImages/E+; serts/iStock Unreleased; SolStock/E+; **LS3:** asiseeit/E+; Tim Graham/Getty Images News; Hero Images; **U13:** Hero Images; Marc Romanelli; **U14:** Leadinglights/E+; Cavan Images; paulprescott72/iStock Editorial/Getty Images Plus; Mixmike/E+; Car Culture ® Collection/Getty Images Plus; simonkr/iStock/Getty Images Plus; © fitopardo.com/Moment; pixdeluxe/E+; Prepelita Eduard Ionut/500px; CRISTINA QUICLER/AFP; Martin Dimitrov/E+; Stefanie Jost/EyeEm; izusek/E+; Adrian Rosu/Eyeem; mapodile/E+; **C4:** sturti/E+; Hero Images; **U15:** Thanatham Piriyakarnjanakul/EyeEm; ArtMarie/E+; Leonid Andronov/iStock/Getty Images Plus; Leontura/DigitalVision Vectors; Photo by Rafa Elias/Moment; Image Source/Photodisc; PeopleImages/E+; mixetto/E+; Tetra Images; **U16:** Arand/E+; Casarsa/iStock/Getty Images Plus; filo/DigitalVision Vectors; BURCU ATALAY TANKUT/Moment; Matt Bird/Corbis/Getty Images Plus; DavidGraham86/iStock/Getty Images Plus; Gordon Esler/Photographer's Choice/Getty Images Plus; **LS4:** JohnnyGreig/E+; Copyright Artem Vorobiev/Moment; **U17:** Justin Paget/The Image Bank/Getty Images Plus; Thomas Trutschel/Photothek; GrapeImages/E+; **U18:** Maskot; ViewStock/China; nortonrsx/iStock/Getty Images Plus; Eva-Katalin/E+; Monty Rakusen/Cultura; Heide Benser/Corbis/Getty Images Plus; Phil Boorman/Cultura; LightFieldStudios/iStock/Getty Images Plus; Westend61; aldomurillo/E+; Caiaimage/Sam Edwards; YinYang/E+; Wavebreakmedia/iStock/Getty Images Plus; Blend Images - Erik Isakson; Philippe TURPIN/Photononstop; Drazen_/E+; DGLimages/iStock/Getty Images Plus; **C5:** Jun Sato/TAS18/Getty Images Entertainment; Charles McQuillan/Getty Images News; icenando/iStock Editorial/Getty Images Plus; gilaxia/E+; **U19:** Westend61; Fuse/Corbis; piranka/E+; Stígur Már Karlsson/Heimsmyndir/E+; PYMCA/Universal Images Group; UHB Trust/The Image Bank/Getty Images Plus; Luca Sage/Stone/Getty Images Plus; kali9/E+; skynesher/E+; **U20:** JGI/Jamie Grill; Plume Creative/DigitalVision; MediaProduction/E+; Justin Lambert/DigitalVision; SolStock/E+; vitranc/E+; **LS5:** David Schaffer/Caiaimage; Westend61; bymuratdeniz/E+; **PE:** Bill Ellman/Mirrorpix; Dong Wenjie/Moment; Ken Kiefer 2/Cultura; takingpics.me/Moment; izusek/E+; Letizia Le Fur/ONOKY; 97/E+; rolfo/Moment; Maskot; Vinit Deekhanu/EyeEm; Carol Yepes/Moment; Ableimages/David Harrigan; Caiaimage/Robert Daly; Caiaimage/Paul Bradbury; Eternity in an Instant/The Image Bank/Getty Images Plus; Thomas Barwick/DigitalVision; SolStock/E+; Leren Lu/Photographer's Choice RF; Daniel Ingold; **EA:** Manuel Hurtado/Moment; Rudi Van Starrex/Photodisc; andresr/E+; Hero Images.

The following photographs have been sourced from other libraries/sources.

U1: © Harpercollins; © Tenith Adithyaa; **C1:** Dvora/Shutterstock; **U4:** BSIP SA/Alamy Stock Photo; Lucky Business/Shutterstock; **LS1:** WAYHOME studio/Shutterstock; **U6:** FGC/Shutterstock; **U8:** nagelestock.com/Alamy Stock Photo; Jack Malipan Travel Photography/Alamy Stock Photo; **U10:** MASSIVE/Stone/Getty Images Plus; Chris Jobs/Alamy Stock Photo; Dean Drobot/Shutterstock; **U11:** Orada Jusatayanond/Alamy Stock Photo; **U12:** imageBROKER/Alamy Stock Photo; Lex and Sten/Shutterstock; Chris Rout/Alamy Stock Photo; john norman/Alamy Stock Photo;